Emerson in Iran

Emerson in Iran

The American Appropriation of Persian Poetry

Roger Sedarat

Credit for Figure 1: Willis Barnstone, *Poetics of Translation: History, Theory, Practice*. Yale UP, 1995, p. 24.

Published by State University of New York Press, Albany

For information, contact State University of New York Press, Albany, NY
www.sunypress.edu

Library of Congress Cataloging-in-Publication Data

Names: Sedarat, Roger, 1971– author.
Title: Emerson in Iran : the American appropriation of Persian poetry / Roger Sedarat.
Description: Albany : State University of New York Press, [2019] | Includes bibliographical references and index.
Identifiers: LCCN 2018035999 | ISBN 9781438474854 (hardcover : alk. paper) | ISBN 9781438474878 (ebook)
Subjects: LCSH: Emerson, Ralph Waldo, 1803–1882—Knowledge—Persian literature. | American poetry—Persian influences. | American poetry—19th century—History and criticism. | Persian literature—Influence.
Classification: LCC PS1642.P47 S43 2019 | DDC 814/.3—dc23
LC record available at https://lccn.loc.gov/2018035999

10 9 8 7 6 5 4 3 2 1

For my two countries

Contents

Acknowledgments

A few mentors early in my academic career instilled in me a lifelong passion for Emerson's writing. More than simply passing down knowledge, the late Americanist Jesper Rosenmeier, along with my former professor and recently retired colleague Harold Schechter, have modeled an especially Emersonian individuality in their lives as well as in their scholarship. I would further include for much the same reason George Held and the late Mario D'Avanzo. Elizabeth Ammons also proved uniquely supportive by encouraging me to bring my Persian background to American literature and culture long before the recent trend in transnational studies. Persis Karim, who significantly positioned Iranian-American studies deeper into the United States through the late twentieth and twenty-first centuries, has greatly helped make this topic relevant. Much like Emerson, Willis Barnstone personally showed me the power of integrating a more inclusive poetic approach to my writing about literary theory and translation, as well as to comparative scholarship, at a time when academia can seem too regressively specialized for its own good. Through his insistence upon my attempting to creatively engage literary theory, as opposed to merely passively apply it to texts, Lee Edelman warrants special mention here as well. The influence of these teachers upon this project and others in formation remains invaluable.

Current Emerson scholars David LaRocca and Ricardo Miguel-Alfonso offered much-needed tangible support of my topic. Their acceptance of a chapter concerned with Emerson's generalized influence from the broader Middle East for *A Power to Translate the World: New Essays on Emerson and International Culture* motivated me to eventually pursue this more specific focus on Iran. The groundbreaking comparative offerings from my fellow contributors to this collection provided a multitude of interdisciplinary approaches to Emerson studies with critical methodologies that led me to radically conceptualize my own original readings in relation to the Persian tradition. David LaRocca,

Dartmouth College/UPNE editor Richard Pult, and Donald Pease—editor of the transnational series that published this collection of essays—gave me helpful notes toward a much-improved revision of this manuscript. Farhang Jahanpour's extensive critique of an early version of my third chapter led to important revisions and redirections. I also want to make special mention of the Ralph Waldo Emerson Society, which granted me a 2018 subvention award in support of this book's publication. That specialists in Emerson studies have found my scholarship worthy of such distinction validates all of the hard work as well as the many critical risks taken throughout the following chapters.

My esteemed colleagues at Queens College have offered comparable critical feedback, along with prodigious encouragement. Duncan Faherty and Annmarie Drury especially extended themselves on behalf of this book. The former spent considerable time with my proposal and compelled me to move forward with my topic, while the latter as a fellow translator-poet-scholar often impressed upon me the value of interrogating the generative role of translation in a nation's poetics. Thanks to our many discussions and my early reading of her scholarship, my study to some extent has become a kind of American counterpart to her groundbreaking, *Translation as Transformation in Victorian Poetry*. The following colleagues, each in their own ways, have also shared their insightful academic work as well as their time and support: Glenn Burger, Steve Kruger, Amy Wan, Richard McCoy, Ryan Black, Andrea Walkden, Talia Schaffer, Kevin Ferguson, Jason Tougaw, Bill Orchard, Gloria Fisk, Miles Grier, Siân Silyn Roberts, Karen Weingarten, Jeff Cassvan, Wayne Moreland, Fred Buell, Christopher Williams, Maaza Mengiste, John Weir, Kimiko Hahn, Nicole Cooley, Ammiel Alcalay, Tom Frosch, and David Richter. I include here as well President Félix Matos Rodríguez and Acting Provost William McClure, administrators who generously support publication by professors at a relatively teaching-intensive institution. Though currently not at my college, former visiting professor Susan Bernofsky's willingness to provide me with a rough trot of an almost indecipherable Saʿdi translation into early nineteenth-century German for this study helped provoke an especially illuminating insight into Emerson's strategic adulterations through English translation.

Friends outside academia on a personal level have given the most time and attention to this project. My best and far longest friend Paul Schneider almost daily reminds me of Emerson's greatest lessons in integrity, aspiration, and intellectual curiosity. Other invaluable friends include Melaine Oster, K Bradford, Steve Sussmann, Gene Pitts, Jesse Garza, Michael Haas, Mark Snow, Dewar MacLeod, Francis Taplin, Joe Regal, Benjamin Selesnick, Justin Morris, Robert Babboni, Elizabeth Cahill, John Younger, Jonathan Fink, Gregg

Popovich, Wes and Rebecca Jones, Nicky and Sara Nodjoumi, Rouhollah Zarei, Till Schauder, James Cox, and Ron Reich.

Family of course even more intimately extends such support. My dear sister Mary Sedarat and her husband William Brick embody the best qualities of the Persian family tradition in the displaced and rather fragmented culture of America's East Coast where we live. My mother Nancy Sedarat, arguably the best teacher I have known, instilled in me a lifelong love of learning as well as the needed discipline to pursue it. Her origins in the American Midwest, combined with those of my late Persian father, Dr. Nassir (Robert) Sedarat from Shiraz, Iran—the "land of the poets"—afforded me perhaps the best personal background for such a comparative interrogation. Growing up memorizing the lines of Hafez, my father's embrace of American literature and culture as an immigrant further prepared me for this work. Significantly, he gave me my first copy of Emerson's collected essays, with his favorite sentences underlined, when I was twelve years old. My Iranian sister-in-law Maria Afsharian and her husband Amir Emdad, along with his late father Hassan Emdad—the estimable scholar of Persian poetry whose early comments to me on Emerson and Hafez first inspired the idea of this book—have also provided much needed advice, encouragement, and love.

Finally, my Iranian-American wife Janette Afsharian, who in the Sufi mystic tradition more than qualifies for the role of the beloved as articulated in this study, has patiently listened to seemingly endless turns, discoveries, and frustrations throughout the process of writing this book. My gratitude for her attention and compassion, often mirrored by our sons Milo and Theo, is best expressed in the lines of Hafez and Sa'di to which Emerson found himself so passionately attracted.

Introduction

Emerson

Closing the heavy volume of Montaigne,
The tall New Englander goes out
Into an evening which exalts the fields.
It is a pleasure worth no less than reading.
He walks toward the final sloping of the sun,
Toward the landscape's gilded edge;
He moves through darkening fields as he moves now
Through the memory of the one who writes this down.
He thinks: I have read the essential books
And written others which oblivion
Will not efface. I have been allowed
That which is given mortal man to know.
The whole continent knows my name.
I have not lived. I want to be someone else.

—Borges (189)

The assumption in Borges's poem that Ralph Waldo Emerson, established as a seminal figure in American literature, longs to become "someone else" might seem little more than a product of the Argentinian writer's wild imagination. However, upon closer reflection Borges introduces a problem at the crux of Emerson's self-identification. The same man who fearlessly states in his famous essay "Self-Reliance" that "imitation is suicide" (*CW* 2:27) relies to a great extent on the ideas, quotations, even the identity of others.

Though a volume of Montaigne is referenced in the poem, Borges might just as well have Emerson close a book of Persian verse, considering that in his entire oeuvre Emerson mentions Saʿdi as many times as the French philosopher. If we add Hafez, then poets from Iran collectively become the sixth

1

most-cited writers in Emerson's work, after Shakespeare, Napoleon, Plato, Plu-
tarch, and Goethe (Holmes 295). Upon his intense reading of thirteenth- and
fourteenth-century Persian poets after the publication of *Nature*, one of the
"essential books" that earned him recognition from "the whole continent" as
Borges describes, Emerson indeed wished to become his foreign predecessors
from Iran. He translated over seven hundred lines of Persian verse through
intermediary German renderings by Joseph von Hammer-Purgstall, and further attempted to imitate in his own poetry the lines and even identities of
classical Sufi masters whom he revered. The same Romantically individualized
American who insists, "I must be myself" (*CW* 2:42) similarly adopts the
name of Saʿdi in his own writing, trying his best to channel his predecessor's
voice. Equally paradoxical, Emerson as the great original American visionary
longs to possess the perspective of Hafez. Defining himself by his desire to
become this fourteenth-century Sufi mystic, he proclaims, "Such is the only
man I wish to see or to be" (*JMN* 10:165).

This study considers how Emerson as seminal poet-translator attempts to
anticipate classical Sufi masters through his appropriative translation practices
of Persian poetry. The following close readings of his rhetoric interrogate his
claim of a radical originality in the figurative formation of American literature,
revealing the extent to which it remains contingent upon his adoption and
accommodation of Persian verse into his writing and translating. In this respect
Emerson as subject of the first thirteen lines of Borges's sonnet can be seen
as embodying the burden of his predecessors' voices. However, as if following the convention of the last line in the Persian form of the *ghazal*, wherein
poets like Hafez attempt to transcend the ego by playful self-objectification
through the use of pseudonyms, Emerson in turn reconciles such influence
by coopting the strategy of becoming someone else by borrowing their names
and poetic styles. In this respect even the final line of the bio-critical poem
by Borges, written in a Western form, follows Emerson's transformative renderings of Eastern verse that reorient the self in his own literary tradition.

Though consideration of the Persian material Emerson translated through
German sources and also read in previous English renderings continues to
build on previous critical insights, a somewhat more radical turn toward his
essential rhetorical foundations attempts to expose the formative effects of
conflating his American tradition with Persian sources through the centrality
of his Romantic vision. The following chapters thus focus as much on the
written expression of his identity as on his practice of translation, both of
which he firmly based in his Platonic understanding of literature. While previous scholarship has consistently gestured toward Emerson's all-encompassing
and accessible literary approach based in Platonic and Neoplatonic philosophy

that enabled him to accommodate foreign influence, the extent to which it poetically emerges from his engagement with Persian verse warrants closer attention. Ironically, from his earliest reading practices of transnational litera- ture, the further he seems to get away from his literary origins, the closer he comes to the performance of an authentic self. To preview from a later chapter perhaps the most dramatic manifestation of this phenomenon in Emerson's well-noted missing grief over the death of his son in "Experience," a recur- ring critical quandary in Emerson studies, he comes to retroactively mourn through the voice of his ideal poet Sa'di in an elegy for the Persian father's own lost boy that he re-translates multiple times in his *Notebook Orientalist*. This connection to Persian verse relatively late in his career in turn connects him back to the development of an earlier way of seeing the world as well as himself beyond his nineteenth-century New England, even prior to his more significant investigation and translation of the Sufi poets he came to revere.

Fully realizing Emerson's Eastern gaze therefore means looking as much toward his vision as at his focus on Iran. Predicating self-depictions on his own elusive rhetoric begins to productively foreground why the influence of Sa'di, Hafez, and others proves especially hard to discern. More than thematic statements of his reading practices and specific signifiers from the foreign tra- dition in his imitations, influence becomes paradoxically both most profound as well as most invisible within Emerson's own disorienting poetry and prose. Attempting however falteringly to identify this process of rhetorical disloca- tion thus serves as an analytical entry point into the American forefather's aesthetic, which extends to his translation and imitative practices.

Insofar as the rhetorical means by which Emerson comes to see himself reflected in poets such as Hafez and Sa'di tend to evade critical recognition, an attempt to follow his appropriation of Persian verse on his own creative terms juxtaposes the ubiquitous trope of the mirror found throughout Sufi mysticism with his elusive "transparent eyeball." Interposing such a metaphor reflective of Sufi philosophy, based on a spiritually esoteric interpretation of Islam that informs much of classical Persian poetry, begins to reveal how Emerson's personal view of an all-unifying Platonism effectively sanctions his temporal, stylistic, and even linguistic equations to foreign sources. His mimicry of Persian verse, based in an originating rhetoric expressive of his Romantic vision, consequently offers a specific comparative perspective on how he renders such a disparate influence into English as if he himself anticipated it.

As progenitor poet-philosopher at a turning point in the foundation of his nation's literature, Emerson encountering his own reflection in Persian poetry that he couldn't read in the original language further supports an argu- ment for his initiating a generative approach in the tradition of American verse translation. Closer attention to his theory and practice of translation necessitates significant revision of previous modernist assumptions about Ezra Pound as first substantial American appropriative translator. Pound has been almost unconditionally credited with establishing the Western tendency to creatively render foreign poetry into English with little regard for literal equivalence. As Steven Yao explains, Pound was the first to have "obviated intimate knowledge of the source language as a precondition for translation by demonstrating in an irrefutable way that successful . . . results could be attained without thorough . . . understanding of the original text translated" (*Languages* 26). Yao further considers Pound as "the first broadly influential writer since at least the seventeenth century to bestow upon translation . . . an explicitly primary and generative . . . role in the process of literary cultural formation" ("Translation" 33–34).

More than influencing the American practice of translation in the twentieth century, Pound's approach to foreign literature from the East has been fundamental in conceptualizing modern poetics in the West, in part by assuming creatively misleading linguistic and temporal equivalence between such radically different traditions as ancient Chinese and contemporary English verse. Emerson through his translation of Persian poetry, however, anticipates by fifty years the literary implications of Pound's claim that "all ages are contemporaneous" (*Romance* 8). Prior to Pound's axioms derived from his appropriative translation practices, Emerson can be seen as a contemporary harbinger of the high modernist's emerging aesthetic. More subtly using translation in the literary formation of his nineteenth century, he relies on his English renderings of Persian verse through German sources to develop a strategic approach that accommodates foreign traditions into his own influential rhetoric.

An initial exploration of Emerson's rhetorical theory as it relates however tangentially to translation helps to further substantiate his having anticipated Pound. His understanding of words as etymologically derived from images in his essay "Language," which reverts back to his consistent reliance upon a Platonic reading of the world, significantly influenced Ernest Fenollosa, the intermediary Asian scholar-translator who like von Hammer-Purgstall for Emerson greatly informed Pound's translations. Pound can be understood as claiming more of his original voice after a long process of translating and imitating Eastern verse—as evidenced by his writing the much more personal and far superior *Pisan Cantos* in confinement for political transgression. Emerson as his most substantial American predecessor begins inversely, within the delimited confines of his original lyric vision expressed through his transparent eyeball, moving outward from the self, and consequently more on his own Romantic terms, to Eastern poetry. With such a trajectory, he precedes Pound along with the Persian masters he transforms through his Platonic a-temporality. As the final two chapters of this study will reveal, by figuratively establishing himself as the first and seemingly all-encompassing poet-translator in his literary tradition, he continues to influence American verse translation into the early twenty-first century.

More than contending with a formidable modernist inheritor, such essays as "Language," when contextualized within a sustained close reading of his engagement with Persian poetry, introduce what can be considered as Emerson's emerging theory of translation. Writings that reflect on his own rhetorical practices do more than merely justify his appropriation of the Persian poets. They effectively foreground an approach to literary translation that invites Pound's comparable rhetorical practices as they further extend their influence upon contemporary verse renderings into English. Extracting and re-categorizing Emerson's key rhetorical concepts based in his Platonic relation to Persian poetry helps to position him as predecessor-translator by showing how his own theorizing allowed him to subvert the limitations of literal equivalences to foreign source texts. Examining his theoretical under-standing of writing that unapologetically advocates for brazen intertextuality reveals the process through which he disregards such linguistic equivalence to more radically equate his rhetorical vision to the foreign source poets themselves. At best the ideal translator is said to remain an invisible agent, seamlessly channeling the voice of the original literary work. Despite the distance of language, culture, and time, Emerson draws so close to Persian poets of the thirteenth and fourteenth centuries that he tends to invert this ideal, often rendering himself indistinguishable from the appearance of his predecessors in the Sufi mirror through his insistence on invisibility. Though various literary theory is used to better identify and examine the implica-tions of Emerson's approach to translation, his own reflections best serve to outline the functioning of his elusive rhetoric that so easily dissembles his assumption of foreign verse.

Recently Lawrence Buell, partly responding to the scholarship of Wai Chee Dimock, has called for moving the discussion of Persian verse as an influence upon Emerson "from the edges of discussion" and more toward "the center" (151). Quite tellingly, Paul Kane, in his comparative study of Hafez and Emerson, has expressed doubt about so positioning Emerson's engage-ment with Persian poetry, remarking, "I'm not convinced there is a center, or at least a stable one" (134). In part to extend the close correspondence of the Persian letter in Emerson's writing to the spirit of Persian influence, Kane begins to show how the foreign verse remains latent in the writing of the American poet, helping to foreground a problematic critical tendency that limits comparative analyses between Emerson's specific translations of Persian poetry and his own writing.

Such repositioning aptly identifies both the necessity and the difficulty of investigating this topic. Emerson's ability to make the Sufi verse of Iran his own through his comparable rhetorical and spiritual sensibility often means that his writing becomes as de-centered as the source texts he translates. Because comparative study necessitates a locus of signifiers from two disparate traditions, his close mirroring of foreign literature makes it hard to differentiate him from his Persian sources. His Romantic individualism relative to his refutation of an inherited Christian tradition, for example, combined with his close relation to the essential rhetorical functioning of English in his prose and poetry, often reads like the Sufi mystic poets' struggle with the hypocrisy of seemingly devout Muslims as well as with the materiality of language itself. Even at the level of identity both Emerson and the Persian poets distance themselves from their names. Ironically, by straying so far from what translation studies terms an equivalence of meaning between two languages, the American poet closely resembles poets like Sa'di and Hafez, making it especially difficult to locate his intervention with the source texts. At times, according to Harold Bloom's understanding of influence, he seems to have anticipated his Persian predecessors.

In this sense Emerson can further be seen as having preceded critical approaches that interpret his use of Persian poetry, which do little more than acknowledge his perceived similarity to his foreign sources by admitting the difficulty of separating him from their influence.[1] Oliver Wendell Holmes, recognizing Emerson's interest in Persian verse, comments: "In many of the shorter poems and fragments published since 'May-Day,' as well as in the 'Quatrains' and others . . . it is sometimes hard to tell what is from the Persian from what is original" (173). Also noting the close resemblance between Emerson and his Persian sources in the nineteenth century, Joel Benton asks, "Shall we say on account of this homogeneity that the Oriental is but another Yankee? Or is it that the Yankee is merely the Oriental moved further west?" (28). Robert Alfred Vaughan, a nineteenth-century scholar who "made comparing mysticisms an art" (Schmidt 47) similarly conflated Emerson with the spiritual underpinnings of the Persian verse tradition, calling him, "chief singer of his time at the high court of Mysticism" and "a true brother of those Sufis of whose doctrine he has so much in common" (8).

Attempts to differentiate Emerson's writing from his Persian sources have required both strict linear considerations of equivalence as well as more speculative readings of literary influence. Though J.D. Yohannan's early scholarship focuses primarily on the former with comparisons of Emerson's translations to German intermediary renderings, it importantly begins inviting further interrogations of the latter by looking at Emerson's conceptualization of Sa'di as his ideal poet. Even so, calling attention to the need of identifying influence in Emerson's decentering rhetoric, Yohannan claims to have left out an examination of the "less tangible effect of Persian poetry on Emerson's philosophy," commenting on how difficult it proves to ascertain ("Influence" 25).

Despite Benton basing some of his comparative assumptions on egregiously sweeping statements about "all oriental verse" (27) without a thorough understanding of his foreign subject matter, he successfully initiates keen insights beyond mere denotative concerns with Emerson's resemblance to his Persian influences, exploring how the Eastern poems tend to share the same "mood, texture, and tune" (28). As one of the earliest scholars to significantly associate rhetorical tendencies in Emerson's poetry and prose relative to his Persian sources, he begins to provide an important foundation on which further scholarship has been built.

Paul Kane's observations that link Emerson's writing to the thematically "inconsecutive ghazals of Hafez" (31), like Charles Ives's early study observing how "Emerson wrote by sentences and phrases" as opposed to "logical sequence" (25), have significantly expanded such critical speculation to include comparative insights relating Persian verse to the disparate tension between Emerson's epigraphs and his essays (130–132). In part to extend the close correspondence of the letter in Emerson's writing to the spirit of foreign verse that he translated, Kane begins to convincingly reveal the greater presence of a latent Persian influence on Emerson than what has been previously acknowledged. Importantly foundational for this study, Kane also moves beyond Sa'di, a Persian influence Western critics tend to privilege as a result of Emerson's more overt identification through his own biographical "portrait" of the poet (*JMN* 9:37), extending his focus to Hafez. As Yohannan has previously commented, "Hafiz, no less than Saadi, contributed to the composite picture" ("Influence" 37).

Considering the interconnectedness of Emerson's poetry and prose to the fourteenth-century classical Persian poet Hafez, Kane demonstrates a subtler yet more pervasive effect of the Persian tradition upon Emerson's sensibility beyond a line-by-line analysis of translations or Emerson's imitations of Persian verse as previously offered by Yohannan. Arguing that Emerson appreciated Hafez as a bridge between the secular and the spiritual, he stresses that the American followed the Iranian in part because Hafez kept mysticism from becoming a mere static concept in his poetry. It remains "vehicular" (119), much like the functioning of metaphor, which seems to considerably

resemble Emerson's rhetoric. Such de-centered literary analysis also leads Kane
to assert that Emerson became especially attracted to Hafez for his spirit of
self-reliance, insofar as he asserted a liberating power within the confines
of religious context (119). To a great extent Kane's study thus offers a way
to move Hafez more toward the center of Persian influence. As he explains,

> It is Hafiz who occupies a key position in Emerson's notion of
> who or what the poet is, and he reflects what Emerson himself
> is attempting to do in his own verse. . . . To understand Hafiz is
> to understand Emerson's poetry. (134)

Essays in the recently published *Sufism and American Literary Masters*
further broaden and deepen such early research by examining the stylistic
and spiritual relationship between Emerson and the Sufi poetic tradition
exemplified by Hafez and Sa'di. Mehdi Aminrazavi's introduction highlights
a correspondence between Emerson's nineteenth century and some central
themes from Sufi philosophy such as "vanity of the world, the analogies
between experience in Nature and in love, and the inability of human reason
to explain or address the world's mysteries" (2). Revisiting Emerson's sustained
interest in Sa'di, Parvin Loloi offers historical context for a convincingly specific
reading of the thirteenth-century Persian poet's influence on the American
author. In addition to a meticulous examination of Emerson's interest in the
Persian poets, she revisits Yohannan's comparison of Emerson's translations
and the German renderings from which he worked. Importantly, she goes on
to analyze the influence of Persian verse on Emerson's own writing, drawing
such strong comparisons between Emerson and the Sufis as their relation to
nature (107).

Specifically tracking Emerson's reading of literature from and about Iran
as well as other Islamic cultures, Mansur Ekhtiyar questions the assumption
that his real interest in Persian poetry begins with his reading of Baron von
Hammer-Purgstall's translations in 1841 (Carpenter 161). Making an even
further-reaching case for Emerson's much earlier introduction to literature from
Iran, Farhang Jahanpour offers a rather exhaustive bibliography of Emerson's
Oriental reading, inviting greater investigation of Emerson's subtler mining of
Eastern influence closer to the onset of his development as a writer. To this
end, it becomes necessary to consider the respective expansions of Phillip
Edmonson and Parvin Loloi on Benton's early work that explicates what first
attracted Emerson to the Iranian poets. Reexamining the similarity between Sufi
mysticism and an American Transcendental Romantic sensibility, Edmonson
discovers a similar linguistic framework relative to an accessible spirituality

that enabled Emerson to easily introduce Persian poetry to America during a period when the country's sensibility became especially receptive to it. As Leigh Eric Schmidt notes, by the time Williams James published *The Variety of Religious Experience*, "American Transcendentalists and their like-minded heirs had created an ahistorical, poetic, essential, intuitive, universal, wildly rhapsodic mysticism" (48). While validating such comparisons as those made by Edmonson and Loloi, Marwan Obeidat importantly reinforces previous critical considerations of Emerson's ambivalent relation to "the Muslim Orient," reading it "as stemming from a mixture of condescension and admiration" (87). This latter summation begins to suggest the recurring critical inability to establish Emerson's stance toward Persian verse, further necessitating closer comparative interrogation.

The importance of Albert von Frank's introduction and notes to Emerson's translations and imitations of Persian verse cannot be overstated. In addition to exacting scholarship that has organized and synthesized previous discoveries, his speculation that Emerson's especially "intense creative outbursts" from 1845 to 1846 "could be attributed to the discovery of Hafez" invites greater investigation. Locating "an oriental influence" (*CW* 9:xvii) in much of Emerson's *Poems* published in 1847, von Frank extends the analysis initiated by such previous critics as Oliver Wendell Holmes. Like Buell, von Frank further foregrounds the significance of Persian influence while stressing that "it has not been adequately explored" (lxvii). Following his scholarly commentary on Emerson's engagement with the verse tradition of Hafez and Sa'di with such a qualification has proven especially motivating to both the research and writing of this study.

Though not specifically invested in the influence of Persian poetry on Emerson's verse, the recent and rather groundbreaking *A Power to Translate the World: New Essays son Emerson and International Culture* has offered several important critical models for a transnational relation to American studies. Varied approaches to Emerson's engagement with different cultures, national traditions, and religions prove especially instructive in how to read the American against, as well as alongside, a plethora of foreign influences. The willingness of David LaRocca and Ricardo Miguel-Alfonso to include a formative chapter, "Middle Eastern-American Literature: A Contemporary Turn in Emerson Studies" (310–325), in which many of the ideas for this book first began to take shape, provided significant motivation and instruction toward further investigation of Emerson's relation to Persian poetry.

Susan Dunston's essay "East of Emerson" in the recently published *Emerson for the Twentieth Century: Global Perspectives on an American Icon* presents further insightful readings into Emerson's specific interest in Persian verse informed by Sufism and its correspondence to his own aesthetic. The following chapters remain indebted to her introductory scholarship, especially for suggesting a similarity between Emerson's transparent eyeball and the Sufi mystics' clearing away of the self as they comparably experience or "see all" (121). Chapter 2 attempts to extend this insightful reading, juxtaposing Emerson's transparent eyeball to the trope of the mirror informed by Sufi mysticism for a sustained comparative analysis. Additional use is made of Dunston's observation of how both Sa'di and Emerson attempt to rhetorically reconcile the loss of their sons (117). Slight repositioning of her reading suggests that Emerson uses translation to identify with another poet-father as a cathartically imitative attempt of an elegy to locate his displaced grief in "Experience," an essay that on closer investigation demonstrates surprisingly more significance to Emerson's appropriation of the Middle East and Islam than has been previously recognized. Other observations by Dunston, such as general Platonic connections between Sa'di and Emerson (123), also prove foundational in more specific comparative readings between the American poet and his Persian predecessors.

Finally, Jeffrey Einboden's recent scholarship addressing in part Emerson's engagement with Islamic sources offers several significant insights that extend to the influence of Persian poetry. His close consideration of Emerson adulterating a quote from the *Qur'an* at the beginning of his scholarly development in a college notebook sets a subtle precedent for a sustained tendency toward appropriative verse translation throughout much of his life. Elsewhere, Einboden's tracking of the layered process through multiple drafts of English renderings from Persian lines in *Notebook Orientalist* practically reveals Emerson's creative interventions in his approach to translation. Perhaps most importantly, Einboden's emerging attention to Emerson's adoption of the Middle Eastern name "Osman" and his consequent change to "Sa'di" as related to the aforementioned translated elegy for the Persian poet's son, help direct even greater critical attention to Emerson's imitation of Persian poets.

This study continues the examination of Emerson's engagement with Sufi mysticism based on these previous analyses of his biography and rhetoric. Revisiting observed similarities between the classical verse of Iran and the conflation of Emerson's prose and poetry by Benton and Kane, it argues that in attempting to translate foreign verse through German intermediary texts without knowledge of the source language, he exposes an overriding aesthetic of global literary appropriation that becomes especially generative for the American literary tradition. His idealized relation to the Persian Sufi poets, which leads him to assume their voices and even identities as he projects himself onto his English renderings, reveals his spiritual and thematic claims upon a well-established foreign poetics. Looking at Emerson's paradoxical anticipation of such an ancient literary tradition through his transformation into a transparent eyeball, which reflects the crux of tension between the materiality of language and the transcendence of spirit in Sufi poetry, close readings of his writing interposed with the mystic's vision demonstrate how he in turn attempts to make the Persian verse he discovered and introduced to America his own through the fantasy of *a-priori* influence.

Such theoretical and practical approaches, which are shown to establish an imaginary transcendent unification to Persian verse through Emerson's reading of Platonic philosophy, come to closely resemble the ubiquitous trope of the mirror in Sufi mysticism. Just as devout Sufis try to rid themselves of ego and reach the clarity of divine reflection, Emerson attempts a self-overcoming through his transformation into "a transparent eyeball" (*CW* 1:10). This idealized and all-encompassing visionary trope reflects the Persian verse he reads and translates as if he somehow originated it. Against the Sufi mirror and his own vision, Asia—representative for Emerson as both "unity" and "infinitude" (*CW* 4:31)—positions him in a kind of Lacanian mirror stage relative to what he sees as the West's more "defining" and "surface seeking" individuated "detail" (*CW* 4:31). In looking East, he thus attempts to realize the fantasy of an all-unifying Platonic ideal. Such reconciliation can be seen in the very first sentence of his essay, "Plato, or the Philosopher," where writing of this ideal thinker from the Western tradition gets compared to the holy text from Islam: "Among secular books, Plato only is entitled to Omar's fanatical compliment to the Koran, when he said: 'Burn the libraries; for their value is in this book'" (*CW* 4:23). Here for Emerson, argues Obeidat, "Plato's work brings East to West whereby certain boundaries and categories are set up, associations and distinctions made." Consequently, "the Orient is given a space where it stands vis-à-vis the Occident" (77).

While contributors of *Sufism and the Literary Masters* as well as other aforementioned scholars have importantly tracked Emerson's encounter with the verse of Hafez and Sa'di, which proved especially significant through the 1840s with his reading of collected translated works that include von Hammer-Purgstall's German anthology (Ekhtiyar 64–65), problematic questions remain as to how and why he comes to see himself in the Persian mirror. More than wishing to write *like* his Persian predecessors, he often longs to write *as* them. His Platonic approach of disavowing linguistic and literary differences to see these foreign poets "vis-à-vis" therefore surfaces as a viable starting point to consider why such a seminal writer in American literature so adamantly insists on being himself while also, as depicted in the last line of the Borges's sonnet, longing to become "someone else."

The somewhat radical claim underpinning this book takes the self-reliant Emerson at his own words, arguing that by willingly trying to become Hafez and Sa'di, the American poet-philosopher effectively attempts imitative "suicide" (*CW* 2:27) according to his own criteria of what constitutes destruction of the authentic self. This appropriative foreign identification paradoxically liberates him through disassociation of his Romantic American identity. Though he mimicked a plethora of other writers from different languages and traditions, isolating his attempted entry into Iran can to some extent specifically exemplify his rhetorical engagement with an important foreign tradition while inviting conjecture as to why he attempted it, thereby better understanding Emerson's tendency toward a general transnational appropriation based on translation. While the amorphous nature of influence eludes complete explication, Emerson's uncanny reproduction of the Sufi mystic poets' spiritual self-obviation without reading knowledge of the language in which their verse was originally written offers a critical trail worth following. To slightly amend Buell's astute observation, it is perhaps not so much the Persian poetry, but Emerson's desire to have both written and translated it, that lies at the center of his oeuvre.

Despite Western Orientalist assumptions of Emerson's appropriative gaze toward the Middle East that previous scholarship has made explicit, a revisionist interrogation of recurring theoretical and critical examinations concerned with literary influence also reveals the figurative and even spiritual effects of Sufi mysticism on Emerson's thinking and writing. The American self-authorizes his use of the Persian material so well it is easy, yet potentially erroneous, to lose sight of the Eastern gaze reflecting back, "vis-à-vis," onto his aesthetic. As examined in chapter 3, for example, encountering through Persian verse the latent influence of Islamic fatalism that he overtly disparages paradoxically reflects his own philosophical ambivalence of freedom versus fate. The Persian tradition informed by a religion that Emerson saw as problematically predicated on pre-determinism can be seen as deterministic of his own spiritual vision. Such an analysis begins to suggest perhaps more of a reciprocal relation of Emerson to his foreign source material than previously realized.

For the purposes of this investigation, a few theoretical approaches are used to consider the implications of influence in Emerson's appropriative translation practices. First, Harold Bloom's *Anxiety of Influence: A Theory of Poetry* allows for a comparative analysis beyond previous scholarly contributions of close linear distinctions between Emerson and his Persian predecessors, helping to demonstrate how he had to reckon with the poetry originating in Iran that he transformed into English through previous German translations. Following Bloom, Emerson is read as progenitor poet of the "American Sublime" (*Anxiety* 103) under the category of *daemonization*, a term aptly taken from "Neo-Platonic usage," considering the American poet-translator's ultimate conception of an all-unifying literary origin. Defined as "an intermediary being, neither divine nor human" that intervenes to enable the writing of verse, the *daemon* helps show how Emerson in his relation to the Sufi mystics exemplifies the "later poet" who "opens himself to what he believes to be a power in the parent poem that does not belong to the parent proper, but to a range of being beyond that precursor." In attempting to make claims upon a transcendent spirit in the verse of Hafez and Saʿdi, Emerson translates Bloom's definition into praxis by positioning his verse against "the parent-poem" in order "to generalize away the uniqueness of the earliest work" (*Anxiety* 15).

However, as helpful as such a theory of influence proves to be for a comparative analysis of verse traditions rooted in vastly different cultures and languages, Emerson's proclivity toward the Persian poets calls such an approach into question. The majority of examples offered in Bloom's influential book focus exclusively on Western models. The Greek terms themselves, as well as the Freudian analysis that greatly informs his theory, demonstrate a recurring critical bias towards Western literary and philosophic origins, as seen in the very etymology of the word used to categorize Emerson. Subtly, much like how anglicizing names in translations of the Bible tend to slight the foundational importance of Jewish culture, Bloom demonstrates a kind of Oedipal breaking from the plethora of foreign traditions and languages that precede and heavily inform the English literature he favors. Like Emerson, he too tends to "generalize away the uniqueness" of foreign work. This in turn reinforces, if not condones, the modernist American move of appropriative translation established so firmly by Pound in the early twentieth century. If only to foreground a discursive space to serve as a continual reminder that writers accommodating the work from foreign sources don't merely attempt to reckon with influence into their own rhetoric but have their own texts transformed into something new, further theoretical understanding that accommodates difference appears necessary.

Partly in response to Bloom, Willis Barnstone begins to offer an alternative approach to influence in translation studies. According to Barnstone, in translating a source text, a literary translator must invent a new voice in the receiving language belonging neither entirely to the original poet nor to his or her own style. By implication, this new voice becomes its own influence with which the poet-translator must now reckon. As Barnstone explains, "the influence of translation in the work of poet translators occurs not so much because of their encounter with an extraordinary source text but through their own transformation of that source text into their own invented language." Consequently, "the poet translator self-reflexively discovers the language of his or her own inventions and borrows or steals it" (23). Here Pound truly excelled, proving "strong enough" (to use Bloom's rhetoric) in overcoming the predecessors he engaged. Though upon cursory observation Emerson relative to Pound at times appears to revert to simpler poetic mimicry of both the Persians and their intermediary German translators, a weaker move according to Bloom (*Anxiety* 5), he too surreptitiously attempts to subvert influence from a foreign tradition.

Barnstone's theory importantly invites needed consideration of intermediary renderings from other languages through which original source poems are brought into English. Though acknowledged by Yohannan and others, Emerson's reliance on German translations of Persian verse remains somewhat critically overlooked, especially insofar as it influences the development of his aesthetic. To some extent failure to more fully consider Emerson's engagement with German renderings exemplifies the frequent disregard of texts beyond those in the originating source or receiving literary traditions. Because intermediary translation, or "relay translation," interposes greater distance between source and translated text, it typically has been seen at best as a "necessary evil." As James St. André explains, "the assumption is that it is always preferable to translate from the original, just as it is always preferable to read the original than the translation" (230). Though generally true, as Gideon Toury correctively argues, such a translation practice "can be taken as evidence of the forces which have shaped the culture in question, along with its concept of translation." In this respect, continues Toury, "mediated translation should be taken as a *syndromic* basis for descriptive-explanatory studies" (129). For Emerson, the intervening German renderings of von Hammer-Purgstall between original Persian and translated English affords a conceptually rich creative realm that shapes much of American translation, wherein he can reconfigure both ideas of poetry and himself as poet-translator. It is less about losing a particular word equivalence—first through Persian into German, then German into English—than gaining a sense of proximity to a more foreign and ancient tradition. Tending to "emphasize the 'messy' nature of the translation process and the blurring of lines between original, translation, ADAPTATION, and PSEUDOTRANSLATION" (St. André 232), relay translation much like the site of Emerson's transparent eyeball opens a formative space for new orientations and interventions. Toury goes so far as to claim that "no *historically* oriented study of a culture where indirect translation was practiced with any regularity can afford to ignore this phenomenon and what it stands for" (130). At an important time in his development as a writer as well as the formation of American literature, Emerson discovered the Persian verse from von Hammer-Purgstall's relayed renderings and also from previous imitations by his Romantic German contemporary Goethe. Consequently, using the etymology of verse to follow the "turns" of the source text, he can be seen as inheriting in English his seemingly original claims upon a re-turn to Hafez and Sa'di around his transition through German. Retranslation thus becomes a means by which he reorients himself through his writing, figuratively renewing his voice and vision as if for the first time in the American tradition.

Significantly, "English's increasing dominance in the world of international exchange" has come to make it the predominant mediating language (St. André 231). Looking back to Emerson in this respect reveals how his early interventions with translation have helped give rise to contemporary Persian translators, covered in chapter 5, who render new Hafez and Rumi poems from English versions. One predominant strain of American translation from the nineteenth into the twenty-first century can be read as originating with Emerson's English reflections on German sources. Much as "it was often common in colonized territories for all knowledge of Europe to be mediated by one language, that of whatever European country happened to have control over the area" (St. André 232), English has come to dominate much of the world. Though various factors account for such a trend in translation, Emerson's all-encompassing vision embodied by what can be taken as the colonizing consciousness of his transparent eyeball effectively sees this dynamic coming.

In the triangle Barnstone draws to conceptualize the range from equivalence to free interpretation when rendering source texts into new languages, both Pound and Emerson as American poet-translators end up egregiously close to the far right of the spectrum, as shown in figure 1. Considering that

source author
originality

servile translator   new author
mechanical reproduction   *originality and imitation*

Figure 1.

Emerson and Pound somewhat ignore the real source poems by going through intermediary texts, in a sense they challenge the originating source author to the point of reinventing the translating self and the culture from which the source poem derives. In Emerson's case, such rebellious translation allegorizes his rejection of the Christian trinity and his incessant struggle with patriarchal literary inheritance. Like his own refusal to participate in communion, Emerson favors Hafez for the Persian poet's seeming rejection of Islamic strictures in a somewhat true though overdetermined reading of wine as metaphor for independence of spirit. "Hafiz does not write of wine and love in any mystical sense," he explains, "further than that he uses wine as the symbol for intellectual freedom" (*TN* 2:120). Emerson's sustained attempt of freeing himself from the original source text and author further demonstrates a patriarchal challenge with Oedipal implications. His opening sentence in the introduction of *Nature* takes aim at the top point of Barnstone's triangle: "Our age is retrospective. It builds the sepulchres of the fathers" (*CW* 1:7). Often Emerson's appropriation of foreign influence becomes so subversive that he appears to completely transcend the triangle. In calling himself Sa'di and claiming the vision of Hafez, he tries to overcome Persian influence, becoming alpha of the American tradition through a Platonic relation to a comparable divine source sought by the Sufi mystics. Instead of aspiring to a translating equivalence of the source text, he equates himself as much as possible to his predecessors' attempts at preceding all temporal and linguistic limitation, sharing their spiritual starting point in the pre-eternal, before and above all writing.

To consider Emerson's attempt at a hegemonic claim upon foreign influence that ultimately transforms his writing in the kind of alternate discursive realm described by Barnstone, wherein the poet-translator must invent a new voice to render the source text in the target language, Homni Bhabha's postcolonial concept of a "third space of enunciation" offers an additional theoretical approach. Applied mainly to traditional formations of hybrid literature, Bhabha's "third space" is understood as the circle embodied by the colonizer's culture and all it entails (language, tradition, etc.), which intersects with part of a circle from the colonized world. The intersection thus becomes a formative third space, embodying the synthesis of different traditions that transform into something new (52–56). While Emerson's America does not literally colonize the cultures it engages, its figurative approach to world literatures attempts to considerably render invisible the foreign through cultural appropriation. Emerson especially looked to various traditions with a kind of colonizing consciousness, subsuming significant difference through his all-encompassing transparent eyeball. Along such lines Mark Paryz argues that in his encounter with a "redefinition of history," Emerson "embodies a kind of postcolonial syndrome, which manifests itself in the writers' inability to express America on its own special terms" (20). Similarly reading Melville as attempting to create a more radical "newness" through an engagement with hybrid traditions, Geoffrey Sanborn locates a comparable analogue in Emerson's contemporary, wherein "the colonist must come into being by way of a postulated native" and vice versa (9).

Harish Trivedi's criticism of cultural translation that he attributes to Bhabha's seminal theory, which he claims has tragically caused "the very extinction and erasure of translation as we have always known and practiced it" (282), all the more necessitates its application to Emerson's frequent translingual claims upon the Persian poets. Closer consideration of Emerson's appropriation suggests that he anticipates and perhaps even initiates in the American tradition such problematic cultural translation. Though Trivedi locates the "postmodern idea of cultural translation" that remains both "nontextual and nonlinguistic" within the realm of contemporary Western literature (283), Emerson's much earlier adoption of foreign sensibilities beyond traditional translation in the very foundation of the American tradition warrants closer consideration. Bhabha's theory helps conceptualize and problematize Emerson's cultural reckoning beyond mere language difference, foregrounding the effects of translation, understood in a much broader sense than word meaning, upon the language and nation in which he wrote.

Intersecting Bhabha's theory with more traditional approaches to translation as well as to Bloom's understanding of influence provides an alternative discursive space to consider how Emerson's voice, predicated on visionary language, might derive both culturally and linguistically from elsewhere. Such interdisciplinary theoretical context thus outlines the presence of a formative influence that otherwise remains hidden. As such, it begins to make visible Emerson's seemingly transparent claims upon a first priority that dissemble important sources outside his assumed sphere of influence. Bhabha's interpretation of disruption in postcolonial hybrid literature, which "reimplicates its identifications in strategies of subversion that turn the gaze of the discriminated back upon the eye of power" (159–160), offers a productive means to interrogate the effect of Emerson's vision on Persian poets. More than investigating a niche influence for its local implications in Emerson's writing, exploring these visual implications allows for a greater meta-analysis of how Emerson clears figurative space to invite, appropriate, and ultimately adopt foreign literature as his own.

Before introducing such necessary theoretical correctives, chapter 1 first outlines the correspondence between Emerson's Platonic view of the world and the Sufism that informs the Persian poets he both translates and imitates.

Though his Platonic and Neoplatonic connection to Persian poetry and other foreign literature has been consistently referenced by scholars, the extent to which it establishes an aesthetic that enables him to claim the verse of Hafez and Sa'di as his own has yet to be fully explored. His emerging and sustained interest in Persian poetry from a young age and through the development of his writing career, juxtaposed with a Platonism that obviated temporal and even linguistic differences of classical foreign verse, reveals how he so easily came to sanction his literary appropriation. More specifically, Emerson's Transcendentalism, best represented by his belief in the Over-Soul, proves so close to the Sufi mystic's relation to nature as well as the insistence on an all-encompassing indivisible unity that at times it seems to have anticipated it. In this respect Emerson's overarching theoretical reach comes before his own more practical poetic attempts to establish himself prior to even the classical Persian verse tradition that he will introduce to America.

To exemplify how Emerson more specifically clears figurative space in the American tradition with such Platonic underpinnings, which in turn enables his attempt to claim as predecessor the Persian poet's mystic vision, chapter 2 introduces the trope of the mirror from Sufi mysticism in comparison to the all-seeing transparent eyeball on Boston Common. Revisiting the rhetorical accounting of Emerson's transformation into visual transparency better allows for theoretically tracking how he attempts to polish away all material distraction to reach an elusively transcendent spirit much like the ancient poets of Iran trying to reach the divine. Using the theories of Bloom, Bhabha, and Barnstone to expose Emerson's appropriative attempts, the transparent eyeball can be seen as an intertextual site subsuming the discovery of Persian poetry into his own far-reaching American sphere of influence.

Essentially declaring himself "nothing" yet able to "see all" (CW 1:10), he makes an early claim upon the Sufi mystic vision of Hafez, anticipating his own discovery of the great poet from Iran, who, he remarks, "sees too far." Though he finds himself so distantly intrigued by Hafez's predecessor vision that he declares, "Such is the only poet I wish to see and be" (JMN 10:165), he still attempts to become him in the Sufi mirror, polishing away as much influence as possible while transforming his predecessor into all-encompassing visual agency. Close consideration of Kane's comparison of the rend in Sufi mysticism to Emerson's rhetorical self-reduction, as well as an examination of the inherently disconnected Persian form of the ghazal in relation to the American poet's fragmented sensibility, invites further correspondence with the Persian poets by revealing how Emerson attempts to obviate influence by rhetorically subverting a fixed or unified identity.

In addition to locating in the transparent eyeball the primal lyric tension that invites yet clears away all predecessors, such a reading further necessitates an examination of what Emerson rhetorically represses to make himself, along with the formative effects of texts he uses for self-definition, so hard to find. Taking the transparent eyeball that inhabits the paradoxical reporting of his invisibility as definitive trope for the transformation of his Romantic identity as well as his relation to influence makes his relative disappearance at such key biographical moments as the death of his own son in "Experience" especially worthy of further interrogation. Using the theoretical framework developed in a close reading of Emerson's transcendence that seemingly erases predecessors, along with the American writer himself, the discovery of multiple drafts of an especially emotional Sa'di poem about the loss of the foreign poet's son begins to foreground how such repression of Persian influence returns much closer to Emerson's life and work. Following the "eye/I" pun in the spirit of the Persian poetic vision that Emerson uses to evade the constraints of his identity while attempting to subvert his role as literary heir to a foreign forefather begins to reveal his displaced grief over the death of Waldo, his literal descendent. Ironically, Emerson most surfaces as himself through the process of evading discovery with his translation of Persian verse.

With the figurative stage set upon which Emerson will begin to perform his Persian identity, chapter 3 offers extensive examination of both his seeming success and failure at Persian imitation by juxtaposing his close imitation of Sa'di, his adopted namesake, with his thwarted attempts to repress the influence of Islamic fatalism that underpins the poetry he translates. Reading Emerson's favorite Sufi poets whose verse derives from their inherited religion against his adamant belief in self-determination presents a contradictory impulse difficult to reconcile. Such symptomatic tension exposes his otherwise rather unrecognizable strategy of incorporating the verse and identity of Sa'di within his Platonically comprehensive vision. Nowhere does Emerson become more paradoxical by depending on quotation in his famous essay "Self-Reliance" than when he quotes a fatalistic proverb of Imam Ali, cousin and son in law of the prophet Muhammad. Esteeming both Hafez and Sa'di for their self-reliant abilities to subvert the fatalistic cosmology of Islam that he disparages, Emerson problematically posits a statement that affirms predestination against his famous insistence upon individual agency.

Words attributed to Ali in this one paragraph as well as in the poem "Saadi," which serves as a model for "Self-Reliance," thus invite closer critical comparison between Emerson and the Sufi poets in their relation to fatalism. Repositioning Bloom's idea of influence in Bhabha's understanding of a hybrid "third space" reveals how Emerson actually locates his own struggle of freedom versus fate, exemplified in his essays "Fate" and "Power," in a dichotomy identified with Sufi philosophy that emerges from the *Qur'an*. The Islamic fatalism that Emerson disparages in his self-reliant praise of Hafez and Sa'di resurfaces in their seemingly more liberated verse, mirroring similar tension at the crux of his own quandary where "fate slides into freedom, and freedom into fate" (*CW* 6:20). Closely tied to the wrestling with language itself in an attempt to precede all determinants of meaning for a glimpse of the divine, the effect of Sufi mysticism upon Persian poets like Hafez further reflects Emerson's will to transcend and "see all" through a translingual gaze predicated on revealed wisdom beyond intellectual knowledge. In addition to explaining his general attraction to the spiritual nature of classical Persian poetry, such an analysis offers a compelling example as to just how close Emerson comes to both style and meaning of his foreign sources.

Following an examination of Emerson's rather uncanny reconciliation with the Islamic underpinnings in the rendering of Persian verse on his own terms, chapter 4 demonstrates just how significant Emerson's appropriative translation practices become in his attempt to transcend the integral importance of the foreign source text. Locating what can be seen as Emerson's emerging theory of translation based in part on the essays "Language," "The Poet," "Persian Poetry," "Quotation and Originality," and others helps account for how the combination of his Platonic and intertextual understandings of literature allows him to better foreground his creative interventions by subverting strict equivalence. Much like Albert von Frank considers Emerson's early understanding of poetics as transformative of his verse (*CW* 9:xxx), his broader rhetorical theories offer a means by which to understand both the radical development of his appropriative translation practices as well as their far-reaching influence upon his inheritors. Emerson's ultimate reversion of sources to a translingual origin based on image further reveals how he manages to deftly negate profound differences between literary traditions. Insofar as Ernest Fenollosa based his interpretation of Chinese writing on Emerson's way of looking at language and literature, which Pound in turn used in his own translation practices, this close reading proves especially foundational to better comprehending a generative theory for American verse starting in the nineteenth century.

The relation of Emerson's theoretical approach as developed in the aforementioned essays proves especially illuminating when applied to how he comes to view Persian poetry in the praxis of translation. The recurring comparative trope of the Sufi mirror used in this study can be seen in Emerson's own "meta-view" of translation via his extended metaphor of a critical telescope at the beginning of his essay "Persian Poetry." Looking as if with the first eye from his "Circles" essay, the expanse of temporal distance from an originating perspective between Emerson's nineteenth century and the classical verse tradition of Hafez and Sa'di becomes negligible. While Emerson filters his critical lens with his concept of "genius" that sanctions a great writer's use of quotation, the return of his gaze back to the ancient Middle East further enables him to thwart translation equivalence on his own appropriative terms. Through his theoretical reckonings, his concept of transcendent truth comes to reflect a translingual spiritual understanding comparable to the Sufi mystics' relation to the divine.

Just as the Persian poetry and its influence affect Emerson in ways previously unrecognized, Emerson in turn forgoes translation equivalence as he tries to see his Persian poets on equal terms in the Sufi mirror, face to face, yet in ways that continue to elude critical detection. Reading his *Notebook Orientalist* that tracks his reflections of Persian verse as well as drafts of his English renderings as a kind of extensive translator's note further reveals his strategic designs upon the fantasy of becoming the foreign poets and writing their poetry. The closer he comes to Persian origins, the further he coopts them for his own aesthetic. Though Emerson's appropriation takes many forms, a survey of how he both contextualizes and anthologizes English renderings of Persian verse in translation offers a representative demonstration of his translation based on his rhetorical theories.

Chapter 5 brings full circle the outline of Emerson's hybrid third space oriented around his transparent eyeball, examining the discursive implications of his influence on American translators of classical Persian verse in the twentieth and twenty-first centuries. Coleman Barks and Daniel Ladinsky, whose translations of Persian poetry remain best-sellers, radically pervert their inheritance of Emerson's appropriative influence. This becomes especially noteworthy in their overt slighting of the religious underpinnings in the source texts. Though Emerson dismisses the fatalism he associates with Islam, his close identification with his Persian predecessor's self-liberation paradoxically renders a relative fidelity to their religious influence. While following much of Emerson's model, his American inheritors often outright dismiss such an integral sense of the foreign verse by straying too far from original sources. As Coleman Barks said of his Rumi renderings in English, "I took the Islam out of it" (Curiel). Both Barks and Ladinsky, who remain rather ignorant of the Persian language, culture, and literary tradition, creatively intervene in their interpretation of the original verse significantly beyond Emerson's established approach. Though the former works more closely with previous English renderings, at times he follows the latter into problematic variances from Persian sources.

Relating these translators' appropriative practices, along with contemporary American poet Matt Rohrer's egregiously loose translations of Hafez, to those previously examined in this study helps to substantiate Emerson as a harbinger of what has become an especially American approach to rendering foreign verse into English. Like Emerson imagining himself as Saʿdi, Barks allegorizes Rumi's love for his great mystic teacher Shams with a translation backstory involving his self-chosen *murshid*, or spiritual Sufi mentor, which justifies his intuitive renderings of Persian verse. Ladinsky actually claims that the fourteenth-century Persian poet came to him in a dream and asked him to translate his work. The selection process by which these contemporaries choose some poems for anthologizing further mirrors Emerson's style of excerpting translated lines according to his own predilections. Reminiscent of Emerson before them, Ladinsky, Barks, and Rohrer also claim a radical creative translators' license in their respectively inventive translations and imitations of Persian poets. Though these three translators initially approach foreign sources in ways seemingly inherited from Emerson, they extend and amplify the potential problems inherent in their predecessor's model for their own aesthetic agendas.

To show how Emerson's especially accommodating rhetorical strate-gies related to translation paradoxically offer their own necessary correctives to such egregious appropriation, the final chapter examines two alternative contemporary approaches that at least in part originate from the progenitor American in the nineteenth century. Critical commentary by poet-translator and esteemed Persian scholar Dick Davis, along with stylistic strictures and examples of the Persian *ghazal* by the Kashmiri-American poet Agha Shahid Ali, follow Emerson by achieving greater integrity of the foreign verse through comparable creative interventions. Despite ample erudition about source texts as well as originating language and culture, both poets often more productively revert to their predecessor's especially liberating influence, following his gaze back to Iran as well as to the origins of the American tradition.

As Davis attempts to qualify the impossibility of an English rendering in his essay "On Not Translating Hafez," well known in translation studies for its articulation of what gets culturally and linguistically lost in translation, he ironically tries to translate the various literary qualities of Persian verse that he claims can't be brought into English. His entire essay significantly challenges his own admonition that his domestic verse tradition fails to offer any comparable model to the panegyric mode of the self-abased Persian poet to his subject matter by debasing his receiving English language and culture while reverentially esteeming the source text of Hafez. In this respect he can be seen as figuratively resisting the all-encompassing translation theory of Emerson, outlined in chapter 4, even as he embodies it. Explicating such paradoxes in Davis's criticism reveals how Emerson's gaze in the Persian mirror at the site of the transparent eyeball, wherein he becomes "nothing" while seeing "all," continues to determine contradictory impulses in the study of translation among even the most erudite of Persian scholars. The greatest example offered in support of Emerson's effect upon poet-translators surfaces in this chapter, when after seemingly irrefutable logic about the inevitable loss of Persian poetry and the impossibility of bringing the foreign verse into English, Davis nevertheless publishes his own renderings of Hafez. At least in part, Emerson's previous demonstration can be seen as sanctioning his creative transcendence over so many linguistic and cultural limitations.

Unlike Davis, who begins by critically disavowing attempts at classical Persian translation, Agha Shahid Ali demonstrates a practical corrective to stylistic appropriation in verse renderings by writing his own English poems in the Persian form of the *ghazal*. As an Eastern poet who immigrated to the United States, Shahid Ali most significantly re-introduced the Persian form (in which many of Emerson's earlier translations first emerged) to American audiences in the late twentieth century. More than literal renderings of Persian sources, his creative introduction of the *ghazal*, both in criticism and in praxis, ironically offers perhaps the most authentically equivalent English translation in spirit as well as in letter thanks in part to Emerson's example. Following his American predecessor's cultural appropriation of Persian verse, Shahid Ali takes his own radical cut-and-paste approach to include disparate multicultural traditions and voices in a form that tends to invite Emerson's intertextuality. Attempting his demonstration of ego-transcendence in English through the paradoxical formation of a Romantically individuated voice contingent on the words of other writers, he mirrors Emerson's spiritual vision, along with the Persian poets to whom he attributes origination of the form.

Poets and translators concluding this chapter ultimately reveal Emerson's early and essential influence on both the American as well as Persian verse traditions. In getting so close to his foreign source material through his subversive rhetorical strategies of literary appropriation, he tends to anticipate his Sufi predecessors. Translators and poets who would offer new renderings or imitations of the old therefore must go through Emerson's writing as much, if not more, than original Persian sources.

Chapter 1

From Plato to Persia

Emerson's Transnational Origins

The unity of Asia and the detail of Europe, the infinitude of the Asiatic soul, and the defining, result-loving, machine-making, surface-seeking, opera going Europe—Plato came to join, and, by contact, to enhance the energy of each . . . In short, a balanced soul was born . . .

—Emerson, *The Collected Works of Ralph Waldo Emerson* (4:31)

For Emerson, Platonic integration of Persian poetry begins at an almost mythic level. Much like Zeus in the *Symposium* split the original two-faced, four-legged, and four-armed human, which then sent the respective halves looking to each other for wholeness, East and West for him provoke sustained lyric tension in an attempt to realize ultimate unity. In his essay on the ideal philosopher from which the above epigraph derives, he attributes Plato's journey beginning in his native Greece, then on to "Egypt" and his "eastern pilgrimages," as having "imbibed the idea of one Deity" (*CW* 4:30–31). According to his own criteria, "Every great artist" achieves such a "synthesis" (*CW* 4:31). While Platonism sanctions Emerson's accommodation of many transnational influences, localizing its implications to his reading of Persian verse proves especially instructive. Insofar as for Emerson, "Man is only half himself . . . the other half his expression" (*CW* 3:4), his romantic embodiment of Hafez and Sa'di in the American Renaissance leads to his figurative rebirth as a "balanced soul" between disparate literary traditions. Taking the East as the site of the beloved, which for the classical Persian poet in the verse form of the *ghazal* becomes the desired object leading to the divine, offers him a kind of aesthetic, if not spiritual, completion.

Lacking knowledge of the source language, Emerson's reading of Persian poetry in translation nevertheless identifies significant stylistic and spiritually thematic correspondences. While chapters that follow qualify the limits of such attempted synthesis, a brief comparative outline instructively foregrounds the extent to which his overarching aesthetic allowed him to so easily accommodate the voices of his classical foreign predecessors. Such an approach importantly heeds Lewisohn's call for a greater investigation of the philosophical underpinnings that inform Emerson's rhetoric as they relate to the Sufism found in Persian poetry:

> Just as the Romantics shared a fascination with Platonic philoso- phy and Neoplatonic esoteric doctrines, so the Persian poets were steeped in Sufi mystical doctrine and symbolism; for this reason any comparative study of Romantic and Sufi poetry must take such forms of esoteric speculation seriously, not dismissing it to the realm of the fanciful and fantastic. ("Romantics" 41)

Lewisohn's reading of Emerson's philosophy as analogous to Sufism impor- tantly emphasizes paralleling tendencies, as opposed to direct connections. Whenever possible, this study tries to foreground such analogous relations, despite the difficult, and at times impossible, task of separating the Ameri- can's Platonic conflation with the Persian's Sufi philosophy. William Chittick's extended metaphor for the religious basis of Sufi mysticism as the outer shell of a walnut, representative of the "ritual, legal, and social teachings of Islam" becomes especially helpful in understanding how Emerson effectively man- ages to capture a distinct yet significantly comparable transcendent spirit in the foreign verse while somewhat disregarding such indigenous influences as Islam. In this respect he resembles his twentieth- and twenty-first-century translating inheritors covered in chapters 5 and 6. With an insistence on an all-encompassing unity best exemplified by the Over-Soul, Emerson manages to crack into what Chittick calls the Sufi's "kernel" of "invisible light" held by the "husk" (424), extracting a spiritual essence that mirrors his own.

Briefly surveying the history of the Persian verse tradition shows how its religious origins risk getting lost in Emerson's translations. Emerging around the twelfth century with "mystical and esoteric interpretations" accompanying the spread of Islam (Katouzian 74), authentic Sufism began by considering the *Qur'an* as its foundational religious book and Muhammad, to whom it was revealed by the divine, as its living example (Geoffrey xvii). As the definitive source text underpinning Sufism, it remains as integral to the translation of Persian poetry as the *Bible* does for English renderings of Saint Augustine.

Though poets informed by Sufism lyrically play with lines and concepts from their religious text against more rigid interpretations by mullahs, they nevertheless tend to follow their mystic practice back to the revealed wisdom of the divine as first transcribed by their illiterate prophet. Hafez, arguably the most rhetorically intransigent of the Sufi poets of Iran and one of two classical masters to whom Emerson most devoted his Persian study, earned his pseudonym as "one who has memorized the Qur'an."

Instead of Emerson's variance from the Islamic underpinnings of the Persian poets inevitably leading to egregious misreading, his attraction to their spiritual transcendence over religious strictures frequently enables his relatively close correspondence to their divine intentions. Hafez proves such an ideal poet for Emerson in part because like the American's relation to Christianity he engages his Islamic tradition through poetic and philosophic subversion. In Emersonian fashion, Hafez in his inspired verse plays against the tension of religious constraint and empty, ritualistic performance. "Hypocrisy is the perpetual butt of his arrows" (CW 8:132), writes Emerson. As if projecting his own rejection of communion in "Bacchus," an imitation of his Persian counterpart, he calls for, "Water and bread, / Food which needs no transmuting" (CW 9:233). Much like Emerson, Hafez alternatively transforms his Islamic influence into original, transcendent verse that makes a religion out of poetry. Named for committing the words of the Qur'an to memory, he wrote the kind of timeless spiritual lines that well into the twentieth century Persian speakers and readers memorize alongside their holy book (Lewisohn "Prolegomenon" 16). Predisposed to verse that challenges established dogma, Emerson naturally could gravitate to the comparable sensibility of Hafez without excessive concern for his relation to Islam. If he misses the significance of specific allusions to the Qur'an in his English translations and imitations, he often captures the greater overall effect of the original Persian poetry.

While Emerson in a general sense tends to parallel the Sufi mystics' trajectory toward divine wisdom, he of course differs from their specific origins. With Muhammad as their first living mentor, the Sufis' ultimate goal from the inception of their practice was to spiritually ascend like the prophet preceding them via a "double ladder" of "spiritual discipleship," which includes a process of "repentance, denunciation, restitution before God" alongside "spiritual states" such as "love, contemplation," and "proximity to God" (Geoffrey 10). To a certain extent, this description begins to summarize an archetypal journey of spiritual development within most any religious practice, further revealing how Emerson could so easily accommodate such an influence. However, the Sufi tradition remains contingent upon the unique transmission of wisdom between mentor and student (Burkhardt XV). Such a relationship stretches

back to the prophet as first teacher. As important, its divinely inspired pedagogical objective substantially differs from Western conceptions of spiritual
instruction more aligned with an individuated experience with the divine,
considering that there is nothing like "the same continuity in Islam between
God and creation." Instead, the Sufi seeks the complete obviation of self
through "*fana*" or "extinction in God" (Geoffrey 14).

Nevertheless, following Lewisohn's example of a critical parallel, Emerson
through his ideal Over-Soul approaches a comparable transcendence with
his American ladder, journeying alongside the Sufis in their ascension by
attempting to reach his own conception of a divine source. Lacking a literal
mentor, he analogously positions himself at times as both teacher and student
of Hafez and Sa'di. As will be shown in chapter 3 with a comparative reading of fatalism connected to a spiritual reckoning with the veil of language,
by both following as well as attempting to precede the lines of the Persian
poets, Emerson Platonically positions himself in the realm of the pre-eternal
much like Hafez through his divine vision aligned with Islam. To return to
Chittick's metaphor of the walnut, Emerson can partially discard the shell of
the foreign religion to share the Sufi's deeper spiritual essence.

Irrespective of such distinctive features and prior to Emerson's syncretic
connections to the general sensibility that he found in the verse of Persian
poets, Sufism's spiritual basis has long been associated with broader religious
and philosophical connections. Its name, referenced by Muhammad, was first
derived from the Arabic word for the wool cloak worn by the early Sufi mystics
as a symbol of "ascetic piety"[1] (Brujin 4), which closely associates with what
the Christian monks wore during the tenth century (Geoffrey 5). Thematically
following such a sartorial thread, there is reasonable speculation that either
the philosophy of Platonus or Philo "indirectly nourished Sufi metaphysics
and cosmology" (Geoffrey 34). Winston Waugh specifically places the reach
of Neoplatonism in sixth-century Persia, and despite its conception of a much
more abstract God, he foregrounds sufficient correspondences with Sufism
such as the "supreme good as the source of all things" and the "ascension to
the true source of being through contemplation" (16–17). Ultimately the first
and fundamental principle of the Islamic faith, "God's unity" (Chittick 423),
resembles the Neoplatonist's tenet that all of reality derives from a unifying
oneness. Insofar as "the idea of the ecstatic union with the One" remained
an especially key teaching for Emerson from Neoplatonic philosophy (Richardson 348), it no doubt made him ready to accommodate this core idea
found in Sufism.

Though the distinction between Platonism and Neoplatonism certainly
warrants extended qualification, this study follows Emerson's tendency to

disregard specific differences in support of the seemingly comprehensive and all-inclusive perspective afforded by his reading of ancient Greek philosophy. As Loloi explains, "Emerson's study of Platonism, Neoplatonism and Orientalism were concurrent" (108). Ekhtiyar further establishes Emerson's Eastern and Western ecumenical bibliography, noting that by 1830 he had been "introduced to the philosophy of the various schools of thought in India and ancient Persia." Around the same time, Emerson was "impressed with the philosophy of Plotinus and by its effect on Oriental thought," wherein Neoplatonism coincides with his interest in Zoroastrianism (57).

While the Neoplatonists might be thought of as more explicitly subsuming all of reality within individual unity, their ultimate variance from their founder was seen by Emerson as relatively negligible and easy to conflate in his rather all-accommodating perspective. Much like how the Neoplatonists introduced a greater syncretism in the Middle Ages that influenced Islamic, Christian, and Jewish thinking, Emerson in his time interposes the Western philosophic tradition within his reading of Eastern religions, most notably his approach to the Vedic texts of Hinduism. His own early reading reinforced such Platonic integration of foreign ideas. Joseph de Gerando's *Historie comparée des systèmes de philosophie*, for example, helped him come

> to the realization that ancient Hindu, Chinese, and Persian thought
> was on a philosophical par with Hebrew, Greek, and Christian
> and that it was not only entitled to serious attention but was a
> probable source for fresh insight. (Richardson 104)[2]

That Sufism from its Islamic basis began moving into poetry as early as the tenth century (Katouzian 74) allowed Emerson an even more accessible Platonic accommodation of its ideas. By the time Sa'di and Hafez emerged in the city of Shiraz, respectively during the thirteenth and fourteenth centuries (the height of what is considered the Persian literary golden age), their verse invited rather inclusive interpretations. A predominant theme of "Unity of Being" established in such poetry (Bayat and Jamnia 11) continues to broaden and accommodate varied Western, Platonically informed influences, as exemplified by how Sufis considered "great figures of the old and new testaments as masters of the path" (Bayat and Jamnia 12). Poets incorporating such allusions with "varying degrees of seriousness," from profound sincerity to "little more than fashionable rhetoric" (Davis, *Faces* xiii), further reveals the ease with which they could engage different traditions. If Hafez, who so closely follows the *Qur'an* in his work, found the greatest "*metaphysical* stumbling block of egocentric vision" to be the binary division of personal identities, then its best antidote became immersion in seemingly inclusive unity (Lewisohn, "Puritans of Islam" 173).

Such appeals to the universal with Islamic underpinnings as well as to comparably all-encompassing Platonic influence respectively position Emerson and the Persian poets in a mutual meaning-making site that seemingly anticipates all differences. With exceeding literary playfulness beyond strict intellectual identification, Sufism's greatest resemblance to Plato coheres around the inclination toward a return to primal origination, the mystic's "stages of the remembrances of the Friend" akin to "true knowledge," which for Plato would be considered "recollection" (Brujin 8). In support of such a lyric drive toward the spiritually ineffable in Sufi verse, Leili Anvar remarks how the poetry of Hafez "produces mirror images that reflect what usually cannot be imagined, vocalized, or remembered" (124). As if further referencing Emerson's figurative rebirth in the union of East and West while conjoining Sufism with Platonism, Anvar claims that the fourteenth-century Persian master's poetry, "aims at reanimating the memory of the soul's preeternal life" (128). Such an ideal return considerably relates to the Sufi mystic's ultimate goal of annihilation that collapses the "false distinction and discrimination of separate personal 'identities' ('you' vs. 'me') . . ." (Lewisohn, "Puritans of Islam" 173).

The implications of such Platonic correspondence, which become clear in close readings of Emerson's verse related to Iran, culminate in radically sanctioning the disregard of differences in language, literary tradition, religion, and even time. The Persian poets inheriting from Sufism an "a-temporal relation to our source of being and the intelligible world to which we once belonged" allows Emerson to project onto them a rather similar Platonic obviation of history. As important as source languages remain in any discussion of literary translation, Emerson further follows the Sufi mystics in his conception of an ideal poet who can "speak through the symbolic language of nature" (Loili 112). Important to an application of Emerson's approach to translation and its early effect on his own verse, such a seemingly translingual symbolic connection helps to build a strong case for his having anticipated Ezra Pound's appropriation of the East in his influence of the American poetic tradition.

Despite distinctive tenets of Sufi philosophy surfacing in Hafez, Lewisohn further views the spirituality in his verse at times as transcending any "theological conflicts" with "an ecumenical call for the unity of religions" ("Puritans of Islam" 187). Similarly, although Sa'di exemplifies specific Sufi teachings with Islamic resonances in his writing, especially with his instructive stories, he too tends toward an all-encompassing unity. His famous "Bani Adam" or "Children of Adam" poem inscribed on the entrance of the United Nations and once read by President Obama in a videotaped message to the Iranian people during the Persian New Year, heeds a comparable "ecumenical call":

> The sons of Adam are limbs of each other,
> Having been created by one essence.
> When the calamity of time affects one limb
> The other limbs cannot remain at rest.
> If you have no sympathy for the calamity of others
> You are unworthy to be called by the name of Human. ("Bani
> Adam")

Despite the *Qur'anic* origins of these lines in Islam, referring back to God breathing life into Adam (*Sura* 15:29), they quite easily extend their reach to encompass broader humanistic themes amenable to the West. Politically bringing Obama's recitation of the Persian tradition full circle, in a 1998 televised good-will address to the United States, then Iranian President Mohammad Khatami recounted early New England history, respectfully identifying the underpinnings of American Christianity that influenced Emerson. In their respective ways both Eastern and Western citations exemplify how an especially accommodating approach much like Emerson's Platonism facilitates the close association, if not conflation, of traditions that seemingly overcome very distinct underlying differences. Echoing a similar correspondence in his journals, Emerson writes, "The heart of Christianity is the heart of all philosophy. It is the sentiment of piety which Stoic and Chinese, Mohometan and Hindoo labor to awaken" (*JMN* 5:478). Jahanpour tellingly summarizes such inclusiveness with reference to the originator of Sufism, writing that Emerson "seems to be echoing the famous sentence of Imam Ali, Prophet Muhammad's son-in-law and the first Shi'i Imam, that 'the ways to God are as numerous as human beings'" ("Emerson and the Sufis"). As will be shown in chapter 3, both in "Self-Reliance" and his Persian imitative poem "Saadi" upon which he projects his well-known American philosophy, Emerson directly quotes words from Ali in attempt to work them into his appropriative Platonic model.

Continuing to follow Lewisohn's analogical analysis between Emerson's relation to Sufism further allows for the suggestion of critical parallels that help explain how despite such transgressions he could so easily connect to his Persian predecessors, rendering them into his literary tradition on his own terms. To take Sa'di's poem featured at the United Nations as a unifying example, Sufi mystics consider Adam, the first man into whom God breathed life, as their ideal human (Schimmel, *Mystical Dimensions* 16). Insofar as the Sufi's ultimate goal is to return to original creation (Geoffrey 4), Adam obviously proves more transnationally inclusive than Muhammad, given the Islamic founder's exclusive predication upon Islam. That Adam in Sa'di's poem can be seen as more generally representative of "man as a revelation of divine attributes" (Loloi 107) appears both easily extractable and relatable to such a Platonic perspective. In this vein Mahnaz Ahmad extends an application of the Sufi "Doctrine of the Universal or Perfect Man" to Walt Whitman, insofar as the progenitor nineteenth-century poet seemingly embodies a comparable ability of the mystic to "realize all possibilities" of the human being in a "total and conscious state," as the "Perfect Man" (154). As will be shown in close readings of Emerson's translations and imitations throughout this study, so too does the American poet-translator whom Whitman revered as a kind of *murshid* or spiritual teacher, attempting to establish himself, even prior to his contemporary, as literary American Adam. Though he does so without the mystic's same spiritual intentions, his figurative trajectory often mirrors that of the Sufi, especially as represented in Persian poetry. Ironically, in attempting to displace much of what informs the foreign poets who he comes to imitate, he ends up establishing himself in his own literary tradition as a Western version of the first man and even a scandalous version of the prophet transcribing his Romantic take on divine revelation.

Such revelation connects Emerson to the Sufi mystic's reliance on inner experience, as opposed to rote knowledge, for divine wisdom. His correspond-ing understanding to the Persian poets can be attributed in part to his early reading of Scottish "Common Sense" philosophy, which argued for an inherent "moral sentiment" within human beings able to discern from within a differ-ence between good and bad (Richardson 32). More than rational deduction or sensual experience, "knowledge of the heart" figures as the greatest source of Sufi wisdom (Schimmel, *Mystical Dimensions* 4). Predicating their com-parison upon such intuition, comparative scholars cite the "close resemblance to Emerson's Transcendentalism and Hafez's mysticism" (Khojastehpour and Fomeshi 116). As Emerson writes, "The soul is the perceiver and reliever of truth" (*CW* 2:166). Like the purification process wherein the Sufi rids himself of ego, Emerson further contends that the revelation "comes to whomsoever will put off what is foreign and proud" (*CW* 2:171). Much like the Sufi's challenge to the strictures of the Islam from which they derive, Emerson's famous divinity address "proposed as counterweight to formal religion not atheism but a personal religious consciousness" (Richardson 288). To get a sense of Emerson's eventual connection of Eastern and Western philosophies at perhaps its most essential level, consider Brujin's observation of how closely Muhammad's words resonate with such a Platonic realization informative of the Over-Soul: "Whosover knows himself knows his Lord; that is, self-knowledge leads to Knowledge of the divine" (6). Emerson comparably claims that "within man is the soul of the whole . . . the eternal ONE" (*CW* 2:160). Here again Ahmad's relation of Sufism to Whitman applies just as much to Emerson, as the doctrine of "transcendent unity of being" defined by a "belief in the interconnectedness of all creation" (154) also sounds remarkably like the "Over-Soul." Read more overtly as influenced by Indian religion, Emerson's 1844 essay nevertheless also encompasses much of what can be considered as thematically relatable to Sufism. Though the mystic practice derived from Islam of course has radically different origination than Emerson's inherited tradition, its reliance on inner wisdom tends to sound in a broad sense rather proto-Romantic. A version of Sufism's most basic definition, found in the early pages of a kind of elementary mystic primer, involves "following the Prophet to denote the heart knowledge as opposed to the mind" (Lings 40). Leaving out the Prophet as medium or teacher, the same could apply to Emerson's search for more meaningfully transcendent realization.

Intellectualization, specifically linked to ponderings of the *Qur'an*, certainly still matters to followers of the mystic path. Emerson of course also greatly prizes reason. Having purchased a copy of the "Alcorn" in 1833, rather early in his Orientalist reading (Einboden, *Islam* 190), he quite possibly began to study it with great interest. Even so, like his Sufi predecessors who attempted to break with traditional modes of learning (Schimmel, *Mystical Dimensions* 18), he tends to favor revealed insight over rational deduction. As his essay "The Over-Soul" explains, "The philosophy of six thousand years has not searched the chambers and magazines of the soul" (*CW* 2:159). In this respect, Emerson's prose as much as his verse frequently begins to sound like followers of Sufism. Lines from this same page, such as "Man is a stream whose source is hidden," might easily have been extracted by Hafez as well as more contemporary Sufi philosophers such as Inyat Khan.

By critical consensus, the intuition of Sufism further connects to Emerson through wisdom predicated on phenomenological insight. Husayn Ilahi-Ghomshei's summation of Hafez's cosmological view could generally apply to Emerson's Over-Soul: "For Hafiz, the entire world reflects the grace and loveliness of the divine countenance" (83). Further assessing Hafez through his reading of the Sufis, Lewisohn explains that it is "through the Romantic experience of becoming ensnared by earthly beauty through contemplation . . . that the mystic paradoxically contains release from the bonds of selfhood" ("Prolegomenon" 51). Though the Persian Sufi poets would specifically look to the beloved, in a broader interpretation they also follow Emerson in his physical engagement with the material world. According to Richardson, for Emerson "the spiritual appears only through the senses" (424), which rather closely relates to how the Sufis also sought an experiential realization of a higher wisdom. Even more specifically like the Sufis, Emerson believed that "the ideal poet should speak through the symbolic language of nature" (Loloi 112). Seemingly articulating a further Platonic connection, Obeidat claims that in addition to Emerson favoring the Sufi poets because of their "mental vastness," he resonated with their ideal of the "perfection of man and nature" (84).

From his earliest interests beyond his inherited European literary tradition, Emerson began to establish a philosophical view of the East in relation to Persian verse informed by Sufism that helped him disregard such essential differences of culture and even language. As Carpenter explains, "for Emerson Neoplatonism opened the door to the study of Oriental literature and philosophy," (43) adding that his initial introduction to Eastern literature "depended on Neoplatonic translation of Thomas Taylor and others" (45). Looking beyond his Western tradition seemed to offer a spiritual expanse that he could attempt to reconcile with his own American positioning. Starting in his college years, he begins to consider the continent that contains both Iran and the farther East as a kind of metonymy for mysticism, expressing the desire to write a long poem called "Asia." At seventeen years old, he looks beyond the English and even the trans-European tradition to what he considered the locus of more formative origins, noting, "all tends to the mysterious east . . ." (*JMN* 1:12). In a letter written at nineteen years old to his Aunt Mary Moody Emerson, who significantly introduced him to both Oriental literature along with works of Plato and Platonius[3] (Versluis 53), he imbues the East with childlike transcendent wonder: "Every man has a fairy compass just beyond his horizon . . . and it is very natural that literature at large should look for some fanciful stories of mind which surpassed example and possibility" (*Letters* 1:117). As a precursor to his deeper reading in literature from the Orient, the ideal function of literature becomes for Emerson a transcendence over the limitations of one's boundaries. More than intellectual intrigue, he begins to position the East as desired object in a kind of foreign romance. Anticipating the role of the beloved in the Persian verse that Emerson will come to translate, for whom the mystic spiritually and physically longs in hopes of ultimate divine unification, he will come to call Lidian, his second wife, "Mine Asia" (Carpenter 30).

Emerson's early and sustained reading of Plato seems to have prepared him for a deeper investigation of Eastern poetry. As "the single most important source of Emerson's lifelong conviction that ideas are real because they are the forms and laws that underlie, precede, and explain appearances"

(Richardson 65), Plato allows the American philosopher to accommodate and often even obviate barriers of understanding between the Persian and his own verse traditions. That Emerson preferred to read Plato in translation despite an ability to read Greek (Richardson 65) proves rather significant, considering how he goes through both German and English translations to access Persian poetry. In this respect, his contextual study of Plato becomes a kind of allegory for his eventual reading of Persian source texts, wherein over the years to access the former he "dug down through successive layers of translation, commentary, and editorial arrangement until he came to the real thing" (Richardson 65).

By 1836, an important year marked by the publication of *Nature* and a little over a decade since he started a more intensive reading of Plato (Richardson 65), Emerson had also come to read the *Zendavesta*, a series of religious texts attributed to the ancient Iranian prophet Zoroaster. At this time he was also reading eighteenth-century English translations of Persian poetry by Sir William Jones. Tracking Emerson's reading practices, which includes in this same period the *Arabian Nights* as well as Arabian proverbs, Arthur Versluis significantly identifies an Eastern "movement through Neoplatonic texts toward more and more Oriental works" (54). Supporting such a trajectory, Jahanpour comparably "charts the journey" of Emerson's Western spiritual sensibility "from a narrow and dogmatic outlook towards a mystical, universal outlook" found in the Orient ("Emerson and the Sufis"). By 1841, Versluis observes Emerson achieving the kind of simultaneous reconciling of differences foregrounded in the Platonically divided self—introduced in the epigraph to this chapter—as extended metaphor for his attempt at unifying East and West, noting how he read "both Neoplatonic and Asian texts," which included "Plotinus, Hermes Trismegistus, Synesius, Proclus, and Olympiadorus" alongside Sa'di and Hafez (55). Even prior to Emerson's direct relation to the Orient, the English Romantics, who as his near contemporaries he of course read with great interest, modeled a similar "conjunction of Platonism, NeoPlatonism, and Eastern teaching or mythology" (34).

After an early aggrandized ideal of the Eastern continent, Emerson soon moves from such meta-reflections to a closer reading of literature from Iran, yet he maintains the same figural relation to Persian verse as he attempts to unify himself and his Western tradition to the more specific Oriental other. Significantly, before his earnest reading of von Hammer-Purgstall's German translations of poetry by the Persian masters, Emerson read W.F. Thomson's translation of Jalal al-Din Davani's *Akhlaq-i Jalali* (*Jalalian Ethics*), a kind of handbook that in part accounts for how Platonism was introduced to Persian mysticism (Ekhtiyar 58). The Islamic scholar Carl Ernst calls the text a "synthesis of Greek philosophical ethics with Islamic values" (121). Emerson's literary encounter with Islam through this accessible Persian book naturally reinforced the recurring theme of conjoining Eastern and Western traditions. As he notes of his reading of it in Alger's translation, *The Practical Philosophy of the Mohammaden People*, the book reconciles Greek Philosophy "with the social and religious system of the Mohammedans" (Carpenter 198–199). Written in the fifteenth century at a time when "cosmopolitan scholars were taking ideas from Plato and Aristotle as well as from the Koran," its English translator comments that it holds "all visible and conceivable objects to be portions of the divine nature." He further wrote that it should have been called "Transcendental Ethics" (Richardson 406), a rather Emersonian summary and title. As to be expected, Emerson favored the concluding lines, which, quoted by Richardson, sound very much like something the American poet-philosopher would have written: "Let it be the object of your constant endeavor to instruct both others and yourself" (406).

From early in his personal development as a writer, Emerson begins to self-identify with such Eastern texts. Prior to his public performance of Sa'di's voice, he adopts in his private journal the name "Osman," an "Islamic alias, mirroring himself in a Muslim persona" (Einboden *Islamic Lineage* 129). Though the direct source from which Emerson derives his first Eastern name remains speculative,[4] its appearance in Alger's published translation that he read a year before his first personal use of the name suggests a strong possibility. Reference to "the infancy of the Osmanly empire" in the book attempts to validate the worthiness of the East for study, if not veneration, especially as such a brief historical tracking a few paragraphs later leads to esteeming the "Augustan age of Persian letters" (XVII). Both a Turkish and Persian translation of the name "Uthman"—one of the earliest converts to Islam—"Osman" remains loaded with linguistic and historical ambiguity. Its resistance to a firm critical conclusion rather deftly extends and exemplifies the figural reach of Emerson's engagement with the East.[5] In one journal entry, Emerson writes as Osman in the third person, noting rather independently that since "no one was there to serve him, he learned to serve himself" (*JMN* 7:503). Further setting a kind of stage for his eventual rhetorical performance of the thirteenth-century poet Sa'di, Emerson's editors of his journal in which he adopts the pseudonym note the inherent self-reliance found in "the isolation revealed by Osman's imagined sociality . . . described paradoxically by the American poet as both his 'doom' as well as his 'strength'" (Einboden, *Islamic Lineage* 129).

Emerson's alternative foreign interiority, representative of a divided self, continues to embody his search for a greater reconciliation between East and

West. Writing as Osman, he describes the individual summoning of what sounds a lot like what he will come to call the "Over-Soul": "Let a man not resist the law of his mind and he will be filled with the divinity which flows through all things" (*JMN* 7:450). Reinforcing this connection, Richardson notes that "at the end of *Nature*, when he was reaching for the highest, most authoritative voice possible, Emerson invoked 'a certain poet,' who was this Osman-self, a sort of personalized 'other.'" Emerson unconsciously identifies with his alter-ego through the recollection of a dream in his journal wherein "he walked with a pundit to whom he gave the name Osman" to write "about the world flowing out as emanation" (Richardson 349). Dramatizing Emerson's claim upon the founder of the Ottoman empire as his personal "daemon," Richardson further recounts Osman's own dream wherein a tree growing from his body begins to transform into a ring encompassing the entire world, reading this as the symbol for which Emerson continues to search (350). Informed by his early global reading and writing, such a psychic exploration can further stand for Emerson's emerging and expansive dream of Platonic unification.

Such assessments of Emerson's Eastern gaze so early in his development significantly define the trajectory of his comparative relation to Persian poetry throughout his career. Seeking to offer the most praise possible upon Plato as the first of his great "Representative Men," Emerson compares his writing to the received words of Allah in Islam's sacred text: "Plato only is entitled to Omar's fanatical compliment to the Koran, when he said: 'Burn the libraries; for their value is in this book'" (*CW* 4:23) Elsewhere, as cited in the epigraph of this chapter, he credits Plato with giving birth to the unification of East and West in the form of a "balanced soul." Taken as literally as possible, these statements begin to postulate an equation between the origins of Western secular philosophy and an Eastern religion that underpins the Sufi mysticism of the Persian poets. In his own writing, he would attempt such a Platonic realization introduced in the epigraph, reconciling "the defining, result-loving" effects of Europe as an elusive fantasy of Asia where signifier once and possibly still could link to the signified. In the epigraph, he begins to articulate an encompassing and holistic Orientalist gaze antithetical to what for him proved a much more differentiated, and therefore intimidatingly closer influence, from Europe. Of the latter, responding to the essay "History," Robert Weisbuch argues that Emerson "refuses the rivalry and substitutes for history the vertical time of the present moment that, rightly seized, leads to overwhelming truth and a nature of transparent magnificence" (203). In such a context, Emerson's relation to Persian poetry surfaces as a transcendent alternative to Western tradition.

This survey of Emerson's emerging bibliography consistently seems to reinforce Lewisohn's identification of "Platonic and neo-Platonic thought" as perhaps "the most important mutual philosophical heritage shared by Christian romantic and Muslim Persian Sufi poets and mystics" (*English Romantics* 17). The Platonic effect upon Emerson's engagement with the Eastern tradition proves so pervasive that it invites, if not insists on, violating the conventional chronological tracking of literary influence. Though up to this point a general linear sense of his early reading development indeed offers critical value to understanding his emerging transnational aesthetic, his own example continues to lead back, as opposed to forward, in time. Important for this study, his furthest reach into the deep past of a global literary tradition conflates the epic adversaries of the Greeks and Persians, connecting Plato to the ancient Persian prophet Zoroaster by as early as 1832, when he began comparing "Platonism to Zoroastrianism" (Ekhtiyar 57). Importantly, around this time Emerson also begins seeing a strong resemblance of Plato's theory of forms to the " 'Fravashi' of Zoroaster, which are the symbols of good action, good thought, and good words" (Ekhtiyar 57).[6]

Emerson's emerging Platonic relation to the oldest Persian writer from thousands of years ago best demonstrates his attempt to link, and at times even conflate, Iran to his Western literary tradition. Significantly, Zoroaster's *Zend-Avesta*, perhaps his earliest introduction to Persian literature (Ekhtiyar 55), is among the first books about Oriental philosophy he is credited with reading, having been exposed to an explication of it from Gibbons's *Decline and Fall of the Roman Empire* as early as 1820 (Ekhtiyar 58). Over the course of his career, he makes more references to Zoroaster than any other Oriental writer except Plotinus (Carpenter 217–218). Such paratactic proximity of the seminal Persian to the Neoplatonist in his citation tendencies significantly exemplifies comparative influence. While the writings attributed to Zoroaster available in the nineteenth century vary in their connection to Platonic thought (Carpenter 227), Emerson most seized on the fusion of Eastern and Western philosophic inheritors, as evidenced by the quote wherein he begins to identify his own poetics:

> Our best definition of poetry is one of the oldest sentences, and claims to come down to us from the Chaldean Zoroaster, who wrote it thus: "Poets are standing transporters, whose employment consists in speaking to the Father and to matter; in producing apparent imitations of unapparent natures, and inscribing things unapparent in the apparent fabrication of the world;" in other words, the world exists for thought: it is to make appear things which hide: mountains, crystals, plants, animals, are seen; that which makes them is not seen: these, then, are "apparent copies of unapparent natures." (*CW* 8:10)

Such a description closely reflects Plato's *Symposium* and *Phaedrus*, with the arts shadowing ideal forms of beauty (Lewisohn, "English Romantics" 21). So too for Hafez does "all creation serve as a mirror reflecting God's beauty and love" (Lewisohn, "English Romantics" 35). Using supposedly "one of the oldest sentences" by a Persian writer who validates a Platonic conception of the material world as copies of *a priori* hidden forms can be seen as effectively establishing Emerson's starting point in American poetry. Predicating his approach to the multitude of writing from all over the world that he directly engaged in his own work upon these words, he obviates the temporal and even linguistic relevance of various literary traditions. By focusing specifically on an ancient Persian text so close to Plato as he uses this quoted sentence for his own claims upon verse, he makes his respective Western relation to Iran especially essential, as though going as far back to Adam as possible. So much of Hafez's poetry "aims at reanimating the memory of the soul's preeternal life" (Anvar 128), a summation that sounds much like Emerson's Platonic view. Just as Hafez or Sa'di might intuit the spirit of the divine, so might Emerson through his own interventions of their verse produce "apparent copies of unapparent natures," a transcendent American Plato reconnecting to poetic inheritors of their Zoroastrian ancestor he claims as his own as if for the first time.

That supposed translations of Zoroaster's words Emerson read have been identified as possible forgeries (Carpenter 217–231) says even more about the American poet-philosopher's emerging interest in Persian literature and his self-sanctioned appropriation of it. As Carpenter has shown, Emerson most likely failed to read authentic renderings from the *Zend-Avesta*, otherwise known as the "Zoroastrian Bible," until as late as 1872. In addition to second-hand accounts and translated fragments, his main sources until that time derived from two spurious books: *The Chaldean Oracles*—significantly translated by Thomas Taylor, who brought works by Plato and NeoPlatonists into English, and *The Desatir, or Sacred Writings of the Ancient Persian Prophets* (*CW* 8:209 n69). Emerson's response to their possible falsity, to which this study will frequently refer in its consideration of his appropriative rhetorical practices, proves especially revealing about his relation to equivalence in translation. While the latter source text had its defenders,[7] in his essay "Books" he includes it within the "Bibles of the World" (*CW* 7:187), seemingly more intrigued with the greater spirit found in the translation and its superior rhetoric than with literal authenticity. As he wrote in his journal, he cared little about

> the question whether the Zend-Avesta or the Desatir are genuine antiques, or modern counterfeits, as I am only concerned with the good sentences; and it is indifferent how old a truth is, whether an hour or five centuries. (*JMN* 16:265)

This brazen claim, underpinned by Platonism, at once dismisses the veracity of source texts as well as the literary, temporal, and linguistic traditions in which they were originally written. About Zoroaster, along with Moses, Socrates, and others, Emerson writes, "I cannot find any antiquity in them" (*CW* 2:16). In what becomes an integral part of his emerging approach to translation and imitation, style proves even more important than factual content in his esteem of the ancient Persian prophet, insofar as statements of inspired "truth" revealed to Emerson transcend "centuries." Anticipating Emerson's later relation to Hafez and Sa'di, effective rhetoric constitutes Zoroaster's genuine value more than the historical integrity of texts ascribed to him. If for Emerson "man is only half himself, the other half his expression" (*CW* 3:4), then an aesthetic and even moral "goodness" can consequently be located in a "good sentence." By further implication, if Emerson himself can embody a comparable spirit found in the letters of others, he in part can inhabit their writing without ethical consequence of forgery or appropriation. The possible origins of the *Desatir* in this respect further support a reading of Emerson's attraction to the rhetorical performance of an Orientalist identity. Tracking the claim by an early nineteenth-century scholar that the seventh-century translator had only pretended to first bring the book from an invented ancient language into Persian, Joseph Slater notes that Emerson would most likely have been more intrigued with the "imposter" offering a false translation than "the authentic words of Zoroaster" (*CW* 3:187 n34–35). This displacement of the writer, relative to a translated text without stable linguistic referents in a source language, allows for radical self-invention. As Slater speculates about the idea of Emerson encountering the faux translator:

> [I]n this modern counterfeiter, a Sufi, in Isfahan, perhaps—forging
> a language, putting speeches into the mouths of mythical prophets,
> inventing commentaries on invented prophecies—he might have
> seen a new inventor, a new poet. (*CW* 3:187 n34–35)

While the extent of Emerson's knowledge about Sufi mysticism had been questioned as early as 1850,[8] "What did not seem to have limits was Emerson's sympathetic appropriations of the Sufi poets . . ." (*CW* 9:lxxii n49). Exploring the implications of such a relation to Emerson's Persian translations and imitations therefore greatly reveals how he appropriates by allowing himself to coopt verse as well as the identities of the poets who write it. Though this brief overview of Emerson's reading both Eastern and Western texts in relation to Platonic thought substantiates an early interest in Persian poetry, Richardson rightly sees his discovery of von Hammer-Purgstall's translations *Der Diwan von Mohammed Schemsed-din Hafis*, which he purchased in 1846 (Packer 101), as his "first real encounter." In the verse he read in German, "All appeals to him," including "directness, fondness for short forms, [and] wit" (Richardson 423). Much like Emerson's own American experiential relation to nature, here too as in earlier Eastern readings he finds that for the Sufi-influenced poets the "spiritual appears only through the senses" (Richardson 424).

To exemplify his identification with the volume from which he will render his English versions, consider how following his purchase of von Hammer-Purgstall's book he "comes to fill 250 pages of his notebook with translations of Persian poets, mostly Hafez." In addition to translating hundreds of his lines, Emerson's own verse becomes influenced by his predecessor (Richardson 425). Persian signifiers such as wine and roses begin to appear more in his writing. Richardson observes such influence surfacing in the conclusion of the poem "World Soul" (428), wherein roses represent nature's resilience:

> Over the winter glaciers,
> I see the summer glow,
> And, through the wild-piled snowdrift,
> The warm rosebuds below. (*CW* 9:40)

When considering the poem in its entirety, these quoted lines further Emerson's conflation of a Persian inheritance with his own New England tradition, represented by the opening setting in New Hampshire (*CW* 9:37). To such Platonically unifying ends, Emerson again posits his dichotomous relation between the spiritual East and the technological West. The effect of an "all-loving Nature" in an earlier stanza, informed by the concluding Persian metaphor of the rose, ultimately overcomes industry through a blissful "smile in a factory" (*CW* 9:38).

Like many scholars before him, Richardson's own comparative study metaphorically begins to reproduce Emerson's mixture of Eastern and Western influences. Emerson's hybrid rhetoric provokes such creatively critical responses, as if subsuming objective assessment with his foreign interventions. Speaking specifically of the poem "Bacchus," an imitation of verse by Hafez, he writes: "Emerson has poured his new Persian wine in an old Greek bottle creating a deliberate opposition and alternative to his earlier, Apollonian strain" (426). Such metaphorizing further reflects Emerson's heretical challenge to the rituals of the Christian tradition, with resonances of Jesus' response to the fasting of the Pharisees:

And no man putteth new wine into old bottles, else the new
wine will burst the bottles, and be spilled, and the bottles shall
perish. But new wine must be put into new bottles; and both
are preserved. No man also having drunk old wine straightway
desireth new: for he saith, the old is better. (Luke 5:36–39, KJV)

Allusions such as this in Emerson scholarship, as well as in the American
poet's own writing, dramatize his disruption of the Western tradition with
his interest in Iran and other Eastern literature. Provocative of lyric tension,
they combine the old and the new in Emerson's reading practices as well as
his approach to his own poetry.

Emerson's attempts to resolve such opposition between East and West
further lead to a transformation of his own voice along the theoretical lines
of Barnstone's aforementioned reading of translation as literary influence.
Paradoxically, such effects of the Persian poetry become most significant
when remaining unrecognizable. The "rosebuds" and other signifiers from the
foreign verse occasionally make explicit an even greater yet much harder to
recognize literary outpouring between Persian and American poetry. Richardson's metaphor of Emerson's wine bottle resurfaces in the Sufi verse tradition
as a definitive trope of divine reflection, another manifestation of the mystic
mirror-polishing so closely positioned against the transparent eyeball in the
following chapter that it frequently seems to disappear. Emerson's rejection
of Christian communion proves relevant in this context when considering
how for Hafez intoxication metaphorically embodies an authentic sense of
God as opposed to the mullah's empty religious rituals that the poet tends to
expose as hypocritical.[9] A couplet from *Ghazal* 10 by Hafez, which displaces
the morning prayer with the wine cup, aptly exemplifies such a rhetorical
tendency: "The seeker to whom they give such a cup at dawn / is an infidel
to love if he will not worship wine" (*Green Sea* 59). Though obviously writing and translating into a much different tradition than his revered Persian
poet's fourteenth century, Emerson reorients his aesthetic at the comparatively
transformative site of wine. His own imitation of Hafez in "Bacchus," which
itself reads as a formal displacement of his origins within a combination of
signifiers from both Greek and Persian verse, violates seemingly prescribed
literary norms as a kind of subversion. Extensively analyzed in the greater
context of his engagement with Hafez in a later chapter, the very title of this
Eastern imitation contains the spirit of Persian verse embodied in its central
and indigenous trope of wine within the name of the Greek god. Along with
such inherent tension between literature representative of ancient enemies,
however, Emerson simultaneously seeks Platonic reconciliation through the
familiar recourse of his Greek philosopher.

As so often with Emerson, his own appeals to original mastery ironically involve his appropriating the voices of others through such unification. In his personal copy of *The Poems*, he inscribes the following from Plato: "The man who is his own master knocks in vain at the doors of poetry" (Ekhtiyar 62). Though seemingly stuck in a heretically mimetic paradigm opposed to his insistence upon originality, subsuming disparate influences under Platonism (much like his cosmological view of the Over-Soul) allows him to see himself in a wine cup of an eternally emerging hybrid tradition. As Ekhtiyar observes, Emerson writing his essay "Persian Poetry" in 1848 allowed him to realize a "collapsing dualism" (68). Aminzavani aptly summarizes this ideal union, while importantly foregrounding the inherent ethical problem of such comprehensive appropriation:

> The fact that there is no such thing as a monolithic East and that the Orient consists of diverse cultures was overshadowed by the interest of European and American literary masters and intellectuals in developing a utopian model inspired by the East . . ." (2)

As in so many exemplary manifestations of his nation's culture, such as his philosophy of self-reliance, Emerson as representative author of a utopian model embodies his nineteenth-century America's rather Platonic approach to foreign verse. In part for Emerson's era this idealized Orientalist depiction of the East "gained popularity due to its compatibility with the spirit of Romanticism" (Aminzavani 2). Culturally, the impulse toward a fantasy of completion kept America looking, like Emerson, across the Atlantic for something analogous to the beloved in classical Persian poetry. As Loloi argues, Emerson and his contemporaries' "interest in Oriental Scriptures, as they called anything with religious and mystical qualities, was part of a desire for Universal Knowledge" (Loloi 113). The same relative ebb of Christianity that helps account for the rise of Transcendentalism in Emerson's New England considerably explains such attraction. Following the devastation of the Civil War, Americans also felt drawn to the spiritually palliative effects of Persian verse, resonating with the theme of "living in the present, accompanied by a lack of concern for the material and a focus on goodness, peace, and love" (Aminazavani 2). Tracking Emerson's selections of von Hammer-Purgstall's Persian translations from German that he brought to English, Yohannan's location of a predominating theme of unity ("Influences," 25) further reinforces the cultural need for an all-encompassing connection in the nineteenth century. As the fifth chapter of this study examining Persian verse translation in America's later twentieth century reveals, the same qualities continue to account for the popularity of Sufi mysticism untethered from its Islamic origins. "The spirit of universalism was so strong" during Emerson's time, explains Aminzavani, "that Islam itself was of little interest to American scholars." Surfacing as mere "context within which Sufi poetry and prose were composed," the religion of Hafez and Sa'di in translation was no longer considered "the true source of its message" (2). Looking so closely at Emerson as timeless American Adam, wherein a Platonic atemporality allows him to equate his verse tradition with that of Sa'di and Hafez from thirteenth- and fourteenth-century Iran, thus demonstrates an early and sustained orientation of a Western imitative gaze toward the East.

That Emerson inherits such an open view of Eastern poetry considerably divorced from its integral cultural sources ironically allows him to more radically claim the foreign tradition as his own. In the late eighteenth century, "Sufi poetry entered Western literary circles as versified adaptations or imitations" (Aminzavani 1), much like Emerson received them in German renderings. Since as early as 1790, among English translations of seminal Persian texts such as the *Divan* (*Collected Works*) of Hafez, Sa'di's *Gulistan,* and Firdousi's epic the *Shahnameh* (or *Book of Kings*), there were "no real attempts for especially faithful renderings" (Aminzavani 1). As Annemarie Schimmel makes clear, most significant knowledge of Sufism came only from the early Western reading of Persian poetry in translation, including Sa'di's *Gulistan* among European intellectuals (*Mystical Dimensions* 8). Romantic predecessors and contemporaries whose verse remained an influence on Emerson took a comparably broad and generalized view of Sufi poets, separating them from culturally specific sources (Loli 93). In this respect, "The image of the East as a place of great wisdom that possessed an esoteric knowledge lacking in the West gained popularity due to its compatibility with the spirit of Romanticism" (Aminzavani 3). In support of such aesthetic attraction, Christy aptly notes that in order to

> understand the "orientalism" of the nineteenth century we must comprehend the Romantic temper, which included more than mere poetic interest in something "far away and long ago." It was the expression of a state of mind rather than a literary movement. (37)

In his inheritance of the Persian verse tradition Emerson thus encounters, like his Romantic predecessors, the trans-humanistic themes corresponding to Sufism with which he closely identifies: "vanity of the world, the analogies between experience in nature and in love, and the inability of human reason to explain or address the worlds mysteries" (Aminzavani 2). Emerson perhaps best represents his nineteenth-century New England in "a search for that which unifies, and the need to discover the common humanity and decency of man," which therefore "made it necessary to break the barriers that religious traditions had imposed upon society." Greatly informed by Emerson's personal Platonic vision that begins with an attempt to unify his Romantic self-conception,

> The spiritual landscape of New England spread throughout the rest of America in the form of inspired movements such as Transcendentalism and Perennialism, which stated that the Muslim Sa'di, the Hindu Rabindranath Tagore, and the other masters of "Eastern" wisdom had access to the same Universal Wisdom. (Aminzavani 3)

This brief survey begins to suggest how by the time Emerson received von Hammer-Purgstall's nineteenth-century German translations, in response to his inherited tradition he had already started to shape his own comprehensively unified gaze at the Persian tradition informed by Sufi mysticism.[10]

Jahanpour's categorization of Emerson's three different approaches to translation further reveals the manifestation of the American poet-translator's emerging transformative Platonic vision of the East. Even his first and most basic "attempt to render a literal translation of the original" ("Emerson on Hafiz" 129) through German intermediary versions reflects the expression of a translingual authority in trying to reach an original literary as well as spiritual sensibility. This approach with his most literal English renderings presumes a connection to a comparable divine source from which the verse originates in Persian. As important, much like the twentieth-century protagonist of Borges's short story "Pierre Menard, author of the *Quixote*" who translates Cervantes's novel verbatim in Spanish, Emerson's equivalence of meaning between languages at the very least changes the source text simply by repositioning it in his receptively syncretic nineteenth-century New England. Emerson's second approach, categorized as combining different poems together to form new verse (Jahanpour, "Emerson on Hafiz" 120), further exteriorizes his Platonic underpinnings. More than tangentially referencing his translation practices as an avocation, such a rhetorical strategy foregrounds the kind of intertextual imitation that proves central to his claims upon originality in his overall aesthetic. The third category, defined as loose imitations (120), further advances his appropriative attempts, while also revealing the extent to which Persian verse influences Emerson's own poetry "in style, imagery, thoughts and feelings" (131). For example, his preference for Hafez's expression "blue horizon's hoop," which he adopted for his own poems (144), brings a simultaneously Platonic and Persian image full circle, back to his own tradition.

That his "most active period of writing coincided with the period that he was studying the Persian poets" (145) necessitates a more extensive comparative study of influence within his broader Platonic framework, where the verse of Sa'di and Hafez coincides with his reengagement through translation as if he himself wrote it.

Emerson's rather well-known translation of the first twenty lines from a Hafez poem serves as a good exemplifying summary of all three approaches, as well as a conclusion of his practical engagement with the Persian verse tradition based on Platonic unification:

The Phoenix

My phoenix long ago secured
His nest in the sky-vault's cope;
In the body's cage immured,
He is weary of life's hope.

Round and round this heap of ashes
Now flies the bird amain,
But in that odorous niche of heaven
Nestles the bird again.

Once flies he upward, he will perch
On Tuba's golden bough;
His home is on that fruited arch
Which cools the blest below.

If over this world of ours
His wings my phoenix spread,
How gracious falls on land and sea
The soul refreshing shade.

Either world inhabits he,
Sees oft below him planets roll;
His body is all of air compact,
Of Allah's love his soul. (CW 9:633)

In his analysis of this poem, Richard Tuerk notes such subtle yet significant changes as "body's eye" from "body's cage" in an 1851 published version (25). Such a revision supports his reading of Emerson as a "truly creative translator" who like Pound found himself "in no way fettered by the original text" (24). Further supporting by implication the transformative freedom found in the transparent eyeball, Tuerk claims that the focus on the eye in this poem "emphasizes vision and introduces the Emersonian distinction between physical and spiritual sight." Just as in the alternative version the bird looks to heaven to overcome von Hammer-Purgstall's limited version of a body tethered to the earthly plane (25), so too does Emerson's translation aesthetic, reflective of his overall rhetorical practices, seek to visually overcome textual influence.

Expectedly, Emerson follows von Hammer-Purgstall's previous changes that allow more freedom from strict adherence to the Eastern tradition. Associating the Persian *huma* with the Greek Phoenix, von Hammer-Purgstall opts for the latter, a displacement equally favored by Emerson's Western sensibility. Neither American nor German translator ought to be slighted for such a decision, considering the correspondence between allusions. Like the Phoenix, the *huma* is also known to consume itself over an extended period of time, often depicted as arising from its own ashes (Bane 164). Even so, this reasonable variation from the original source text proves considerable on closer examination. Distinctive in the Persian legend, the *huma* never lands on the ground (Nile 27–28). Also, the Sufi tradition believes that one sighting of the *huma* in the sky suffices for a lifelong blessing (Sari 157). Most significantly, the purported eternal recurrence of the Persian bird by way of comparative metaphor returns to the myth from Plato's *Symposium* cited at the start of this chapter: the *huma* is both male and female, each side divided by a wing and leg (Bane 164). Emerson through his German intermediary thus captures such essence with an even greater meta-union of Greek and Persian traditions. Following his translation choice, he joins ancient enemies through English translation in America.

Both birds embody obvious Platonic associations, especially insofar as they derive from "a time long ago," impossible to assess and therefore suggestive of eternity. Born and reborn unto themselves, they further seem to emerge as an ideal form, possibly to the point of settling the age-old argument as to which came first, the chicken or the egg. Though for the most part relying on his German source for the poem, Emerson just by carrying over the verse of Hafez into English introduces a plethora of dichotomous Platonic reconciliations into his poetry and, by extension, the Romantic tradition he helps establish in the nineteenth century: Greek/Persian (represented by Phoenix/Huma), male/female, and Heaven/Earth. His translations further conflate source text / receiving texts, the languages of Persian/German, as well as writer/translator (Hafez/von Hammer-Purgstall) and German translator / English translator (von Hammer-Purgstall/Emerson). Repositioning the mythical bird in more of a Western context, the Phoenix overcoming the earthly plane and even death itself as he rises to heaven also juxtaposes a suggestion of Christ[11] with Islamic allusions such as *Allah* and *Tuba* from the *Qur'an*.

Following the bird's lead in blanketing the material world of forms in Platonic shadow, Emerson further conflates such binaries by re-accommodating the lines of Hafez in his use of the ballad "stanza" (which etymologically derives from "room"). In his English form and language as well as with his rhymes, despite following many of his German predecessor's translation choices of meaning, he begins to take possession of the Persian poem, domesticating it in his English tradition. Twice he claims the bird as his own, calling it "My Phoenix." Of course, von Hammer-Purgstall does the same in German with "*Mein Phönix*," but here too just by carrying over the same expression into his English language and American tradition it begins to belong more to him, especially given his own aforementioned subversive visual claim through the change to "body's eye." If in Sufism one glimpse of the *huma* translates into a lifetime of blessings for the beholder, Emerson taking rhetorical ownership of the bird like a domesticated pet to the point of his renaming it grants him the fantasy of its transcendental and regenerative powers.

The Platonic atemporality of the original poem as well as its recurrence, like the Phoenix rising from the ashes as it undergoes the kind of death and "afterlife" in translation described by Walter Benjamin in his famous "Task of the Translator" essay (254), gets further reinforced by Emerson's choice to insert the *Tuba* tree missing in von Hammer-Purgstall's version. Tuerk's speculation that Emerson most likely borrowed the allusion from elsewhere in the German translator's renderings (25) further reinforces a reading of the nineteenth-century American poet-translator anticipating Pound in his comparable reinventions based on the notes of his intermediary translating-scholar Fenollosa. This single change in the tree radically transforms the meaning of the poem in English appropriation, making it simultaneously more Islamic and American. Referenced in the *Qur'an* only as the spiritual concept of blessedness, the *Tuba* surfaces as an actual tree in a *hadith*. In Persian literature the *simurgh*, equated with the *huma*, lays its eggs within its branches (Suhrawardi 113). So expansive that it can't be crossed in over one hundred years of travel, this tree "has breasts that nurse the children of the people of Paradise" and "the clothes of the people of Paradise are taken from its bark." (Q*Tasafir*). Though obviously ancient in the Islamic, and by extension Persian verse tradition, the eternal newness of the tree becomes vegetative counterpart to Adam as the new man. While only one signifier from the Middle East among so many used by Emerson in his translations and imitations, the *Tuba*, like the *huma* in this respect, effectively demonstrates how the American achieves a greater figurative renewal relative to Iran than his more proximate European contemporaries.

In his comparative reading, Russian poet Joseph Brodsky offers a brief allegory of poetry in Europe versus the United States, derived in part from his interpretation of Auden's perspective on American verse:

> [W]hen a European conceives of confronting nature, he walks out of his cottage or inn, filled with either friends or family, and goes for an evening stroll. If he encounters a tree, it's a tree made familiar by history, to which it's been a witness. This or that king sat underneath it, laying down this or that law—something of that sort. A tree stands there rustling, as it were, with allusions. Whereas when an American walks out of his house and encounters a tree it is a meeting of equals. Man and tree face each other in their respective primal power, free of references: neither has a past, and as to whose future is greater, it is a toss up. Basically, it's epidermis meeting bark. (225–226)

While Emerson often seeks such an equal relationship to nature, as evidenced by his solitary and rather personally transformative "stroll" through New England early in *Nature,* his greater rhetorical feat involves his intertextual step toward a tree rooted with ancient allusions to the foreignness of Islam onto which, in yet another change from von Hammer-Purgstall's version, he grafts a limb ("golden bough") from Virgil's *Aeneid.* Concluding his close reading of Emerson's version, Tuerk begins to offer a deft summary of the American's approach to Persian translation:

> Thus, rather than closely following the German version, Emerson weaves together imagery drawn from Hafiz' other poems, from the Koran, and from classical literature to produce an image startlingly similar to ones Yeats later uses in "Byzantium" and "Sailing to Byzantium." (25)

The comparison to Yeats's eternal artifice seems particularly apt in this context, considering that Emerson has been leading American Romantic poetry toward a comparable atemporal and all-unifying Platonic ideal throughout his approach to writing and reading in foreign traditions as well as his own.

In light of such an introduction, the process underpinned by Platonism that allows Emerson to come so close to his Persian predecessors that he appropriates their identities along with their verse, as if sharing their origins,

suggests a need for further investigation. With an adherence to his own rhetorical theory, he reflects a recurring attempt to reconcile difference through
the practice of a transnational, translingual, and transliterary union. Since for
Emerson, "Man is only half himself . . . the other half his expression" (*CW*:
3:4), looking as closely as possible at his own formative romantic origins
reveals much about how he comes to include the Persian tradition in his own
work. The influence of Hafez and Sa'di proves so hard to critically discern in
Emerson because he assimilates it in his writing from his own most essential
beginnings, rivaling the Sufi's "first man" as American Adam.

For this reason, the next chapter turns to the formation of his "transparent
eyeball," where he seemingly hides his first and most significant attempts to
fuse himself with his Eastern gaze. The *huma*/Phoenix, born from an East/West
division that Emerson longs to unify, emerges from such primal figuration.
The transparent eyeball effectively subsumes the bird's shadow, which spans
the globe from America across the Atlantic to Iran. Through his approach to
foreign texts in theory and praxis, Emerson can thus be seen in the following
chapters as rendering his Phoenix so timeless and transnational that it has
seemingly hatched prior to the one depicted by his Persian predecessor, as if
from his own Platonic egg.

Chapter 2

Transparent Eyeball / Persian Mirror

The Renewal of American Vision

> Who dedicates himself to the glass
> Wherein the world mirrors itself
> Lifts securely the veil
> Which separates the worlds.
>
> —Hafez (Translated by Emerson [*PN* 308])

Prior to translating and imitating the Persian Sufi masters, Emerson expressed a way of seeing remarkably like one of his eventual poetic influences, Hafez. Though from a vastly different national tradition, time period, and language, he indeed shared much of his fourteenth-century predecessor's perspective. As Jahanpour explains, "In Hafiz, Emerson found many of the qualities that we admire in him; his self-reliance, his rejection of dogmatism, his break from tradition, his feeling of universal love, his belief in the oneness of truth." Representative of Sufism in his native Iran by his reaction against both the "prevailing religious orthodoxy . . . and a growing tide of materialism," Hafez also strongly appealed to Emerson's reaction against the Christianity of his time ("Emerson and the Sufis"). Lewisohn's summary of the fourteenth-century Persian poet's aesthetic makes Emerson's intense and sustained attraction to it rather understandable:

> [M]uch of Ḥāfiẓ's genius is devoted to dissecting the psychopathology of religious hypocrisy, to composing lampoons in verse on spiritual materialism, and deriding the literalistic religious perspective based on rote learning and devotion by the book. ("Puritans of Islam" 172)

While such comparative scholarship has become well established, surfacing even in Emerson's own writing about Hafez, the rhetorical manifestation of a relatively similar perspective invites further discovery. Beyond comparable critiques of valuing character over crass commercialism or authentic spiritual insight above hypocritical religious ritual, Emerson appears to do more than merely share his Persian predecessor's cultural critiques. He actually looks *like* Hafez, mimicking the stylistic means of his figurative vision to similar Romantically transcendent ends. Before actually attempting to translate Hafez, his famous transformation into a "transparent eyeball" on Boston Common presciently captures his own future assessment of the fourteenth-century poet from Shiraz whom he will render into English from German: "He sees too far, he sees throughout; such is the only man I wish to see and to be" (*JMN* 10:165). In addition to anticipating his discovery of Hafez, he begins in Bloom's terminology to "clear imaginative space" by "misreading" his predecessor (*Anxiety* 5).

Tellingly, he desires both "to see and to be" Hafez, making the transformation into his idol contingent upon the sight of him, as if visual recognition of the Persian poet can lead to his spiritual way of seeing. For Emerson especially, vision remains fundamental to the individual's relation to the world. Insofar as he himself attempts to embody perceptual origins in his essay "Circles," wherein "The eye is the first circle" upon which what follows remains predicated (*CW* 2:179), he would as American Adam preemptively see all who come before him into being. His longing to become Hafez thus translates into his desire to assert himself as his literary tradition's first man figuratively cleared of foreign influence. Near the beginning of *Nature*, when he turns into a transparent eyeball, he claims to see through all that precedes his vision, including himself:

> Crossing a bare common, in snow puddles, at twilight, under a clouded sky, without having in my thoughts any occurrence of special good fortune, I have enjoyed a perfect exhilaration . . . Standing on the bare ground,—my head bathed by the blithe air, and uplifted into infinite space,—all mean egotism vanishes. I become a transparent eyeball; I am nothing; I see all; the currents of the Universal Being circulate through me; I am part or particle of God. (*CW* 1:10)

At its most reductive reading, this passage, which Bloom has called central to the American tradition (*Climate* 60–61), means that Emerson's attempt at becoming the first to arrive in nature obviates even his own presence. As "nothing," devoid of all "mean egotism," he resembles the gap or lacuna in deconstructive theory around which words themselves arbitrarily cohere. This site of radically de-centered meaning both attracts the projection of a plethora of influences while resisting them by claiming authority over all visual and rhetorical imagination. Consequently, it helps to exemplify Emerson as "the unsurpassable prophet of the American Sublime." Such an ideal, of course, proves illusory. As Emerson resists even "the universe of death" by insisting that he makes his own "circumstance," Bloom's "student of misprision" counters with the reply:

> "You do, you do, but if that circumstance is the poet's stance, ringed about by the living circumference of the precursors, then the shadow of your substance meets and mingles with a greater shadow." (*Anxiety* 103)

The following chapter attempts to examine the effects of foreign influence in the textual shadows surrounding Emerson's presumed transparency. Seeking to identify one of the many outside sources considered marginal to his hegemonic claim upon origins, it argues that Persian verse subtly informs the shaping of Emerson's voice and vision to become significantly generative in the early development of the American literary tradition.

Though Bloom's theory of influence offers a way to begin interrogating Emerson's denial of precursors in his shadow, its disregard of foreign literature as well as translation limits a thorough approach to the American writer who he offers as his supreme example of *Daemonization*. Introducing a chapter under this category with an excerpt from "Self-Reliance" to begin demonstrating Emerson's attempt at the erasure of influence on a Romantic path devoid of previous "footprints" (*Anxiety* 98), Bloom offers a rather convincing argument against such a fantasy with an extended quotation of Percy Shelley, Emerson's near contemporary. Despite poets' intentions as original "creators," continues Bloom, they nevertheless remain "creations of their age" (*Anxiety* 103–104). No account is given, however, beyond the poet's specific English tradition. In addition to neglecting such foreign influence in the author's own literary age, such a comparative reading fails to consider how a strong poet such as Emerson can extend his reach back in time and through traditions in order to agelessly negate all difference. His seemingly eternal lyric moment comparably heeds the admonition of a modern mystic teacher: "The Sufi lives in the present. To live in the present, the basic need is to withdraw yourself from the past . . ." (Rajneesh 3). In this respect Emerson's transparent eyeball threatens to limit or even dismiss the breadth and depth of Bloom's own analysis, much like Bloom has shown the progenitor American poet does with his predecessors.

Bhabha's theory of a "third space of enunciation," intersected with Bloom's argument, offers a better way of discerning the "shadow" of foreign influence that seemingly disappears into the strength of Emerson's *a priori* and all-consuming transparency. Bloom himself qualifies the difficulty of positioning Emerson's eyeball in the center of American literature, writing that "there is not too much to say (nor very original to say) about such an observation" ("Central Man" 30). Though applying Bhabha's conceptualization of hybrid literary formation from a colonizing power's engagement with foreign sources to the origins of an American poet-translator appropriating the Persian verse tradition seems critically unorthodox, especially considering that Iran was never colonized by America, it effectively offers a means by which to outline the presence of a transformative influence arising in rhetoric informed between traditions that otherwise would remain hidden by Emerson's Orientalist appropriation. As Bhabha writes:

> The theoretical recognition of the split-space of enunciation may open the way to conceptualizing an international culture, based not on the exoticism of multiculturalism or the diversity of cultures but on the inscription and articulation of culture's hybridity. It is the in between space that carries the burden of the meaning of culture . . . (209)

Rather than resisting such theoretical application, Emerson's reversal of the assumed trajectory of colonization—wherein instead of physically traveling to a foreign land and controlling its indigenous people, he appropriates their language and literature on his own terms—invites comparable interrogation of culture hybridity. Though Emerson appears the antithesis of a colonizer, he posits a domestic starting point presumably devoid of all influence, best summarized by his depiction of a widely read American scholar who looks abroad from his "empty continent" to "fill it with wit" (*JMN* 8:292). The emptying gaze of his American eye toward foreign traditions it attempts to subsume represents a kind of "colonizing consciousness." The "third space" offers a means by which to highlight latent Persian texts that his presumed clarity dissembles within his Western sphere, foregrounding a comparative shadow between East and West. Importantly, such an approach calls into question hegemonic interjections of multicultural exoticism, revealing ways in which Iran proves equally transformative of American literature and philosophy.

By reenvisioning Emerson's eyeball as the trope of a Sufi mystic's mirror reflecting the divine, Bhabha's hybrid theoretical crossing productively inverts typical considerations of influence studies. This approach appears especially necessary to assess Emerson's effect on previous critical readings, which tend to thwart interrogation by imposing its seemingly infinite visual reach. Despite using the seminal American poet as a default example in his attempt to expose influence, Bloom himself reverts to making his own problematic Emersonian demonstration, attempting to subvert daunting writers such as Shakespeare by ignoring them altogether, while concluding his study with an original poem as epilogue that mimics Emerson's de-centered presence he elsewhere critiques. Further influenced by Emerson as predecessor, Bloom disregards any anxiety of foreign influence whatsoever by failing to consider the implications of translation on English writing from other literary traditions. As a necessary corrective, Bhabha's interpretation of postcolonial hybrid literature's disruptive presence, which "reimplicates its identifications in strategies of subversion that turn the gaze of the discriminated back upon the eye of power" (159–160), therefore helps avoid mere reiteration of meta-analytical Western approaches.

Since Emerson as American Romantic of what Bloom calls the "counter-sublime" insists on embodying all predecessors through an essential relation to them that tends to elude discovery, his transformation into a transparent eyeball serves as an apt site to interrogate his attempt to overcome influence. Rather than overt reference to Persian signifiers in later writing, Emerson's rhetorical manifestation of Romantic vision serves as a more seminal entry point for his engagement with foreign literature. Though seemingly unified and all seeing, his eyeball is indeed "ringed about by the living circumference of the precursors." Eluding detection, their "shadows" begin to emanate from the "first circle" of his eye, which fills his own transparent "I" with the shadow of ambiguity. Inherently self-divided by the articulation of his visual transcendence, he wrestles with the materiality of language itself as if to reflect the aesthetic of the Sufi mystics. In an even closer correspondence with the Persian poets, he paradoxically tries to overcome the presence of his ego by insisting upon it.[1] Crossing traditions as he voices his transparency, he becomes his own mirror, both subject and object. "Man is only half himself," he writes, "the other half his expression" (*CW* 3:4). This de-centering at the most essential level ensures that from the "first circle" of the eye he remains always in formation, so close to his own reduction that he appears to subsume any outside sources, especially those like the Persian Sufi poets who uncannily mirror his rhetoric. As Dunston explains, "Emerson did not lose himself on the Boston Common. He found himself and found himself able to contribute to a body of work" (121).

Looking to the unlimited vastness beyond him from his "mean egotism," Emerson's relation to influence nevertheless proves so hard to identify because

he positions himself in a kind of Lacanian mirror stage. The formative effects
of his ego transformation both unite and divide the "I," rendering much lyric
tension in the infinite regression of a *méconnaissance*, or "misrecognition" of
himself. According to Lacan, "The mirror stage is far from a mere phenomenon
which occurs in the development of the child. It illustrates the conflictual
dual relationship" of the subject (*Le Séminaire* 17). As an inhabitant of the
symbolic, he or she remains divided by speech (*Écrits* 269). Observing the
fundamental level of disconnectedness in Emerson's figurative subject formation, Donald Pease has called Emerson's transparent eyeball a "catachresis"
(59), a rather telling summation of such rhetorical self-division. Reinforcing
such a connection to the mirror stage, Pease further argues how Emerson's
eyeball eludes both "the child's prereflexive relation with nature" as well as
"idealist abstractions," positioning formative tension "between the gaps" (50).

Bhabha's theoretical intervention begins to allow for the textual spot-
ting of Emerson's transparent eyeball, the site at which meaning begins its
metaphoric break down, exposing Emerson's imagined self-identification
to interrogate how he in turn attempts to cohere around disparate literary
constructs of verse and the foreign poets who write it. Returning to Bhabha's
description, the figurative eyeball both takes shapes and threatens to disrupt
identity in a "split space of enunciation." Though the actual writing of *Nature*
predates Emerson's deeper reading and translating of Persian verse, considering
his eventual attempts to anticipate Sa'di and Hafez, analysis at such a primal
formative site of meaning appears warranted. It is here that he begins to first
preempt the poets who precede him.

The "mean egotism" of the "I" that seemingly disappears in the invisibility
of the "eye" aptly surfaces in the textual third space of a pun, foregrounding the
irreconcilable self-union through homonym. Puns in classical Persian poetry,
especially in the verse of Hafez, liberate as they contain. Like Emerson's attempt
at transparency, they try to out-metaphorize the very metaphor they posit.
Pease effectively deconstructs the essence of Emerson's punning to show how
the well-known passage about his transformative vision ultimately embodies
the process from which metaphor emerges: ". . . the eyeball is trans-parent,
trans-individual, trans-objective . . . undefinable as either subject or object,
God or nature . . . like the living glance exchanged when God and nature
look face to face" (59). Inadvertently, as though influenced by Emerson's
rhetorical effects that help him appropriate foreign predecessors, Pease by
this assessment also offers an exceptional description of Persian Sufi poetry
invested in paradoxically liberating yet confining puns that tend to read the
book of nature as divine. To this figurative end, in an essay on the difficulty
of translating Hafez, Dick Davis cites a representative pun from the Persian

tradition by Masud Sa'd: "*Nalam bedel chu nai man andar hesar-e nai.*" As Davis explains:

> Only in Persian can this line be evocative. The pun is on the word *nai*, which means a reed flute, and also alludes to the name of a fortress used as a prison. Hence the line means, "While I am (imprisoned) in *nai* (the fortress), I complain in my heart like a *nai* (reed flute)." (*Not Translating* 8)

Emerson could hardly come as close to Davis, an esteemed Persian translator with expansive knowledge of the source language and tradition, in his own English pun. Yet he has approximated the spirit of Sufi poetry by attempting to turn an imprisoning "I" into liberating visual transcendence with the all-seeing "eye." In the praxis of literary translation, his pun would be considered an excellent demonstration of a compensation strategy, the displaced yet relative compromise that captures in the receiving language something lost from the source text. In the hybrid comparative theory used for this study, such an American pun can further double as Bloom's textual shadowing that impedes the poet's fantasy of originating Romantic presence. An enunciation of essential identity at the point of the subject's visual differentiation reflects the Sufi mystic poet's similar rhetorical attempt to reach the divine. As von Hammer-Purgstall significantly noted, Hafez was commonly known as " 'Tongue of the Secret' " (*CW* 9:255), paradoxically articulating that which could not be seen. Such a metaphor giving voice to the invisible closely resembles the function of Emerson's transparent eyeball that becomes a primary statement on an attempt to transcend self-identification. Emerson's personal veneration of Hafez reinforces this comparison, especially as he references the Persian poet as master of an encompassing vision that he above all desires.

For greater comparative understanding, the ubiquitous trope of the Sufi mirror offers a new way of seeing Emerson's fundamental attraction to the verse of Hafez and Sa'di. "An important multivalent symbol in Sufi poetry," much like Emerson's transparent eyeball, the mirror for the Persian mystic poet can stand for "the whole person in relation to others" (Renard 205). Anvar's explanation of Sufi poetry seems to define Emerson's eyeball in relation to such reflection: "Where words fail around the 'invisible' or 'the realm of inner realities' poetry produces mirror images that reflect what usually cannot be imagined, vocalized, or remembered" (124). The rhetorical functioning as extended metaphor in the Sufi tradition, wherein "Polishing the mirror from raw iron into a highly reflective surface is also a metaphor for spiritual ascent" (Renard 205), further resembles Emerson's transformation into transparency as he attempts to rid himself of "all mean egotism." Similar to Emerson's transcendence that would erase any human intervention, the mystic's trope represents "the highest human perfection" where "Adam was 'the limitless mirror' of God's attributes" (Renard 206). Such a description imitates the stated function of Emerson's eyeball, which, explains James Cox, involves not just seeing the material world but attempting to see through it (78). The process of Sufi mirror-polishing so closely reveals a correspondence to Emerson's attempt at visual transcendence that it can even be taken as its description:

> While looking at a smudged mirror the viewer sees the glass. If the mirror is polished, a shift occurs. The glass becomes invisible, with only the viewer's image reflected. Vision has become self-vision. Sufi mystics used the polishing of the mirror as a symbol beyond the distinction between subject and object, self and others. (Sells 63)

Ultimately, both the Sufis and Emerson attempt to penetrate beyond the veil of language itself as they seek to visually transform into something like pure agency. What Michael Sells says of the Sufi mystic Ibn Arabi's language proves applicable both to the verse of Persian poets like Sa'di and Hafez as well as to Emerson's rhetoric. Seeking to continuously

> "polish the mirror," it resists a stable reference to mystical union. The moment of transformation from nonreflexive to reflexive constitutes a "meaning event," which "struggles against the dualistic nature of language." (63)

Ego-reduction at the site of reflection attempts to become a function of metaphorical invisibility. Much like Bloom's category of the counter-sublime as exemplified in Emerson's transparent eyeball, the Sufi seeks the fantasy of overcoming bifurcation through vision, wherein the mirror becomes "a symbol of the shift beyond the distinction between subject and object, self and others" (Sells 63).

Such seeming infinitude embodied in the fantasy of a unified self reflects Emerson's impossible to reach ideal. Much like Jalauddin Rumi saying that the words of his poetry proved a poor substitute to the spiritual realm he'd come to inhabit (Baldock 101), Emerson predicates his seeming transcendence on the paradoxically textual reporting of it. In this respect his self-definition through the expression of visual transparency reflects the Sufi's own problematic relation to figurative mirror polishing, as they too in a sense reductively attempt to free themselves from the very words used to overcome the material world. This accounts for the crux of lyric tension in the Persian verse to which Emerson found himself so passionately attracted. Divided between himself and his expression, he looks to classical masters like Hafez as the lover to the beloved, yet another referent for the metaphor of the mirror in Sufi mysticism (Renard 205). Much like the Platonism that Emerson associated with Persian poetry, this spiritual aesthetic underpinning the foreign verse he discovered came to sanction his appropriation. "Half himself," he longs to find his "other half" in the expressed identities of Sufi poets before him who ultimately reflect his way of seeing and their own ideal for *a priori* unification.

To exemplify this comparative analysis with Emerson's own translation of Hafez, consider the following lines he rendered into English through von Hammer-Purgstall's German version: "Take my heart in thy hand, O beautiful boy of Schiraz! / I would give for the mole on thy cheek Samarcand and Buchara!" (*CW* 8:134). The poet here attempts to sacrifice the material world for a vision of the beloved which, for the Persian Sufis, leads to a realization of the divine. According to legend, Tamerlane, a native of Samarkand, confronted Hafez for the blasphemy of offering his land for the mole of the beloved's face. Hafez is said to have replied, "Your Majesty, it is because of such prodigality that I have fallen into such poverty" (Kashani 7). This self-inflicted poverty through the trope of the mole in Sufi poetry exemplifies the return to the most primal source of material origins from which to access a spiritual experience. As Florence Lederer writes in the introduction to another Persian poet in the same tradition of Hafez, "The mole on the cheek is the point of indivisible Unity," (15) adding that "the heart and soul of Adam evolved from there" (29). Syed Mumtaz Ali's description of the mole for Sufis could just as well apply to Emerson's eyeball as the embodiment of material reduction toward liberating vision:

> The mole on her face signify [*sic*] that when the pupil, at times, beholds the total absence of all worldly want on the part of the preceptor, he also abandons all the desires of both worlds—he perhaps even goes so far as to desire nothing else in life than his preceptor. ("Sama")

In another poem by Hafez, the mole becomes a mirror of the perceiver's pupil: "Her cheek's a mirror of all my vision / My pupil in her mole is seen (subtly)."[2]

Like the paradoxically opaque mole on the face of the beloved that opens to a seemingly infinite world for Hafez, Emerson experiences his visionary transformation to an Adamic state devoid of influence on a dirty puddle that appears to metonymically displace the pupil as part of his entry into an all-seeing transparency. The "common" landscape that Emerson crosses as well as the smaller microcosm of space in the puddle where he stands gets subsumed by the comprehensive vision of the eye, an inversion of his expanding "Circles" essay wherein the eye as the first circle goes out to define the world. Dunston significantly locates the relation of Emerson's "inconsecutiveness" in this essay to the Persian poetry he engaged (117). Visually, this gets reinforced in the American's attempt to clear away all sullying influence, based in the process of his own ego reduction. To the extent that Emerson would overcome his predecessors via the "trans-parent eyeball," he attempts to experience like Hafez before him "a living glance" wherein "God and nature look face to face." Comparing Hafez's "circular becoming" to Emerson's rhetoric in "Circles" and elsewhere, Dunston claims that they both "sing the same song." Comparable to the Sufi mystic's complete surrender for ultimate spiritual inheritance, Dunston further explains how the American at the site of the transparent eyeball becomes "nothing" to "see all" (118). In this respect Emerson makes as much of the Persian poet's demonstration at the site of his visual transformation as he does in his translations and imitations of Hafez or Sa'di. To quote the contemporary Sufi teacher Inyat Khan:

> To become something is a limitation, whatever one may become.
> Even if a person were to be called king of the world, he would still
> not be the emperor of the universe. If he were the master of the
> earth, he would still be the slave of Heaven. It is the person who is
> no one, no one and yet all. . . . The Sufi, therefore, takes the path
> of being nothing instead of being something. It is this feeling of
> nothingness which turns the human heart into an empty cup into
> which the wine of immortality is poured. It is this state of bliss
> which every truth-seeking soul yearns to attain. ("Selflessness")

Extending and somewhat redirecting Dunston's comparative point, Emerson can be seen as emptying the self to accommodate a plethora of voices in his intertextual reinvention of the American tradition. Though Bloom may prove correct in his claim that little can be said about the transparent eyeball, Emerson shows that much can be said through it. Buell tends to support such reinvention through displacement in Emerson's rhetoric, arguing that "discontinuity" ironically helps him remain true to his self-reliant aesthetic (572).

One of the main forms of Persian poetry, underpinned by Sufi philosophy, seems to further reflect Emerson's de-centering rhetoric that continually places and displaces him. Like the Persian *ghazal*, comprised of a series of disparate couplets that cohere through a recurring rhyme and word or phrase in each second line, "Emerson opts for a series of particular aspects of a subject, rather than on the continuity of expression" (Ives 25). Also similar to Emerson's verse, as well as his prose, the form invites literary appropriation. Favored by classical masters such as Hafez, it inherently anticipates by several centuries what poststructural theorists come to call intertexuality. A single *ghazal* may quote lines of the *Qur'an*, excerpted narrative from well-known myth or folklore, the words of predecessor poets, and even verse from other traditions. Much of Emerson's writing style mirrors this form. In addition to relying on varied allusions from foreign sources, he comprises essays "with passages gleaned from other lectures and from his journals, as well as with newly written material" (*CW* 3:xlvii). Much like disparate *ghazal* couplets constitute a unified poem, his two series of essays were

> conceived of and composed as books, as orchestrated volumes in which parts would create dialectical wholes, in which separate essays would reflect on, balance, or rhetorically counter other essays. (*CW* 3:xlvii)

To show the extent to which Emerson's own rhetoric mirrors one of the two Persian poets he would most attempt to imitate, consider Lewisohn's description:

> As a poet, Hafiz was a genius of transformative appropriation, supreme connoisseur of verse-aphorisms and epigrams, who specialized in selecting the choicest verses from the past masters of Persian and Arabic poetry, transcreating their imagery, improvising and improving on their ideas in his own original manner. ("Prolegomenon" 6)

Emerson's specific approach to translation further interlinguistically mirrors the original Persian verse, insofar as he brings the source poems into English through German intermediary renderings. He also fragmentizes already fragmented couplets by cutting and pasting select lines with his own recreated rhymes that he opts to present in English outside formal strictures of the source text with assumed editorial authority. Significantly, Emerson "sometimes combined fragments of different *ghazals* in passages intended for publication or his own translations of those of Hammer-Purgstall" (Aminrazavi 6).

Paul Kane compellingly compares the *ghazal*'s contained couplets that resist coherence of Western poetics to the tension between Emerson's epigraphs

and the essays to which they seem disjointedly attached (130–132). Often a
given speaker in the *ghazal*, much like the litany of quoted voices in Emerson's
essays, gets positioned against other preceding voices. The inherent disparate
nature of the form invites such interjections of lines from many sources, much
like Kane shows Emerson using quotations as epigraphs to which he both
responds as well as thematically resists by breaking away from such citations.
Kane's dialogic reading of the epigraphs "as if the little poems were written
in a different mood or by someone other than the author of the essays"
(112) closely corresponds to what Persian scholar and translator Dick Davis
observes in the *ghazal* as "the shifting from second person to third person
then back again" (*Faces* xxii). Such a comparative reading by Kane further
suggests the Persian form as an analogous model for how Emerson's voice
emerges from an amalgamation of other voices. As Pease observes, "Emerson
turns his writing into the equivalent of quoting" (67), an apt summation of
the classical Persian masters of the *ghazal* who, also like Emerson, quote other
texts against their own verse to increase dialogic tension while simultaneously
distancing themselves from fixed subjectivity.

The convention of the Persian poet "signing" the *ghazal* in the last
couplet, often with an assumed name, presents a means by which to extend
the paradox of naming the transparent self at the point of Emerson's figurative origins. Referencing a somewhat displaced persona at the conclusion
of seemingly displaced couplets, the Persian poet simultaneously identifies
with and detaches himself from his identity. This stylistic predilection proves
especially significant in both traditions. In the Persian form, the brief series
of disjointed couplets concludes with the poet's self-identification (or at least
the performance of it), which, like Emerson's naming of "mean egotism,"
paradoxically gets undercut by self-diminishment. He reduces his name to
nothing, much like his own translation of a couplet by Hafez: "I am: what I
am / My dust will be again" (*CW* 8:133).

This common self-"rending" via self-referencing helps to exemplify
Ricardo Miguel-Alfonso's observation of how Emerson differs from European
influences "by a greater acceptance or affirmation of discontinuities of self"
(55). Though less frequently associated with the East, Emerson in this respect
may indeed belong more to it relative to the West. Considering that American Romanticism remains rather predicated upon his voice and vision, this
association becomes significant, though often too elusive to critically develop.
Emerson as speaker foregrounding his presence in an attempt to transcend
it also follows a pattern of ego-disruption through the interposition of other
voices seen in the verse of Hafez, wherein objectifying a variety of disparate
and foreign texts helps disrupt a subjective presence. "When 'I' quote, then

'I' am speaking by another who speaks through me when I assume his word,"
writes Pease in his close reading of Emerson's response to his transparent
eyeball (67). Such a rhetorical strategy in the *ghazal*—with the poet inhabit-
ing ubiquitous shifts from the first to second and third person—reflects in
Emerson's prose another means of both ego displacement and reduction. At
significant lyric moments, the self literally as well as visually disappears from
texts in the writing of the American and his Persian predecessors. Such self-
erasure in the *ghazal* as in Emerson's rhetoric tends to suspend meaning as
if through recurring ellipses, wherein gaps between sentences and couplets
invite if not trap the reader into that same sense of absence that relays such
an inexplicable spiritual tone. Holding a mirror up to Emerson's writing, the
Persian form thus helps account for how he "abrogates the privileged position
of ego" (Pease 51). In much the same way, Emerson inserts the Persian poetic
tradition into his own rhetorical self-displacement. Richardson's location of
what he considers the crux of the "Over-Soul" essay as well as a few other
related poems suggests Emerson's need to displace himself—and the reader
along with him—by claiming the voice of other Persian poets:

> Emerson's point of view, his procedures, his method of composi-
> tion, and his main convictions all rest on the perception that the
> world of differences can and must be resolved into a world not
> only of similarity but of identity. (334)

Such identification remains predicated upon a kind of transparent overcoming of the self that supports Marietta Stepaniants's assessment of the Sufi's
ideal for "perfection," which involves "annihilation of an individual self in
the Divine Self" (80)

The Persian Sufi poets in turn seem to invite Emerson into comparable
transparent spaces. Because he looks for himself elsewhere, attracted to the
foreign, he begins to surface in a version of Bhabha's "third space of enunciation." As "half himself," at times he dislocates his "other half" in Hafez
and Sa'di. Outlines of the Sufi mirror and his transparent eyeball intersect
to comparatively reveal how Emerson identifies with the disidentification of
poets who would transcend their own subjective presences through their verse.
Related to the aforementioned mirror stage, Lacan's example of the gaze in this
respect offers an allegory of how Emerson, looking to the East, reveals both
his self-division as well as his formative imagining of an all-encompassing
unification with hybrid influence. Seeing a sardine can floating far from the
shore in the sunlight, a native fisherman teases Lacan, "You see that can?
Do you see it? Well, it doesn't see you!" (*Four Concepts* 95). According to

Lacan, the scene eludes his mastery: "[The light] grasps me, solicits me at every moment, and makes of the landscape something other than the landscape . . ." (96). Emerson similarly looks across the Atlantic as well as back through several centuries, seeing a tradition that fails to see him. To use Freud's German word for translation (rendered into English to partly follow Emerson's own linguistic trajectory), his Orientalist gaze undergoes a kind of "distortion" through the Persian language and the German intermediary rendering from which he accesses it. As Jahanpour notes, at times Emerson actually attempted exact translations but misunderstood German and therefore changed the Persian text in English (*Emerson on Hafiz* 129). Dislocated from the foreign source of a comparable mirror, he ultimately envisions the fantasy of himself belonging to it, or rather, it belonging to him. In an inimitable feat of overcoming his predecessors with an all-encompassing authoritatively personal as well as national claim, and in the Persian spirit of a pun, he figuratively transforms "a mirror can" into something "American." His voice and vision thus become generative of his tradition founded in part on his attempt to subvert it.

Here again the fundamental problem of locating Persian influence in Emerson's rhetoric resides in his Romantic visual transcendence. Bloom's statement that "there is not too much to say (nor very original to say)" about the transparent eyeball transformation, which he considers "the central passage in American literature" ("Central Man" 30), applies further to the spiritual vision of the Sufi. In a story related by Hazrat Inayat Khan, the ones who scale "the wall of mystery" never returned to tell their countrymen what they discovered beyond it. Those on the side of the material world decided to tie a willing explorer with a chain. They let him climb to the top, and as he smiled in wonder, they pulled him back down to their side. Unfortunately, "to their great disappointment, when he came back they found he had lost his speech" (Khan, "Sufi Message" 173). The greatest lyric tension, as well as the crux of Emerson's problem of literary influence, is located at a similar threshold of unknowing, which explains in part why Bloom's interrogation of it reverts to mirroring his own Emersonian performance in his theory.

The closest analysis possible for both Emerson and his Sufi predecessors remains the rhetorical entry point into seeming self-obviation, wherein the small puddle on Boston Common mirrors the symbolic mole of the Persian poet. While Emerson returns from mounting the wall of reason, he thereafter only talks *around* his absence. Tracking instead the chain of signification leading to his seeming transcendence best accounts for the primal tension he exerts on himself, which tends to parallel (like the aforementioned "double ladder" of "spiritual discipleship" leading Sufis to the divine) the rhetorical pull upon

Hafez and Sa'di in their original Persian language. Inadvertently, Emerson's self-reduction to the point of near disappearance comes to resemble the Sufi poetry he translates and imitates into English, tethering lines originating from foreign couplets like umbilical cords to his Adamic spiritual presence in his figuratively new America. Rather than climbing up, however, he apparently uses them to descend to a point of performing humility reminiscent of the mystic poets. Sells effectively summarizes the fundamental doctrine of pan-Sufism as "the annihilation (fana) and subsequent abiding (baqa) of the self," both of which surface in comparison to the mirror. When "the ego-self of the Sufi passes away, the divine is said . . . to reveal to Him / him through Him / him his mystery." It is at this point, continues Sells, that "the referential distinction between reflexive and nonreflexive, self and other, human and divine, breaks down" (132). Such a description rather eloquently describes the poetry and prose of Emerson, who seeks a similar self-annihilation and begins his American vision on the metaphoric breakdown of transparency, as observed by Pease.

Kane's most original claim, which provides a point of departure for this study when applied to the passage of the transparent eyeball, connects Emerson's liberation through self-reduction to Lewisohn's observation of *malámati* (self-censure) found in the Sufi mysticism that underpins much of the verse by Hafez. Drawing on lines from "Self-Reliance," such as, "For nonconformity the world whips you with its displeasure," Kane locates a Western analogue to the Persian poet's inversion of power in the "rend" that diminishes his self-importance as he challenges hypocrisy (123). Kane aptly reads this as Hafez's most predominant theme (125). The rend, according to Lewisohn, encapsulates the "whole spiritual universe of Persian Sufism" since it rejects the posturing of the religious, their supposed "propriety and right way of living" ("Prolegomenon" 75).

Further referencing Emerson's description of Hafez in Emerson's journals, Kane notes how this could easily serve as Emerson's self-reliant man, particularly in his insistence on his own fearless way of seeing the world (123). Kane's analysis astutely predicates his reading of the "rend" in the vision of both writers: "The Emersonian *rend*, like Hafiz, is fearless because he *sees*; he is a visionary in both a religious and secular sense: the clarity of his perception penetrates the world" (123).

This metaphorical or "vehicular" nature of Hafez's de-centered verse, combined with the positioning of the diminished self through the "rend," which, like Hafez, Kane finds operating in Emerson "through a disinterested and visionary gaze" (122) offers an alternative means of considering influence in Emerson's rhetoric. The rend for Emerson connects to his self-proclaimed transcendent vision, as dramatized in his own time by publication of a famous cartoon by the illustrator Christopher Cranch that lampoons the writer's outlandish transformative claim, depicting him as a giant eyeball on stick legs. Emerson especially exemplifies Lewisohn's reading of the *malámati* in Hafez, wherein the libertine comes to outwardly "incur blame" from the community despite "inwardly" being of "sound character" ("Prolegomenon" 36). "His spiritual task," explains Lewisohn, "is to take roads for which others will blame him. Hafez thus submits himself to public censure and blame . . ." ("Hafez and his Genius" 75). Noting how foreign such conceptions appear to Western sensibilities, Lewisohn in his study of Hafez suggests Emerson as perhaps the best comparative English example, quoting these lines from his essay "Compensation":

> The wise man throws himself on the side of his assailants. It is more
> in his interest than it is in theirs to find his weak point . . . Blame
> is safer than praise. I hate to be defended in a newspaper. As long
> as all this is said is said against me, I feel a certain assurance of
> success . . . in general, every evil to which we do not succumb
> is a benefactor.[3] (*CW* 2:68–69)

Further following Kane's analysis, such a caricature embodies related self-diminishing moves by Hafez who would playfully objectify himself in the final couplets of his *ghazals* or, at the very least, announce his eventual return to the dust. In this respect the humiliation becomes a process of abandoning the ego, a means by which the mirror between the self and the divine can be scrubbed pure. As Lewisohn explains:

> Blame gradually strips the lover of his egocentric selfhood and
> forces him to abandon all secular support: blame turns the lover
> away from the world first and then from himself. Indeed, without
> blame, no love affair ever truly begins or ends. ("Hafez and his
> Genius" 78)

Emerson's comparable *rend* connects humility to humiliation. Melville's description of him as "cracked right across the brow" (121–122) and his satirizing of him as Mark Winsome, a character in his novel *The Confidence Man*, derives from his pollyanna optimism exemplified by his claims upon spiritual vision. Though perhaps setting himself up for such ridicule by proclaiming that all egotism "vanishes," his impulse toward a clearing away of egocentric claims on the world has led to his self-reduction and deeper into *humilitas*, Latin for "of the Earth," upon Boston Common. Such a seemingly abased position in turn affords him visual transcendence.

Though the Persian word was somewhat mistranslated as the equivalent of mere drunkenness or drinking in the German renderings of von Hammer-Purgstall (Verma 47), Emerson in English tends to capture the spirit of the *rend* from the original concept as demonstrated by his expressed affinity to the Sufi poets. The "rend" or "debauchee" in the poetry of Hafez is associated with hoodlums and other outcasts, including those affiliated with wine such as tavern keepers and their *saki* (wine servers). Their relevance derives in relation to those supposedly pious in society whose hypocrisy Hafez attempts to expose. Putting the significance of wine in the context of fourteenth-century Iran, Jahanpour writes:

> At a time of religious fanaticism and bigotry when drinking wine could result in harsh penalties, Hafiz uses wine as a way of transcending religious strictures and expressing his disgust of hypocrisy and sanctimonious religiosity" ("Emerson on Hafiz" 128).

"To irk and humiliate the hypocrites," writes Ehsan Yarshater, "Hafez puts the men of ill-repute on a pedestal, almost sanctifies them, and attributes to them all the virtues absent in the hypocrites" (498). The Persian Sufi poet in this respect offers a dramatic example of Emerson's own location of a greater faith outside the church, best exemplified in his claim that "in order to be a good minister it was necessary to leave the ministry" (*JMN* 4:27). Richardson's summation of critical judgments that Emerson received following his "Divinity School Address" also makes the American sound like one of Hafez's outcasts, insofar as he was accused of "impiety . . . infidelity, blasphemy, and 'foulest atheism'" (299). In Emerson's own translation of verses by Hafez, he follows his Persian poet's depiction of wine as the speaker's mirror where truth gets revealed through such inversion:

> Lo, this mirror shows me all!
> Drunk, I speak of purity,
> Beggar, I of lordship speak. (*CW* 9:257)

Because Emerson sees a reflection of himself as American outcast in the foreign trope, he further captures much of the true spirit of wine in the original source poems despite his Persian illiteracy. As he records in his journals: "Hafiz does not write of wine and love in any mystical sense further than that he uses wine as the symbol of intellectual freedom" (*TN* 2:120). Carpenter's early scholarship aptly positioned Emerson's treatment of wine from Persian verse in the context of a transcendent Platonism (46), which in a broad sense supports the American poet-translator's attempt to transcend limitations of language and literary traditions. Ekhtiyar, tracking the metaphor of wine beyond Persian translation in Emerson's own essays, poetry, and journals, concludes that the allusion invariably "suggests divine ecstasy" (62). Though wine in Sufi poetry has the added association of mystic intoxication, which Davis argues invariably gets lost in English translation ("Not Translating" 315), Emerson demonstrates an uncanny analogue in his own tradition through his inversion of drunkenness and spiritual sobriety when compared to Hafez. Here again he becomes a mirror for his Persian predecessor, opposing in his discussion of Hafez the mere alcohol found in "Devil's wine" to "God's wine," representative of spiritual verse (CW 3:17). Paradoxically, Emerson's sobriety comes quite close to the Persian mystic's drunkenness. In part his contradictory impulses that take a "rational view of Hafez" regarding wine but "elsewhere leaves him ambiguously mystical" (Kane 118) can be explained as reflecting the Western perception of his Eastern predecessor, wherein sobriety can lead to the kind of intoxicated divine connection of Hafez. "The sublime vision," he writes, "comes to the pure and simple soul." To exemplify this claim, he juxtaposes "the lyric poet" as wine drinker against Milton as the superior "epic poet" who "shall sing of the gods" and "must drink water out of a wooden bowl" (CW 3:17).While noting Emerson's reluctance to identify with mysticism in his essay "The Poet," Kane offers an important rhetorical qualification on his tempering approach, arguing that for him, "poetry ought to proceed naturally from mysticism, and that poetry is what keeps mystical perception vehicular and transitive" (119). In this respect Emerson in English ironically exposes Davis's possibly too rigid insistence on an equivalence of meaning regarding wine, a version of the kind of literal religiousness antithetical to him as well as the Sufi mystics.

While dismissing traditional notions of literary influence, Emerson further challenges received assumptions about their translation through the vision of Hafez relative to his own culture and tradition. Like Hafez, "Emerson's religious vision is inseparable from his skepticism" (Kane 120). In his own self-reliant way, he further insists on freedom from American religious strictures, an independence best exemplified by his early refusal of the holy sacrament, wherein the wine cup represents for him an empty symbol of formality devoid of true divine spirit. A key signifier of his turn against formal Unitarianism and toward Transcendentalism, his rejection of wine in Christian communion anticipates the problem of translation cited by Davis. Part of his arguing against the sacrament in his sermon "The Lord's Supper" is that it represents a "local custom," which like the Passover fails to help an American audience in the nineteenth century understand what it once "signified." In asking the church "to make communion less a matter of ritual and more a spontaneous 'commemoration' of the life of faith" (Geldard 129), Emerson resembles a translator creatively rendering a foreign text in his attempt to better reach the spirit of the original Judeo-Christian origins as opposed to their superficial literal meaning. Though quite different from the Sufi's "mystic intoxication," a Western translator couldn't offer a better metaphor to carry over comparable Eastern understanding. The Biblical quote that Emerson chooses for an epigraph comes as close as possible to re-presenting what Hafez and other Persian poets mean by being drunk on spiritual revelation versus rote performance of the Islamic religion: "The Kingdom of God is not meat and drink, but righteousness, and peace, and joy in the Holy Ghost.—ROMANS XIV.17" (186). Such a comparative analysis exemplifies Kane's assessment of Emerson's Hafez translations as "polyvalent," showing "a sensitive engagement with the poet and an appreciation for his complex, paradoxical and antitheti- cal stances" (131). Freed from comparable linear constraints, the American identifies with Hafez's "antinomian and self-reliant qualities associated with the rend" as well as his "condensed, elliptical style" and "apparent discontinuity of sense" from consecutive stanzas (132).

Since the inception of *Nature*, which positions a somewhat negated self that remains opposed to the material world on a transcendent pedestal, Emerson insists on his outsider status relative to formal institutions and rituals that he deems as empty in signification as the sacrament. In this way especially he aligns himself to Hafez. "What have I to do with the sacredness of traditions, if I live wholly from within?" he writes in "Self-Reliance," going so far as to answer a friend who questions his operating from bad impulses as though appealing to the debauchery of Hafez by proclaiming, "if I am the Devil's child, I will be then from the devil" (*CW* 2:30). Later in the same essay, Emerson relates a fable about "the sot who was picked up dead drunk in the street, carried to the duke's house, and treated like royalty to the point that he realizes his true nature as a prince" (*CW* 2:36). Such an example could easily have derived from Sa'di's *Gulistan* (*Rose Garden*) a book based on the natural world comprised of moralizing poems and stories that Emerson favored because it so resonated with his own rhetoric,[4] which places nature as his "main source of effective imagery in writing and speech" (Richardson 155). In one brief vignette, Sa'di offers an inversion of Emerson's story toward the same end, wherein a vizier fired from his post finds new meaning in a life among dervishes. Offered reinstatement from the king, he refuses, explaining, "Retirement is better than occupation" (*Gulistan* 39).

Far from occasional comparative coincidence, when examined further Emerson, like Hafez and Saʿdi, consistently juxtaposes the independent outsider to the assumed authority of the status quo, invariably attempting to take down the latter through critical inversion. In the very beginning of his introduction to *Nature*, he offers a critique of established institutions and customs, which includes the influence of predecessors. While for Hafez such elders appear as learned and pious mullahs of the mosque who hypocritically sneak off to the tavern, Emerson locates comparable analogues with ministers of the Unitarian church and academics at Harvard who privilege the relative emptiness of formality over a genuine integrity of spirit. As if reinforcing Hafez's attempt to expose the hypocrisy of those like the learned mullahs whom society elevates by positioning them against the more lowly wine-serving *saki*—who are often just boys—Emerson esteems the "nonchalance of boys" to "the man . . . clapped into jail by his consciousness" (*CW* 2:29). Relative to Hafez, Emerson goes as far, if not further, as esteeming the wine drinker and tavern owner, an exaggerated dramatization of the *saki* represented as intoxicating agency opposed to intellectualization. Consider that his ultimate ideal appears as an unintelligible baby: "Infancy conforms to nobody: all conform to it" (*CW* 2:28). The aforementioned transparent eyeball, which has previously been compared to the infant in a Lacanian mirror stage, ultimately warrants the reader's adherence to the birth of primal and unadulterated vision akin to that attempted by the Sufi mystics.

Thus far this comparative approach between Emerson and the Persian poets he came to translate has remained largely theoretical. Before turning in the next chapter to Emerson's encounter with a seemingly irreconcilable influence of Islamic fatalism in "Self-Reliance," one of Emerson's most recurring translation choices read against one of the most significant events in his biography can now be considered as revealing the practical return of a Persian poet whose identity he attempts to adopt as his own. His recurring attempt at overcoming all influence, predicated on self-evasion, makes tracking the return of a foreign predecessor contingent on such recognition of his rhetorical presence. Ironically, however, Emerson renders the construction of a Romantic American self so transparent that the critic tends to look through, as opposed to at, his personal life. A Saʿdi poem that Emerson suspiciously keeps retranslating about the loss of his predecessor-namesake's son, compared with his seeming denial of grief over the death of his own son Waldo in "Experience" (an essay subtly informed in key moments by the same religious origins as verse of the Persian poets), begins to highlight the shadow of textual influence around his seeming invisibility.

Emerson's ubiquitously cited repression of his son's death in this essay, which strangely culminates in an expression of mystic intoxication so divine that it rivals lines by Rumi, introduces the centrality of the Persian poet's vision referenced by Buell as well as the means by which Emerson attempts to render it invisible from critical identification. Rather than mourning for him, he mourns his inability to mourn. "The only thing grief has taught me," he writes, "is to know how shallow it is." Like so much of life, his sorrow "plays about the surface" (CW 3:29). Quite significantly, in his essay Emerson never names his son. As Sharon Cameron explains in an analysis of grief in "Experience," he "struggles not to mourn," ultimately displacing his emotion over the course of the essay by "converting grief to analysis" (140).

An alternative Freudian reading of influence that considers Emerson's Persian influence, however, suggests that repression remains all the more present elsewhere, manifesting in the poet Sa'di with whom the American mimetically identified to the point of calling himself by his name. In Emerson's *Notebook Orientalist*, a record of his original poems and translations as well as quotes related to Middle Eastern literature (explicated in chapter 4 to support the development of Emerson's emerging theory of translation), he curiously displays excessive concern with the rendering of Sa'di's poem about the death of his young son. Given its biocritical implications, Einboden seems justified in his claim that this translation "perhaps best expresses his personal engagement with Persian poetry" (*Islamic Lineage* 152).

As Dunston points out, Emerson would have learned about the death of Sa'di's son from James Ross's biographical essay on the poet (117), included in the *Gulistan* translation for which he wrote the introduction. Given the relative wealth of von Hammer-Purgstall's Persian poems in German from which Emerson could choose to translate, his opting to draft four different versions of this poem by Sa'di in his *Notebook Orientalist* (*TN* 2:70, 77, 79, 83) suggests that he remained especially interested in its content. Of course he had a plethora of reasons to find interest in Sa'di, yet considering his problematic stated abstention from grief in "Experience," his identification with the Persian poet and his verse proves especially noteworthy. Referencing the translation, Dunston begins to make a reasonable case for Emerson in "Experience" following Sa'di's philosophy of objectifying loss, "even to the unbearable point of knowing that a son's life is not, after all, a father's to own" (117).

Looking more closely at Emerson's interest in rendering Sa'di's poem into English, however, suggests an alternative reading. First translating this poem almost a decade after writing "Experience" (which was published two years after the death of his son), Emerson seemingly allows his grief to resurface

through these words of Saʿdi and cathartically free himself from the extreme
emotional constraints cited in the original essay:

> In Senahar, my first born sleeps;
> Stunned with the blow, poor Saadi weeps;
> Tho' youth more fresh than Jussuf blooms,
> The charnelworm his pink cheek consumes.
> Where is the palm, star-topped, earth-footed,
> Which the brute storm has not uprooted?
> I muttered,—"Perish God on high,
> Since pure youth dies as greybeards die!"
> I staggered to my darling's tomb,
> And tore the sealed stone therefrom,
> Then frantic, tottering, void of wit,
> Groped down into that marble pit.
> When grief was spent, & reason came,
> Methought I heard my son exclaim
> 'If my dark house thy heart affright
> 'Saadi strive upwards to the light
> 'Wilt though give graves the blaze of noon
> 'High hearts can work that wonder soon
> The crowd believe that harvests grow
> Where never man did barely sow.
> But Saadi saw the fruit enchanted
> By bending sower truly planted. (*Poems* 492)

Even the first two lines of Saʿdi's poem, quoted above from "Manuscript
Translations" to offer a cleaner version devoid of editorial markings, begin
to compete with Emerson's expression of grief over his lost son in both his
journals as well as his elegy "Threnody." An earlier version in his "Notebook
Orientalist" directly addresses the loss in the first person: In Sanaa <Senahar>
I lost my son; / <<How can I tell how> I>↑my head↓ was stunned ↑by the
blow↓!" (*TN* 2:70). Such an emphatic expression of emotion reads as antithetical to Emerson's "Experience," wherein he displaces sorrow beneath both
cold objective reason as well as transcendent expressions of self-overcoming.
At least in this respective section, the Persian poet's emotive lament, which
proves retrospectively cathartic for Emerson as translator, produces a metaphorically comparable cry of the "gazelle," which Agha Shahid Ali claims gives
the Persian form its name and sensibility (*Ravishing Disunities* 3). Emerson's
quoted version, noteworthy for the change from having directly "lost" to "my

first born son sleeps" as well as the inability to express sorrow in the first person to the third person of "poor Saadi weeps" (492), curiously sanitizes more emotive early drafts. Nevertheless, it still retains the kind of substantial grief missing from his personal narrative.

Extending Saʿdi's own metaphor from his poem in this comparison, it is as though Emerson endeavors to "transplant" the materiality of the son through his translated text with lines such as these:

> "The crowd believe that harvest grow
> Where never man did barely sow.
> But Saadi saw the fruit enchanted
> By bending sower truly planted." (*Poems* 492)

More than simply carrying over words of the poem into English, Emerson through translation adopts the voice of Saʿdi's son. In an imagined encounter with his child from beyond the grave after his "grief was spent and reason came," Saʿdi writes, "Methought I heard my son exclaim . . ." At this point the boy begins to address his poet-father. This transromantic connection, wherein the child fathers the man, inverts in *Nature* Emerson's first and arguably most important aesthetic, as well as one of his greatest philosophical problems, centered on influence: "Our age is retrospective. It builds the sepulchres of the fathers" (*CW* 1:17). In this sense Barnstone's theory of reckoning with the original source author in translation proves personally applicable:

> [T]here is an anxiety-ridden conflict between originality and translation in which the paternal source of a translation must be killed or at least concealed in order to grant the translated child the dignity of originality. Hence the aim of the child is self-disguisement so that the translated self can pass as self-created and original, with minimal reference to transition and its modeling force. The source should be buried. If the burial is complete, with nothing showing, then the shadow of translation is forgotten (95).

Retrospectively, Emerson's early claims on Saʿdi's name relative to what would become his "translated self" has enabled him to become "self-created and original." Einboden significantly points out how in a notebook inherited by his father, Emerson "repeatedly inscribes the name 'Saadi' on its flyleaves, tracing in stylized calligraphy this single identity" (*Islamic Lineage* 130). Such biographical repositioning has even deeper roots in Emerson's own American family tree than may be apparent on mere surface-level inscription. Einboden's

extended analysis of inscribing Saʿdi on his father's notebook begins to shed
light on how Emerson's subtle use of the Persian poet's name will help him
achieve a "burial" of the source text within what Barnstone calls the "shadow
of translation":

> Writing in pages passed down from the American deceased,
> Emerson births his new Islamic name, his "sublimed self," pivoting
> between discrete paternities, reaching back to rebrand a notebook
> owned by his own father while offering private material for his
> son and grandson to recover, annotating for the twentieth cen-
> tury public their famous father's evolving Islamic alias. (*Islamic
> Lineage* 130)

Having biographically displaced the words of his actual father with the
adoption of Saʿdi's name early in his development as a writer, Emerson through
translation assumes the voice of his namesake's original source text. He tears
away the figural gravestone much like "flyleaves" from his re-possessed father's
notebook as he displaces or "transplants" Saʿdi's son to follow the Persian poet
into the boy's grave: "I staggered to my darling's tomb / And tore the sealed
stone therefrom" (*Poems* 492). Taking the etymology of "verse" as "turn"
derived from the movement of the plow in farming, and considering the
poem's concluding couplet, Emerson reaps the harvest of his predecessor's
buried son: "But Saadi saw the fruit enchanted / By bending sower truly
planted" (492). Reworking his appropriative poetic labor into English, the
American translator-poet thus resurrects the theme of his own lost son as
if to overcome it, along with his assumption of an ancient literary tradition.
   More than a few mere words or the application of a certain passing
sensibility, Emerson attempts to coopt through translation the integral essence
of his predecessor's verse. Walter Benjamin's famously esoteric "Task of the
Translator" essay, wherein the source text dies and experiences an "afterlife"
in the target language (254), helps accounts for the transfer of spirit as well
as letter embodied in the original poem. Though originally written by a poet
based in Islam, the verse relating the death of Saʿdi's son uncannily resonates
with the story of Jesus' resurrection. Consequently, it remains amenable for
Emerson's typical syncretic approach to global literatures. One of Emerson's
trots of the original poem reads,

> despairing I gathered down to <the grave/ stone/ mouth/>his tomb
> and tore the <grave> stone away from <his grave> its mouth
> I <wandered> entered into that narrow place <of terror,>
> with enflamed eyes quite out of my senses. (*TN* 2:70)

Given Emerson's intertextual proclivities, it's worth noting the possibility of a displaced Christian resurrection here as well. Even if the original source poem partly derives from the gospel story, it would come as no surprise, considering how Sufis like Saʿdi at times make good use of Jesus' teaching. As Ilahi-Ghomshei explains, "the Sufi poets consider the appearance of Jesus as an ever recurring event sustaining them in the present . . ." (101). Regardless of literal origins, this correspondence to Christ for Emerson can be seen as allegorically allowing him to further assume the resurrected voice of Saʿdi's son as his own rendering gets figuratively reborn into English.

In 1857, fifteen years after the death of his son and around the time he most likely would have been translating this Saʿdi poem, Emerson opened Waldo's tomb. He records the following in his journal:

> This morning I had the remains of my mother and of my son Waldo removed from the tomb of Mrs. Ripley to my lot in "Sleepy Hollow." The sun shone brightly on the coffins, of which Waldo's was well-preserved—now fifteen years. I ventured to look into the coffin. (*JMN* 14:154)

"In that flatly declarative last sentence," writes Cameron, "Emerson records his sense of the risk associated with looking for the child . . . or the child's remains . . . or . . . into the space where the child is or was" (137). While such an entry begins to foreground Emerson's emotional search for his son, Saʿdi's poem displays even greater displaced feeling relative to his more objectified, empirical investigation of the tomb. Toward such a reading of the translation, Einboden finds Emerson "enacting a type of unconscious translation, physically repeating in America an act poetically reported in Persia eight centuries earlier." Noting how the "sun shone brightly on the coffins" in Emerson's prose echoes how Saʿdi's verse renders the light to "blaze like noon,"[5] Einboden substantiates rhetorical parallels wherein "Emerson recovers his son through surrogate Persian rendition and physical American 'removal.' . . ." For Emerson, however, Einboden concludes that only a "half-translation" occurs, since unlike "the revelatory words that culminate Saʿdi's painful silence," the American seals his experience "with a quiet 'vault' conclusively 'covered with slabs of granite'" (*Islamic Lineage* 153).

However, insofar as Persian verse so often allows him to voice the "other half" of himself in expression, the idea of a "half translation" especially suggests a pressing need to further reconcile personal closure in his Saʿdi translation. Though sealing his son's tomb, his English renderings of the Persian poem should therefore remain open to further interrogation. More than locating his deferred feelings over his great loss in the lines of Saʿdi, Emerson finds in his translation an echo of his frequent denial of agency to express his profound grief, followed by his subtle reclaiming of it in writing. Much like Cameron reads the trajectory of Emerson's "Experience" as the deferral of emotion from grief to analysis, in the translated Sa'di poem the "despairing" father goes into the "grave" or "mouth" of his son's tomb, facing the "terror" that drives him "out of his senses." After such terrible disturbance, he rather suddenly experiences mental restoration, explaining, "back from grief my reason came." Reverting to reticence more akin to his treatment of his son's death in "Experience," Emerson suspiciously contains emotion even as he expresses it, a common rhetorical pattern even in his early letters following the immediate death of his son. After stressing to the reader in a letter how he can say little if nothing of the loss (*Letters* 3:7), "he goes on to glorify the boy in sentimental terms . . ." (Schneider 100). In another letter, again as in "Experience," he states, "Alas! I chiefly grieve that I cannot grieve" (*Letters* 3:9) before going on to express intense emotion in subsequent correspondences about his great loss. This makes his seeming emotional closure in the translation along with his son's actual tomb rather suspect, suggestive of repression.

One small yet significant translation choice by Emerson begins to reveal his continued attempt to reconcile his son's loss by domesticating the Persian poetic tradition in English. The term "darling," with no equivalent found in the German intermediary source from which he translated, can be taken as a symptom of his personal relation to loss that he paradoxically begins to express through containment. Though also used in Emerson's translations of Hafez as well as in his own poetry, the word never appears in the entirety of Gladstone's rendering of Sa'di's *Gulistan*, for which Emerson wrote an introduction. To dramatize the notable changes he makes by inserting the word in Sa'di's elegy for his son, consider acclaimed German translator Susan's Bernofsky's literal English trot of von Hammer-Purgstall's rendering from Persian:[6] "Despairing I went down to the tomb." Emerson opts to change this line to "I staggered to my darling's tomb" (*TN* 2:83, 86). In Emerson's multiple versions of the same poem, "darling" continues to appear: "my darling sleeps" "Methought my darling <cried out>" (*TN* 2:70, 77), "my darling did exclaim" (*TN* 2:79, 83), and "my darling did" (*TN* 2:97). Notably, nowhere does von Hammer-Purgstall use the German equivalent in the rendering Emerson worked into his translation. Other changes—such as the first line, closer to the literal German meaning "At Sana I lost a son," to his "In Senahar, my firstborn sleeps,—" (*TN* 2:83), further support a reading of his interventions as translator to recreate this Persian poet's comparable loss more in the image of his own son.

Without reference to the Sa'di translations, Schneider notes that generally in his writing "Emerson's sentimental characterization of his son as a 'darling'" becomes "a common feature of his journal entries and letters about Waldo"

(99). In this sense the return of the term years later in the Sa'di rendering, which models the earlier journal entries that tend to sentimentally "memorialize Waldo" (Schneider 100), dramatize Emerson's recurrent attempts of collapsing the temporal, linguistic, and literary distance of personal loss. On the night of young Waldo's death, Emerson wrote four letters to friends and family, then at least six more the following day (Richardson 359). "Darling" recurs in his brief, emotional messages: "Dear Lucy, Our darling is dead" (*Letters* 3:6); "My darling & the world's wonderful child . . . has fled out of my arms like a dream" (*Letters* 3:7); "Dear Elizabeth[,] Everything wakes this morning but my darling Boy" (*Letters* 3:8).

In light of this analysis, it is worth noting that the first stanza of "Threnody," which has been "praised as one of Emerson's finest poems" and remains "arguably one of the great nineteenth-century elegies" (*CW* 9: 290), concludes with the lines: "And, looking over the hills, I mourn / The darling who shall not return" (*CW* 9:290). Too long to quote in full or to sufficiently analyze in this study, the poem demonstrates enough of a connection with Emerson's later translated poem as to warrant further comparative investigation. The "tears of ancient sorrow" (*CW* 9:298) in the final lines anticipate his eventual reckoning of profound loss through the classical Persian verse tradition in both "Experience" as well as his Persian namesake's thirteenth-century elegy. Young Waldo's "ominous hole he dug in the sand" (*CW* 9:292) in "Threnody" prefigures not only the boy's impeding death, but the hole into which his poet-father will descend in physical and spiritual search for him through a German translation of an original Persian poem. That the latter's allusion to the story of "Yusuf" from the twelfth sura of the *Qur'an* (Einboden, *Islamic Heritage* 153) carries over into Emerson's translation with the anglicized name change of "Joseph" (bringing with it even more Biblical associations) deftly unifies the underpinnings of the two poets' religious backgrounds. This in turn lays the groundwork for the figural resurrection of domestic and foreign sons in their respective elegies. Questioning the worth of the earth's "harvests" in his own verse and upon American soil where his child has been buried (*CW* 9:293), Emerson ascribes to nature his inability to reconcile loss:

> Was there no star that could be sent,
> No watcher in the firmament,
> No angel from the countless host
> Could stoop to heal that only child,
> Nature's sweet marvel undefiled,
> And keep the blossom of the earth,
> Which all her harvests were not worth? (*CW* 9:293)

Much like Saʿdi arrives at "the end of wit" before hearing the transcendent
voice of his son calling him into the light, Emerson exhausts reasoned
possibilities in an apparent conclusion to his elegy. He declares, "I am too
much bereft" and laments Waldo having been, "Born for the future, to the
future lost!" (*CW* 9:294–295). However, the "ominous hole" that Waldo dug
in an anticipation of his own grave becomes, in Emerson's Saʿdi translation,
a "mouth"[7] (*TN* 2:77). Such an opening gives the son, as well as the father
who channels him, a renewed voice. While the "deep Heart" in "Threnody"
responds to Emerson with a consoling reminder of the "mysteries of Nature's
heart" beyond "utterance, and past belief," Saʿdi receives a redeeming message
from his son through the opening of the grave:

> I heard my son exclaim
> 'If my dark house thy heart affright
> 'Saadi strive upwards to the light
> 'Wilt though give graves the blaze of noon
> 'High hearts can work that wonder soon

Relocating his lost child into Saʿdi's poem, Emerson gets paradoxically closer
to Waldo by moving farther away. Despite the linguistic differences of German and the original Persian, as well as the temporal and physical distance
between America and Iran, his displaced grief through translation begins to
change the nameless heart to the voice of his son. Emerson thus discovers
through Saʿdi the absent, repressed "angel" in his own elegy, who speaks to the
father from above.[8] Reconfiguring the aforementioned comparison between
the light upon the Persian and American sons' graves, "Threnody" achieves
a retrospective illumination of both poets' progeny: "Light is light which
radiates, / Blood is blood which circulates" (*CW* 9:297).

Returning to "Experience" with the comparison to his translated Saʿdi
poem in mind, Emerson tends to rhetorically supplant his first-born son by
different yet relatable means. Failing to reconcile his grief through a redeeming cycle of "harvests" (*Poems* 492), as in Saʿdi's poem where grief gets transformed into joy, he returns later in his essay to the ultimate "unhappy cause":
the predecessor source of "The Fall of Man" (*CW* 3:43). Using the diction of
fallen nature to describe his personal loss, he calls it "caducous," a term from
botany referring to the premature dropping of leaves, while further noting
that it "falls off from me, and leaves no scar" (*CW* 3:29). The true loss for
Emerson occurs fourteen pages after citing his son's death in this reference
of the Fall, not out of a Christian Eden, but from the primal vision he once
claimed in his personally Edenic "transparent eyeball." As he explains in
"Experience": "Once we lived in what we saw . . ." Just as he seems to have

forgotten his son, like the loss of land, he further relates: "People forget that it is the eye which makes the horizon . . ." (*CW* 3: 293–294).

Like Emerson's claim upon Sa'di's poem through translation, his essay displaces the son in an attempt to precede him as ambiguous "eye/I," arriving before the first and more tragic Fall of man. To conclude this cursory introduction of Emerson's engagement with Iran, consider his attempt to ground himself in the deepest roots of the Islamic religion while returning, as though transplanted, back to his pre-Fallen, Romantically *a priori* America:

> But every insight from this realm of thought is felt as initial, and promises a sequel. I do not make it; I arrive there, and behold what was there already. I make! O no! I clap my hands in infantine joy and amazement, before the first opening to me of this august magnificence, old with the love and homage of innumerable ages, young with the life of life, the sunbright Mecca of the desert. And what a future it opens! I feel a new heart beating with the love of the new beauty. I am ready to die out of nature, and be born again into this new yet unapproachable America I have found in the West. (*CW* 3:41)

Regressing to an "infantine joy and amazement," he conflates his appropriative translation practices with "innumerable ages" and the fantasy of a transcendent present. Such ecstatic joy is reminiscent of Emerson's critique of life as too often impinging on the true "intellectual freedom," which he comes to associate with Hafez's Persian wine. As he writes in "Experience": "So much of our time is preparation, so much routine, and so much retrospect, that the pith of each man's genius contracts itself to a very few hours" (*CW* 3:29). In his own way, he calls for transcendent intoxication like Hafez: "Last night in the rose garden the bird sang: / "Wine boy! Help these drinkers reach ecstasy!"[9]

Again following the death of his son and the repressed burial of emotions over his loss, in "Experience" he feels "a new heart beating" (like the return of the heart in "Threnody") as a kind of mystical awakening. To "die out of nature" in the context of this essay means to preempt the Fall and the mourning over the fact that "Once we lived in what we saw." Like Hafez before him who claimed "a vision of an event that took place in eternity" (Anvar 125), Emerson sees again as if for the first time, embracing his originating arrival at a "Mecca" that he has discovered in the "yet unapproachable America I have found in the West."

The birthplace of Muhammad and not far from where he received his first revelation of the *Qur'an*, Mecca remains the principal locus for the religion of Islam, which underpins the mysticism of Persian Sufi poets Emerson

renders into English and attempts to imitate. Replacing this sacred place of
great historical and religious resonance with the "desert" of his own country
through approximate rhyme ("Mecca/America"), Emerson aptly introduces
the core foundations of his Persian appropriative translation practices. Considering his ignorance of the Persian language (as well as Arabic, in which
the Qur'an is written), his will to a pre-verbal "infantine joy" in the passage
above proves particularly apt for this comparison. Much like the revelation
of words from the divine to an illiterate Muhammad, Emerson will come to
channel original verse from Persian he fails to understand into English as
he pretends to be Sa'di and Hafez. He receives poetic inspiration the way he
claims in "Experience" to achieve spiritual insight: "I do not make it. I arrive
there." Insofar as he further relies on his secretary to make trots from von
Hammer-Purgstall's intermediary German versions (Verma 47), he doubles his
prophetic power as translator-poet, mirroring the transcription of the Islamic
holy book's divinely revealed words. By going back through one European
language to access classical Persian verse as well as returning to Mecca in
"Experience" for his own figural reinventions, he positions his own Western
golden age of the pastoral in the new tradition he claims for himself, "whereon
flocks graze, and shepherds pipe and dance" (CW 3:41).

Of course, none of this is to argue that Emerson makes Persian verse
or the Islam from which it derives overtly central to his personal vision,
best exemplified by his transparent eyeball. Following the quote about his
regression to infantine joy in an American Mecca, he goes on to articulate
the "unbounded substance," a "cause" that paradoxically reiterates his will
towards a translingual ideal insofar as it "refuses to be named." As he explains,
it manifests in various material forms: "Jesus and the moderns by love" and
"Thales by water." For Emerson, "Zoroaster," the prophetic founder of the first
religion in Iran, arrives "by fire" as one among many assigned to a specific
"national religion" (CW 3:41). Following the comparative threads between
Emerson and the Persian tradition, however, leads to a better understanding of how he rhetorically inserts himself into a nonlinear, fragmented, and
circulating aesthetic predicated in part on the influence of Persian poetry in
an attempt to overcome it. This in turn makes a fundamental demonstration
of his American aesthetic that would accommodate all retrospective ages and
traditions through negation.

Returning to his displacement of the buried child in both Sa'di's poem
as translator and his own prose in "Experience" as essayist, Emerson himself
opts for a position between originating father and son. Ironically, he locates
emotion not by a quintessential desire for "unmediated experience," as Richardson claims in his reading of Emerson's journal about opening his son's

tomb (3), but through the mediation of a Persian predecessor poet accessed via an intermediary German translation. "The mid-world is best" (*CW* 3:31) he reiterates throughout "Experience." Though on one level he references "the middle region of our being" between the "realm of . . . lifeless science" and "that of sensation" (*CW* 3:36), figuratively he puts himself into the center of a recurring absence ephemerally marked by the fire of Zoroaster's "unbounded substance," an alternative or Bhabhaian "third space" between past and future, Mecca and America, and father and son. Along what he calls "the equator of life" (*CW* 3:36), he insists on his own transparent vision, "the eye which makes the horizon," as he writes a few pages later in "Experience." Part of his arriving at a Mecca of his own invention means clearing away the space of the predecessor, emptying the sepulchres both of forefathers like Sa'di as well as their offspring. In this respect, by his own claim upon "middles," he himself effectively replaces his son, "Waldo," which of course is the American poet-translator's own middle name.

Chapter 3

Imitation as Suicide

Islamic Fatalism
and the Paradox of Self-Reliance

"Not one is among you," said Mahomet, "to
whom is not already appointed his seat in fire
or his seat in bliss."

—Sa'di, *Gulistan* (1)

Much like Sa'di offers a mediating voice for such a personal theme as the loss
of a child, along with Hafez he further provides Emerson a means by which
to interrogate and even help to reconcile one of his central philosophical
problems. Persian poets who through the free-play of their verse subvert what
Emerson views as the predetermination of Islam return him to his comparable
approach to fate. That the religious underpinnings of his Persian influences
potentially threaten his self-determination in his own writing paradoxically
reveals the interdependence of his presumably individualistic and original
American perspective with a foreign verse tradition. Projecting the essence
of his most well-known argument in "Self-Reliance" upon the imitation of
his ideal Persian persona in a poem he makes adoptively eponymous through
the name and identity of "Sa'di" reinforces such a connection, especially as
an Islamic source in both the essay and exemplifying verse seems to oppose
Emerson's insistence upon himself. Ironically, he must in part rely on the
example of his Persian namesake to transcend fatalistic limitation and achieve
his definitive American independence.

   Before extracting comparable ideas of pre-determinism from the respective writings of the American and his foreign predecessors, a closer reading
of Emerson's identification with Sa'di and Hafez begins to show how he comes

to conflate their fatalistic reckonings with his own. Unlike his passing citation of the epic poet "Firdousi," who he calls simply "the Persian Homer" (*CW* 8:126) while moving on to other more lyrical authors, he curiously makes his critical discovery of Sa'di a matter of personal destiny. Prior to his actual 1848 reading of the poet in translation (Ekhtiyar 60), he claims to have anticipated him. "In Saadi's *Gulistan*," he writes, "I find many traits which comport with the portrait I drew" (*JMN* 9:37). Having coopted the fragmented voice of Sa'di's son through translation, Emerson also embodies the father's biography by adopting his name, ultimately replacing his predecessor's self-portrait in the Persian mirror. Insofar as Emerson considered the poet's conventional "signing" of the *ghazal's* last couplet as a kind of Persian "copyright" wherein identification gets romantically "interwoven more or less closely with the subject of the piece" (*CW* 8:134–135), he begins taking ownership of the thirteenth-century poet's identity by imitating it under his chosen pseudonym. That he possibly changed his predecessor's name to "Seyd" or "Said" out of metrical convenience in English (Edward Emerson 414) further constitutes an act of appropriative translation, an attempt to fashion himself into the Persian poet on his own rhetorical terms.

While such attempts to precede Sa'di demonstrate tremendous agency as well as considerable hubristic presumption, they ultimately draw so close to the poet who he replaces that the influence can't help but appear as reciprocal. From a psychoanalytic perspective, supported by Emerson's own reflection on his prescient discovery of his poetic ideal, his sustained interest in Sa'di can be interrogated as a kind of biographical determinism emerging from his formative gaze toward the Middle East. Early in his development, he had a plethora of choices for a persona in his journals. Why did he opt first for "Osman," derived from the founder of the Ottoman Empire? Soon after, in his more public writing, why did he then come to claim a Persian poet from the same era, as if desiring to viscerally establish the literary equivalent of a seminal dynasty? In Alger's aforementioned translated anthology that Emerson read, "the infancy of the Osmanly empire" extends in the following page to the "Augustan age of Persian letters" (XVII). Such an exemplifying allegory of Emerson's literary development reveals his early attempt to imaginatively inhabit the history of a foreign region through its central political and artistic figures. Both his initial look toward the Middle East as well as his later and more specific focus on Iran constitute a kind of psychological projection. His superficial gaze across the Atlantic thus appears worthy of further examination for what it reflects of his own identity. While Emerson seemingly chose to read the Persian poets, in a sense they first decided to read him, provoking his desire for self-evasion while also providing the means to achieve it. In this respect, just as much as Emerson envisions Sa'di's portrait before his respective biographical discovery of the Persian poet, Sa'di too sees Emerson coming.

A plethora of reasons account for Emerson's attraction to Sa'di, helping to explain why he was destined to find his way to this poet. In addition to allowing for the cathartic grieving of his own son in the Persian poem he translates, he views Sa'di as reflecting his Romantic insights of the natural world in his writing. Noticing how Emerson cites Sa'di more than Hafez as his ideal poet, Carpenter reasons that he found greater identification with his overall sensibility, as evidenced by his description in the introduction that he wrote to the Persian masterpiece known as the *Gulistan* (129). This book, which translates as "Rose Garden," uses the figuration of the ubiquitous rose and other natural imagery in Persian literature to interrogate deep philosophical truths, much like Emerson's own book, *Nature*. The introductory poem as epigraph to this book aptly captures the aesthetic of Sa'di: "The eye reads omens where it goes, / And speaks all languages the rose . . ." (*CW* 1:7). Stylistically similar to the fragmented lyricism of Emerson's essays, much of the text combines poetry and prose to the point of calling the strict division of genres into question. Optimistic as well as sarcastic in tone, it further thrives, as does Emerson's writing, on aphorisms. Thematically, spiritual teachings rooted in Sufi mysticism also resemble Emerson's transcendent observations and informed moralizing.

Noting the Persian poet's "wit, practical sense, and just moral sentiments," as well as his "instinct to teach" in his introduction to his verse (*Gulistan* Preface v), Emerson naturally begins to locate his own self-portrait in his adopted namesake. David Maulsby observes that as in Sa'di, "In Emerson also is the unusual concurrence of ecstasy and prudence" (149). Emerson further praises Sa'di's lack of old-world superstition (*Gulistan* Preface x) and rhetorically values his "inconsecutiveness," which he finds in the form of the Persian *ghazal* (*Gulistan* Preface xi), and which Benton has shown applies just as well to Emerson's rhetoric (33). Like Emerson, the writing of the Persian poet with whom he most identified resists stable signification, as evidenced by Katouzian's assessment: "it is virtually impossible to fit Sa'di's ideas into a system of thought, or easily locate him in a given category of classical Persian poets" (71). Add to this the ancient poet following a tradition of highlighting "legends of typical men" (*Gulistan* Preface xii), much like Emerson's frequent appeals to examples of greatness. While the American wrote of "Representative Men" who embody admirable qualities as he encouraged their examples for his reading audience, the Persian gave advice to rulers of his day to better perfect the administration of their appointed positions. To this end both poets also offer frequent reflections on human psychology. In an extended study of

what attracted Emerson to Saˈdi, Loloi considers Emerson's nineteenth-century
America as being especially receptive to the Persian poet, finding the aesthetics between traditions linked, as did Emerson himself, through Platonism
and Neoplatonism (106–111). Importantly, it is at this earliest philosophical
point of origin where he first seems to significantly make a connection to
Persian poetry.

To best exemplify the extent of the reciprocal influence between Emerson and Saˈdi, wherein the two disparate poets become especially connected,
consider William Alger's introduction of the Persian poet in his previously
cited anthology *Poetry of the East*:

> Saadi was asked what he, an ideal poet, was good for. In turn he
> inquired what was the use of the rose; and on being told it was
> good to be smelled, replied, "And I am good to smell it!" So our
> Concord Saadi sings, as if resounding from to-day and America,
> over the ages and the sea, the dead lyrist of Persia . . . (77)

As Einboden explains, by giving this "Concord Saadi" the power to "dialog
with the dead," Alger's subtle reference "recalls Emerson's own earliest strategies
of Muslim pseudonym" (*Islamic Lineage* 154). Alger's critical transformation
of Emerson into a hybrid American / Persian poet also recalls earlier critics
such as Oliver Wendell Holmes conflating the two men, finding it "hard to tell
what is from the Persian and from what is original" (173). Circling back to a
question of origins, Alger tellingly begins to turn Emerson into Saˈdi through
the physical connection to his New England town. Such a site of reconfiguration comparably reinforces the clearing of figurative space in "Experience,"
which facilitated Emerson transplanting "Mecca" on American soil.

To fully appreciate how Emerson makes such an audacious claim upon a
predecessor, it becomes necessary to revisit the radical usurpation of influence
he attempts on a foreign nation's literature and its integral foundation in a
very different religion from his Christian background. Uprooting the Persian
tradition and all that sustains it, Emerson effectively transplants himself as
Saˈdi, its prize Shirazi rose and author of the *Gulistan*, or *The Rose Garden*.
To do so, he must pre-determine the Persian poet's arrival in America. More
than passively receiving him as an imitative model, Emerson reconfigures
him into his own version of a poetic ideal. Fiercely self-reliant to the point
of thwarting any impediments to creation in his own image, Emerson must
anticipate Saˈdi by seeing him into being. Through Platonic unification previously outlined in chapter 1, he therefore demonstrates an appropriative
tendency to disavow temporal and linguistic difference as he equates his

tradition and his own Romantic identity to the identity of the Persian poet as well as the verse he wrote in his respective age. While revering religious texts from various cultures, he ultimately asserts his own Romantic originality, best expressed in his "Self-Reliance" essay: "What have I to do with the sacredness of traditions, if I live holy from within?" (*CW* 2:30). As he affirms, "you shall not discern the foot-prints of any other . . . you shall not hear any name" (*CW* 2:39). More than progenitors, Emerson echoes himself in "Experience" by figuratively clearing away the essence of all Middle Eastern influence. "Mecca," after displacing "America," remains so new that even he finds it "unapproachable" (*CW* 3:41), as if from previous metrical "feet" (to again use the ubiquitous convention of the pun from Persian poetry in English). If even divine tradition housed in the holiest site of Islam that greatly informs Sufi poetry fails to remain sacrosanct, personal lyric influence appears easily refuted, if not erasable.

Establishing himself *a priori* the religion of his classical literary inheritors, Emerson effectively empties out integral linguistic and cultural foundations of his source author, resurrecting the Persian poet in his own name and on his own American terms. "Our Age is retrospective," he declares at the beginning of *Nature*, a book similar to one based on a metaphorical rendering of roses by his Persian predecessor. Disavowing what precedes him, he would empty the "sepulchres of the fathers" (*CW* 1:7), playing on his own Christian inheritance that he resurrects to transcend other established traditions. Henry David Thoreau, Emerson's Romantic contemporary, dramatizes his comparably radical usurpation of Sa'di's verse and identity:

> I know, for instance, that Sadi once entertained identically the same thought that I do, and thereafter I can find no essential difference between Sadi and myself. He is not Persian, he is not ancient, he is not strange to me . . . He had no more interior and essential and sacred self than can come naked into my thought this moment. . . . If Sadi were to come back to claim a *personal* identity with the historical Sadi, he would find there were too many of us; he could not get a skin that would contain us all. The symbol of a personal identity in this sense is a mummy from the catacombs,—a whole skin it may [be], but no life within it. By living the life of a man is made common property. By sympathy with Sadi I have emboweled him. In his thought I have a sample of *him*, a slice from his core, which makes it unimportant where certain bones which the thinker once employed may lie . . . (*Writings* 290)

The personal sense of the ancient poet from Iran, like his body, has presumably been emptied of its original cultural and historical identification. Like Emerson's cooptation of Persian verse by naming himself as the author of his imitations as well as inserting his own English language and literary allusions in translation, Thoreau claims the same predecessor as "common property." No longer "Persian," "ancient," or even "strange" in his foreignness, Sa'di has been rendered into America from his corpse. He remains subjected to appropriation by anyone currently "living the life of a man." "The symbol" of the predecessor remains preserved as "a mummy from the catacombs," but only upon the surface level, much like Emerson's "sepulchres of the fathers." Similar to Thoreau, Emerson thus finds himself free to inhabit both the name and identity of Sa'di.

Such a manifestation of Emerson's persona surfaces relatively early in his writing with the character of 'SAID' in the poem "Uriel," which anticipates his later, more developed poem titled with his adopted namesake. Like Bloom's *daemon* of the counter-sublime, "SAID" challenges all surrounding influence of "the young gods," significantly positioned in an ancient Greek universe of "Pleiades" comprised of Atlas's seven daughters. The Persian poet alone becomes privy to Uriel's disruption of Western order, represented by "Time" with the division of the "calendar," as well as by poetics with "Laws of form, and metre . . ." Through his lyric reflection as Persian/American, or American/Persian, Emerson as SAID thus exemplifies Bloom's process of *daemonization*, defined as a "revisionary ratio of de-individuating the precursor" (*Anxiety* 107). Self-divided by imitation, he locates much of the Western tradition, along with himself, in a Persian poet upon whom he predicates his transcendent vision.

The outlier, self-reliant young god whose words Emerson's "SAID" transcribes introduces an antithetical Eastern aesthetic: "Line in nature is not found; / Unit and universe are round" (*CW* 9:34). Violating linearity, such a summary speaks for Emerson's rhetorical attraction to, and frequent modeling of, Persian verse, which he summarizes in his introduction of the Eastern tradition as the "inconsecutiveness quite alarming to western logic" (*CW* 8:127). There is scholarly consensus that Emerson deliberately relates his own heretical stance in his famous "Divinity School Address" against Unitarians to Sa'di's contrarian announcement of an "Uranometrical truth to an audience of Geometrical fabulists" (*CW* 9:32). The Persian poet as represented in "Uriel" further invites broader comparisons to Emerson's greater aesthetic. Observing how such fragmented logic resonates with Emerson's sensibility, Dunston notes how he "is comforted, not alarmed, by this inconsecutiveness, because it speaks the truth about life's surprises" (117). Further justifying

Emerson's fragmented rhetoric, Buell argues that his "self-reliance can't be achieved at the level of conventional linear expression," hence his "shifts of focus, intuitive leaps, self-corrective backtracking" as well as a "discontinuous" and "hyperbolic" writing style (572). In this respect Emerson relies on "Eastern mysticism" that can help him "move poetry constantly further from the linear, not to say mechanical logic of the Understanding which, as in the 'Rational Religion' of Anglo-American Unitarianism, obscured the truths that he felt were available only to reason" (CW 9:lxxii). Here again critical description of Emerson proves equally applicable to the Persian poets, especially the discontinuity that allows them to embrace, rather than resist, life's mysterious turns in their verse. A greater spiritual sensibility infuses the Persian form, as noted by Robert Bly when comparing the more logical or "thinking poems" of Stevens and Wordsworth that "proceed in a gentlemanly way down the page" to the lines of Hafez that "move in a jagged manner" (ix). Uriel's final paradoxical line in the next couplet, which further contradicts assumed laws of causation, could easily have been written by Sa'di or Hafez: "In vain produced, all rays return; / Evil will bless, and ice will burn" (CW 9:34). While "SAID" in this poem at times may sound Persian, he more often resembles Emerson, exemplifying the American's ubiquitous claim upon his foreign ideal. Having recorded Uriel's challenging "the bounds of good and ill," SAID presumably remains the sole, self-reliant witness to the young god's "sad-self-knowledge," noting how he "Withdrew, that hour, into his cloud" (CW 9:34). To some extent, the poem concludes with an ambiguous speaker, meaning the reader can't know if Emerson or "SAID" writes of Uriel's extreme and rather fearless isolation, much like Alger conflates both American and Persian in his introduction of "our Concord Saadi." In this respect, the former inhabits a position analogous to intermediary translator.

Rather than going "through" the source poem, however, Emerson channels the source poet himself. Consequently, Bloom's quotation of Emerson, "The Daemons lurk and are dumb," speaks to the latent effects of appropriative influence, an ephemeral "context against which the numinous shines forth. This context is a void," continues Bloom, "emptied or estranged by the poets themselves, while the shining-forth returns us to all the sorrows of divination" (Anxiety 101). The poem's ending further reinforces Emerson's resistance to Western linearity, insofar as the lines read more like a recurring refusal to voice a conventional conclusion, "a forgetting wind / Stole over the celestial kind" (CW 9:34). Nobody knows for sure the location of Uriel, and by implication, of the poet who once articulated his presence. It is as if he inhabits the transformative site between Emerson's Concord and his reconfiguration of Mecca. Further highlighting the nebulous context that Bloom describes, which thus becomes a conflation of the ambiguous Bhabhaian "third space" shadowing of hybrid literary influence around Emerson's transparent eyeball, "Uriel's voice" surfaces "now and then." He "shines forth," to use Bloom's rhetoric, illuminating his elusive effects that subtly disrupt assumed authority, even while remaining hidden: "And a blush tinged the upper sky / And the gods shook, they knew not why" (*CW* 9:35).

By the time Emerson writes his poem "Saadi," he has come much closer to his Persian namesake and consequently attempts to draw at least partially away from his own identity. This becomes yet another rhetorical move toward a kind of discontinuity of self that could be added to Buell's categorization, especially as it further allows Emerson to achieve a greater self-reliance in such radically foreign identification. Taking Bloom's "revisionary ratio" between poet and precursor as Persian reflection, Emerson identifies so strongly with the thirteenth-century Sufi poet that they effectively become one, an equivalence of poet/poem as seen in the Sufi mirror. Spanning both East and West, Emerson conflates disparate traditions through a foreign voice he claims in his own language: "Suns rise and set in Saadi's speech!" (*CW* 9:247). Though containing Persian signifiers representative of Sa'di's originating culture and verse, Emerson's poem more completely embodies his self-reliant philosophy. Just as Emerson believed he anticipated Sa'di's portrait prior to discovering his biography, he seems to consider himself as having anticipated representation of his poetic sensibility. "Thou shalt leave the world, and know the muse only," he writes in "The Poet" (*CW* 3:23). In "Saadi," his isolated Persian subject has direct communication from the "Muse" while removed from the masses behind his "cottage wall" (*CW* 9:247). As one of Emerson's "liberating gods" who "are free" and "make free" (*CW* 3:18), Sa'di in tune with the fact that "Man in man is imprisonèd" (*CW* 9:246) opens "innumerable doors" of humankind. An "unveiled Allah" liberates man from "Fraudulent time," allowing "gray haired crones" to transcend death at "the height of mighty Nature . . ." (*CW* 9:247).

While in the previous chapter Sa'di's poem about the loss of a son returns Emerson's own repressed grief through translation, his overt claim upon his ideal poet through this imitation embodies a resurrected rhetorical performance of his predecessor. "Well or poorly known," argues von Frank, "Saadi remained to Emerson for a very long time a sort of allegorical representation of what an Emersonian poet might be" (*CW* 9:lxix). Seemingly looking at the Persian mirror with his more universal and all-encompassing transparency, Emerson attempts to find "the other half" of himself in Sa'di through his performance of the foreign poet's "expression." Though he based his own poem with the Persian poet's name as title in part on his knowledge of his predecessor's background and literary tradition, he ultimately projects his most definitive philosophy as articulated in "Self-Reliance" onto the biographical reconfiguration of the first "half" of his American self. Richardson to this end finds the message "that the true poet must keep to his own affairs" as the "unmistakable main point of the poem" (388). As an early discoverer of Saʿdi for the American tradition who boasts having correctly imagined his portrait prior to his actual reading his work in translation,[1] Emerson found himself searching beyond the European tradition as he continued to "look in vain for the poet" (*CW* 3:21) who he fantasizes will emerge in his country. "Saadi" in his eponymous-persona poem therefore has "the Muse" decree, "Ere one man my hill may climb / Who can turn the golden rhyme." As if to resurrect himself from the "sepulchres of the Fathers," Emerson further has the same muse, who significantly seems to derive from the West, anoint the Persian poet to "Seek the living among the dead" (*CW* 9:246). Such an admonition follows Thoreau's claims on foreign identity by "living the life" of the same "man." The remnants of the Persian language and its poetic tradition, exemplified by the very name of "Saadi," surfaces like the mere "skin" of a lifeless literary ancestor for both Americans to embody.

Seemingly emerging directly out of "Self-Reliance," where Emerson proclaims, "the great man is he who in the midst of the crowd keeps with perfect sweetness the independence of solitude" (*CW* 2:31), his poem insists that "Saadi loved the race of men," even as multiple stanzas end with slight variations of the recurring refrain, ". . . Saadi dwells alone" (*CW* 9:243–244). As Buell observes, for Emerson "the first requirement for self-reliance is to have distance from others" (557). Emerson's depiction of a poet able to "sit aloof" for the maintenance of his spiritual integrity further demonstrates what Schmidt sees as "One of the most important Transcendentalist innovations . . . the remaking of the hermit's solitude into a much more expansive spiritual trope." Emerging from the enlightenment as a negative stereotype, solitude in the nineteenth century became "an oasis of redemptive isolation amid the myriad alienations of modernity" (15–16). Emerson's affirmation of the hermit through Saʿdi thus carries a Persian figure into his contemporary American ideal of artistic and spiritual independence.

Yet while affirming his ability to stand apart from the social order, Emerson paradoxically relies on a fusion of Eastern and Western influences to assert his individuality. He predicates much of his American identity in both his essay "Self-Reliance" as well as in his persona poem "Saadi" on different verse traditions. Positioning his Persian poet in a Greco-Roman pastoral with "kine in droves," Emerson has him receive "the lyre" from "God," effectively making him Apollo. A few stanzas later in "Saadi," he is said to possess the wisdom of "the gods" (243–244), casually interjecting what would prove unimaginable polytheism in the Persian poet's Islam.[2] Sa'di even reaches an Emersonian insistence on American optimism, along with his ideal of visually overcoming his rhetorical presence: "Sunshine in his heart transferred / Lighted each transparent word." He is also rendered *sui generis* among any competing influence, much like Emerson's self-reliant ideal: "For Saadi's nightly stars did burn / Brighter than Dschami's day" (*CW* 9:245). It is worth noting that following the typical approach to his English renderings, Emerson uses the German spelling for "Jami," a contemporary of Sa'di. Having started his poem in ancient Greek origins, he then subtly approaches, as if to outshine by a reflection of American self-reliance, the romantic German tradition of von Hammer-Purgstall and Goethe who precede him as translators and imitators of Persian verse.

Localizing such imitation begins to exemplify how Emerson ironically becomes most like himself by mimicking or quoting others, even while approaching the limits of such appropriation. There arguably has never been a more outsourcing writer, philosopher, and poet in any tradition who so adamantly disavows dependence on anyone else, famously stating, "imitation is suicide" (*CW* 2:27). Just a few paragraphs before he adamantly advises fierce self-assertion in the present life of the individual, proclaiming, "Insist on yourself, never imitate!" (*CW* 2:47), he relies on words of the ancient Persian prophet: "to the preserving mortals, said Zoroaster, the blessed mortals are swift" (*CW* 2:45). Despite citing a predecessor, Emerson ultimately attempts to obviate influence in his self-assertion by making claims upon the words of other writers he deems worthy of replacing. To this end, like Thoreau, he has made Sa'di a mere "symbol" to re-create himself and his voice in his predecessor's image.

While Emerson claims through quotation and imitation a plethora of writers as his own, a rhetorical approach so central to his translation practices that it figures into what will be examined in the following chapter as constitutive of an emerging translation theory, his example of Sa'di offers a unique entry point into how his attempt to anticipate a foreign predecessor at the essence of his and their respective origins necessitates a radical accommodation of integral differences. Considering that he projects his ideal philosophy in "Self-Reliance" onto his ideal poet in "Saadi," the interjection of similar quotes by the same Islamic source that underpin the Sufi mysticism of the Persian poet surfaces in English, threatening to invert Emerson's imitative process by making fatalistic claims on his own self-determination.

Published the same year that his son died (Einboden, *Islamic Lineage* 153), this poem much like the translated elegy invites further readings of biographical determinism, which in turn inform Emerson's view of fate.

For example, the Persian poet's resistance to "Wormwood" sent from the "sad-eyed Fakirs" (244–245) echoes Emerson writing to Lidian about their "eating of this everlasting wormwood" (*Letters* 3:11) over Waldo's death. In addition to such personal reckoning with loss, Emerson imagining himself as Saʾdi in his poem begins to locate a more expansive means by which to transcend the idea of a universe dooming the poet to eternal suffering. Saʾdi getting praised for "Sunshine in his heart" (*CW* 9:245) seemingly subverts the fatalistic cosmology of Islam so disdained by Emerson. Opposing Saʾdi to the "Sad-eyed Fakirs" who sing "endless dirges to decay," he celebrates his ideal poet's self-determined happiness, like his "Self-Reliance" essay that best defines him, by resisting such physical impingements as "haircloth" and "bloody whips" (*CW* 9:244–245).

However, in "Self-Reliance" Emerson includes the following statement that problematically affirms Islamic predestination, which he views as opposed to his self-determined philosophy: " 'Thy lot or portion of life,' said the Caliph Ali, 'is seeking after thee; therefore be at rest from seeking after it' " (*CW* 2:50). Comparable Islamic fatalism surfaces in the poem "Saadi": "Seek nothing,—Fortune seeketh thee . . ."[3] (*CW* 9:249). Though seemingly spoken by an ambiguous "Muse," who like "Uriel" channels both Eastern and Western sensibilities, the same voice cites Ali a few lines later: "Wise Ali's sunbright sayings pass / For proverbs in the marketplace . . ." (*CW* 9:247). The fatalism in the poem attributable to Imam Ali, cousin and son in law of the prophet Muhammad, threatens to return the eastern gaze back on Emerson's Romantically independent "eye." The original religious source from Arabic seems to reveal the kind of blind faith associated with Islamic fatalism that he overtly disliked in Persian poetry.

Such an interjection of Islamic fate, which Emerson locates in his ideal Persian poet, exemplifies how he must attempt to reconcile his own philosophic problem in the disparate religious underpinnings of a foreign verse tradition. As Carpenter states in his early scholarship, "Emerson distrusts Mohammadism" (212). Reinforcing his aversion to the religion as represented by the "sad eyed Fakirs" in "Saadi," Emerson further argues, " 'Tis weak and vicious people who cast the blame on Fate" (*CW* 6:13). Even so, the repression of Islamic fatalism that Emerson finds so anathema to the fantasy of his ideal poet nevertheless seems to insist on returning, even in his own poetic depiction of Saʾdi. Both in "Self-Reliance" as well as its exemplifying imitative Persian poem, the idea of a divinely scripted plan for the individual that he would divorce from his reading of the Sufi mystics seems to somewhat thwart his attempts at appropriation. Before subverting it through his critical reinvention of Saʾdi, Emerson makes general assessments of what most problematizes his claims upon the influence of Sufi poetry:

In common with countrymen, Saadi gives prominence to fatalism,—
a doctrine which, in Persia, in Arabia, and in India, has had, in
all ages, a dreadful charm. "To all men," says the Koran, "is their
day of death appointed and they cannot postpone or advance it
one hour. Wilt thou govern the world which God governs? Thy
lot is cast beforehand and whithersoever it leads, thou must follow." (Preface *Gulistan* ix).

Emerson seemingly foregrounds such determinism in his introduction
of Sa'di to overcome it through his writing under his Persian persona, yet it's
difficult to reconcile his competing assessments of his ideal poet. A page later
in his introduction to Sa'di's verse, he places the Sufi poet more safely into
the fantasy of his own Transcendental aesthetic, observing how "the Sheik's
mantle sits loosely on Saadi's shoulders." He further notes that "I find in him
a pure theism." Supporting such a reading, he continues in his essay by noting
that Sa'di "celebrates the omnipotence of a virtuous soul" adding that he is
"so little clogged with the superstition of his country" (Preface *Gulistan* x).
Continuing to fashion Sa'di into something akin to his version of the "Over-
Soul" and away from the Islamic religion that insists above all on monothe-
ism, Emerson in his imitative verse imbues his Persian poet with "Wisdom
of the gods" (*CW* 9:244), channeling inspiration through polytheistic nature.
        True to his own attempt to reconcile constraints on self-determinism,
Emerson has his ideal poet somewhat paradoxically both concede the role of
fatalism while still retaining the power of free will. Such an approach closely
corresponds to his "Fate" essay, which foregrounds the struggle between
self-determination and the submission to circumstances beyond one's control
that dictate life: "If we must accept Fate, we are not less compelled to affirm
liberty, the significance of the individual . . ." (*CW* 6:2). The human being
thus becomes "a stupendous antagonism, a dragging together of the poles of
the Universe" (*CW* 6:12). Much like Emerson personally identifies himself
and his verse to his ideal Persian poet, he begins conflating "eastern and
western speculation" into fate on a greater cosmological scale with a quote
from Schelling: "There is in every man a certain feeling, that he has been
what he is for all eternity, and by no means became such in time." Offering
his own paraphrase in conclusion, he writes, "in the history of the individual
is always an account of his condition, and he knows himself to be a party
to his present estate" (*CW* 6:7). As a counterbalance to a fatalistic universe,
what seemingly "lames" or "paralyzes" can provide a means of compensatory
"power" (*CW* 6:26). Especially fitting for this study, Emerson in "Fate" reaffirms
a metaphysical relation to determinism by quoting Hafez: "We learn that the

soul of Fate is the soul of us, as Hafiz sings: Alas! till now I had not known / My guide and fortune's guide are one" (*CW* 6:22). Locating a comparable liberating presence in Hafez's reconciliation with fatalistic forces, he relishes the "sallies of freedom" in his esteem of the Persian poet's lines.

Such contradictory ideas of fate cohering so closely to the Persian poets show that the American poet-translator did more than merely carry meaning over from German intermediary sources into English. His early understanding of their comparable relation to pre-determinism in a certain sense positions him within their aesthetic associated with Islam in ways beyond what his Western perspective may indicate. More than specific translation choices that concern equivalence of meaning, the question of fatalism perhaps brings Emerson the closest to Saʿdi and Hafez, which is to say back to their reckoning with their own religious influence. Both to better understand why he comes to so personally identify with the Persian poets (as previously outlined in his translation and imitation of Saʿdi), as well as his attempt to precede language difference in his theoretical conception of translation (as introduced in the following chapter), the comparative question of fatalism through the words of Ali and elsewhere warrants closer study. Interrogation toward where and how the "poles of the universe" representative of freedom and fate extend back to both Platonic and Islamic origins begins to reveal the broad reach of Emerson's engagement with a foreign influence, while further helping to identify a fundamental source of his own lyric power.

Ekhtiyar tellingly observes Emerson's idea about predestination changing from his earlier treatment of it in "Compensation" to his later "Fate" essay "due to the progress of his Oriental reading" (59).[4] Noting that Emerson "was quite aware of the fact that 'fate' and 'no free will' had different connotations to a Persian mystic," he further cites the Sufi's variance from traditional Islamic interpretation by translating the "will of God" as "love." Since "a lover follows the will of the Beloved," continues Ekhtiyar, "his 'will' is always the 'will of the Divine'" (59). Much like Emerson's conception of the Over-Soul, the Sufi mystics distinguish "between 'private will,' which is, in reality, 'willingness and self-annihilation,' and the 'Divine will,' which is the 'eternal tendency to the good of the whole . . .'" (59). Avery's accounting of the Sufis' relation to Islamic fatalism, offered in his introduction for a study of mystic philosophy in the poetry of Hafez, supports Ekhtiyar's summary, further suggesting why the Persian poets' origins proved so appealing to Emerson. While "Sufism is totally hinged on Islam," it predicates the "Written Decree" forged in the originating "Covenant" between "Adam and God" upon love (xiv). This redirection for Sufis "of Man's returning to his true self through unity with God" implies the possibility of human perfection, which proves "incompatible with the traditional thesis of God's absolute transcendence" as understood by the Muslim religion (Stepaniants 66).

Taking Emerson at his own words in wishing to claim the vision of Hafez to the point of becoming him—"He sees too far, he sees throughout; such is the only man I wish to see and to be" (*JMN* 10:165)—his attempts to mirror his Persian predecessor's origins replicate the Sufi's ultimate longing of returning to "Oneness." Consequently, he inherits the problem of human agency versus divine determination. In this respect, much like Emerson's comparable divergence from his Christian origins, wherein he extracts what most serves his transcendent predilections, Sufis "believe that the references to love in the Qur'an indicate the special love relationship between man and his creator, in which God functions as the Lover" (Seyed-Gohrab 108). Following Hafez in his desire to unify with God as the Absolute Beloved" (Seyed-Gohrab 111), despite the cultural difference of a divine conception, Emerson upon his Platonic basis displays a similar "passion," which he analogously seems to sense "was enkindled in pre-Eternity when the uncreated souls of men first professed divine love for their Lord" (Ilahi-Gohmshei 93). Seeking to so essentially emulate the origins of Sa'di and Hafez, he thus makes these poets his own manifestations of the Beloved, representative of his ultimate longing for a comparable "Pre-eternity." In this way he attempts to surrender himself to the vision of Hafez, for whom "it is only through the romantic experience of becoming ensnared by earthly beauty through contemplation of the theophanic witness (*shāhid*) that the mystic paradoxically obtains release from the bonds of selfhood" (Avar 51). By relying in part on the pre-eternal origins of Hafez, Emerson even while attempting to transcend literary influence and time itself must follow the light of the Persian poet's burning flame, which, according to his own lines of verse, have been burning: "for now, for always—and since pre-Eternity" (Ilahi-Ghomshei 93).

Emerson's pre-determined biographical discovery of Persian poets with whom he closely identifies thus begins to reflect a paradoxical freedom of original self-expression contingent on foreign influence associated with fate. Considering the religious origins of Hafez and Sa'di as relative draws him much closer to their lyric freedom, consequently helping him to find his own "release from the bonds of selfhood" (and therefore a greater sense of the eternal) by relying on the words, and even the names, of these poets. "Hafez," which means "one who has memorized the Qur'an," indeed makes what can be considered Emersonian demonstrations of self-reliance to his native Islam. Ubiquitously using words from the Qur'an in his poetry, he significantly deviates from the diction of the holy book when he attempts to "depict man's relationships with the divine in erotic terms" (Seyed-Gohrab 108). Emerson's interpretation of his own Christian tradition, such as his reinvention of the religious sermon to forge a spiritual and intellectual connection with his audience on his secular basis, supports such a general comparison. He goes much further, however, by following Hafez into his Islamic origins, even in his relation to the holy book that Hafez knew "by heart." Setting up his essay "Love" with a quote as though to explicate it in imitation of a Christian sermon, he begins with an epigraph from the *Qur'an*: "I was as a gem concealed / Me my burning ray revealed" (*CW* 2:97). As Einboden discovers, this epigraph "is not a simple citation, but is itself a revision, representing a loose paraphrase from lines spoken by the Muslim Prophet in *The Practical Philosophy of the Muhammadan People*" (*Islamic Lineage* 133), a Persian source translated into English.[5] Emerson, reminiscent of Hafez subverting *Qur'anic* diction to express love, adulterates the quote to serve his own rhetorical purposes. "Endowed with pseudo-epigraphic authority, the '*Koran*' is ascribed verses that are instead adapted by Emerson himself, his 'Love' entitled with the Muslim scripture yet reflecting his own first-person participation" (*Islamic Lineage* 133). Rhetorically personalizing the original religious text, "Emerson's opening to 'Love' emphasizes the disclosure of a divine subjectivity, a triplicate of first-person pronouns punctuating these two short lines, with Emerson's 'I,' 'Me,' and 'my' deepening the 'autobiographic' resonance of his Islamic interests" (*Islamic Lineage* 132). Such intense first-person lyrical subjectivity further transforms Emerson into what looks much like the Sufi's individualistic relation to the beauty of the "beloved" in Persian poetry, tellingly within lines first derived from the *Qur'an*.

Coming this close to his Persian inheritors' religious influence, Emerson discovers his own struggle between free will and fate in their poetry. Much as he finds Sa'di contradictorily giving "prominence to fatalism" (*Gulistan* ix) while remaining "so little clogged with the superstition of his country" (*Gulistan* x), he himself demonstrates a certain ambivalence to the pre-determinism that he claims to oppose in his own cultural and religious traditions. Early in his "Fate" essay, while criticizing America for its "superficialness," he contrasts its "boasters and buffoons" to the more courageous "perceivers of the terror of life." Among the latter he praises the "Turk, the Arab, the Persian" who "accepts the foreordained fate" (*CW* 6:2). In the next paragraph, as he includes "[T]he Hindoo" in the vein of such Orientalist esteem, he draws on the same religious comparison of Islamic fatalism to pre-destined Calvinism made by Avery (xiii). However, instead of seeing it as comparable limitation, he rather surprisingly seems to embrace it:

Our Calvinists, in the last generation, had something of the same
dignity. They felt that the weight of the Universe held them down
to their place. What could *they* do? Wise men feel that there is
something which cannot be talked or voted away,—a strap or belt
which girds the world. (*CW* 6:3)

Comparing Emerson's struggle with fate from his tradition to that of Sa'di
and Hafez, Carpenter's qualifying adverb in his statement about the American
finding himself attracted to the Sufi poets because they had "*partially* freed
themselves from Mohmmedanism" (179; emphasis added) proves especially
insightful. Following Ahmad Kasravi's nineteenth-century reading that finds
contradictory and inconsistent themes in Sa'di's writing (55), Iraj Parsinejad
challenges the firm assumptions made by his critical predecessor about the
poet's "fatalism," arguing that it "is equally amenable to interpretation and
self-control . . ." (*History* 182). This ambiguity extends to Emerson's assertion
of self-determination into a fatalistic world:

Fate is unpenetrated causes. The water drowns ship and sailor,
like a grain of dust. But learn to swim trim your bark, and the
wave which drowned it, will be cloven by it, and carry it, like its
own foam, a plume and a power. (*CW* 6:17)

Sa'di similarly cites the role of fate in such lines as "Wealth and power depend
not upon skill, and cannot be obtained without the assistance of Heaven"
(*Gulistan* 165) while also asserting the need for human agency: "Without toil
there can be no treasure / For he alone receives wages who work" (Kasravi
55). Sounding especially like the fatalistic lines of Ali in "Self-Reliance" as
well as Emerson's persona poem "Saadi" that exemplifies the essay, the actual
Sa'di writes in his *Gulistan*: "That which is not allotted, the hand cannot reach;
and what is allotted will find you wherever you may be" (362).

     Much like Emerson returns to the Calvinist underpinnings of his inher-
ited Christianity, Sa'di's cited lines emphasizing the need for self-assertion can
be considered as having a basis in the *Qur'an*: "Man shall achieve nothing
except what he strives for" (53:39), "God will not change the condition of a
people until they change what is in themselves" (13:11), and "Whoever does
an atom's weight of good will see it, and whoever does an atom's weight of evil
will see it" (99:7–99:8). Sa'di therefore begins to expose the question of free
will deeply embedded in his native religion. "As early as the time of the first
caliphs," explains Stepaniants, "there arose disputes and contentions among
the concerning predestination. The notion's inherent contradiction consisted

in its being incompatible with the principle of Man's responsibility for his actions" (66). Favoring the liberating words of poetry over ritualistic obedience that he associates with Islam, Emerson understandably gravitates somewhat away from Islam as well as his own Christian origins to the more spiritual verse of Sa'di and Hafez, even to the point of perhaps over-idealizing their severance from religion. The Islamic fatalism that Emerson resists, however, at least to a certain extent, resurfaces in his Persian inheritor's attempts to reconcile their own free will.

These corresponding examples lead to a closer consideration of Emerson's return to Sa'di's fatalistic origins, all the way back to Islam, represented through imitation by channeling words of the Imam Ali in English. Accommodating his Persian influence allows him to better reconcile the dichotomy of fate versus freedom. The very resurfacing of Sa'di in his nineteenth-century New England begins to invite the liberating return of what Emerson considers the "law" (*CW* 6:28), a universal and atemporal force that for him must ideally become reconciled with fate. Comparative origins for Emerson and his foreign influences prove so hard to locate because his understanding of such a force extends seemingly through all languages and traditions. Supportive of his Platonic reading, he effectively obviates differences among literary traditions, languages, and even religion. Just as Emerson disdains a superficial relation to fate among his Americans, he penetrates his own surface level assimilation of Sa'di by reaching further back to originating deterministic energy. In his essay "Power," he precedes even the influence of Islam to arrive at such an effect, summoning the words attributed to the first Persian prophet Zoroaster: "Enlarge not thy destiny, said the oracle: [E]ndeavor not to do more than is given thee in charge" (*CW* 6:39). In harmony with Sa'di, Ali, and Zoroaster, he includes himself as belonging among "All successful men" who "have agreed in one thing;—they are *causationists*. They believe that things went not by luck, but by law" (*CW* 6:28). Among the Persians, as among a plethora of other foreign influences, Emerson incessantly attempts to locate and channel a collective "mind that is parallel with the laws of nature" (*CW* 6:30). No one writer from any nation in this broader understanding can claim a monopoly upon influencing Emerson. As he proclaims: "'Tis hard to find the right Homer, Zoroaster, or Menu . . . There are scores and centuries of them" (*CW* 6:9). Far-reaching and endlessly accommodating, such a law emanates through his conception of the "Over-Soul" beyond the more direct and obvious influence of Indian spirituality typically ascribed it. The following passage, excerpted from this essay, could easily have been written by Ali, based on his words that Emerson brings into "Self-Reliance" (" 'Thy lot or portion of life,' said the Caliph Ali, 'is seeking after thee; therefore be at rest from seeking after it' "):

The things that are really for thee, gravitate to thee. You are
running to seek your friend. Let your feet run, but your mind
need not. If you do not find him, will not you acquiesce that it
is best you should not find him? for there is a power, which, as
it is in you, is in him also, and could therefore very well bring
you together, if it were for the best . . . Has it not occurred to
you, that you have no right to go, unless you are equally willing
to be prevented from going?" (CW 2:173)

It is in this context that the reception of literature, and consequently of
the authors who wrote it, is considered preordained by Emerson: "Every
proverb, every book, every byword that belongs to thee for aid or comfort,
shall surely come home through open or winding passages." Demonstrating
Lacan's famous axiom that "a letter always arrives at its destination" (Écrits
41), Emerson presciently sees Sa'di's portrait before his actual reading of his
biography, just as the Persian poet according to his comparable American
visionary foresees the great classical Western poets: "Saadi, without having
read Horace or Homer, says the same things" (TN 2:126).

The transcendent and preordained potency found in the verse of such
foreign writers that Emerson considers himself especially anointed to receive (as
if transforming the remnants of the Calvinist tradition for his self-sanctioned
appropriation) rather easily manifests in his own language and American perspective. In "Power," remarking on how the "affirmative force is in one, and
is not in another," Emerson cites Hafez in words especially close to his own:
" 'On the neck of the young man,' said Hafiz, 'sparkles no gem so gracious
as enterprise' " (CW 6:30). Commenting on this quote, Slater exclaims: "This
sounds more like Benjamin Franklin than Hafiz!" He then goes on to cite the
process by which Emerson altered the intermediary translation from German
(CW 6:199 n8). Following the quote from Hafez in the essay, Emerson quickly
transitions into praising the industriousness of his native New Englanders, "a
colony of hardy Yankees, with seething brains, heads full of steam-hammer,
pulley, crank, and toothed wheel . . ." (CW 6:30). Both Emerson's writing
as well as Slater's critical commentary on it paratactically exemplify a kind
of Franklinesque American discovery, as opposed to outright invention, of
pre-existing power. Channeled into a new context through translation, previous ideas along with language itself become electrically charged. Even the
semblance of Franklin, who Melville assesses as "everything but a poet" (Fifty
Years 66) gets converted into the process of moving Persian poetry into an
English imitation. This is seen both in the noted "enterprise" of the Hafez
rendering, as well as elsewhere in Emerson's slight attempt to remake Sa'di

into the famous American by his stated comparison to "Franklin" insofar as the Persian too "draws the moral" (*Gulistan* vii). In this way the predecessor force of a Persian poet both reconfirms the spirit of truth-making in two disparate traditions while redirecting and renewing poetic energy through the American discoverer of electricity.

Though the reckoning of power with fate manifests for Emerson in various ways, including actual industry, he makes his most integral demonstration through inspired verse that shifts an experience of the divine away from religion. In his essay "Persian Poetry," he tellingly juxtaposes his less favorable view of Islamic fatalism to the literary medium through which he accesses kindred poets from their literary tradition:

> Religion and poetry are all their civilization. The religion teaches an inexorable Destiny. It distinguishes only two days in each man's history: his birthday, called *the Day of the Lot*, and the Day of Judgment. Courage and absolute submission to what is appointed him are his virtues. (*CW* 8:125)

While Emerson "never ceased to identify the power of his own poetic eloquence with the religious sentiment" (*CW* 9:lxx) he tends to privilege in his strong identification with Saʾdi and Hafez a transcendent expression over rigid intellectualization. For example, he reads in the former poet a more authentic spiritual truth "lost to modern religion by the preference of orthodoxy for ritual and ceremony" (*CW* 9:lxx). Even when not specifically referencing the Sufis, he favors an inspired truth akin to their esteem of the heart, as opposed to what he disdainfully sees as a less inspired reliance on their Islamic origins.

> But there will dawn ere long on our politics, on our modes of living, a nobler morning than that Arabian faith, in the sentiment of love . . . We must be lovers, and instantly the impossible becomes possible. (*CW* 1:158)

Much as Obediat points out how Emerson locates such love as emerging from his "dead" Christian tradition (86), in a greater sense he offers in his presentation of a new "lover of mankind" (158) a comparative resurrection from both religions. Rather than scripture, as for the Sufis, such spiritual freedom indeed better surfaces for him through poetry. For further comparative understanding in his own tradition, consider how as a Transcendentalist he feels a mystical connection to Swedenborg "for his elaborate view of spiritual correspondences." However, he can only go so far with such a religious and

intellectual influence, finding his theology "too subservient to the Bible and
Christian symbolism" while somewhat disdainfully concluding that his writings
were "without poetry" (Schmidt 43). Both the fact that "the dīvān of Hafiz
has been canonized as chief among three books of poetry used in Persianate
societies for the purposes of divination . . ." and Hafez opts to write under a
name meaning "Memorizer of the Qu'rān" (Lewisohn, "Prolegomenon" 16)
exemplify how the Persian poet making poetry out of religion would prove
so appealing to Emerson.

To this end, the Sufi underpinnings of Persian verse, informed by
Islam but seemingly redirected toward greater figurative freedom, helps lead
Emerson to his own spiritual reckoning with fate. Anathema to static forms
much like his own stance against established Christianity, the Persian poets'
more dynamic attempt to reach the divine that ultimately exposed the question of fate represents his comparable dynamic reconciliation. As Stepaniants writes, "Sufism—, cursed blind imitation and repetition of theological
maxims. It declared itself solely the captive of the Beloved, God; at the same
time it could not get rid of supernaturalistic determinism" (74). In his essay
intended to introduce Persian verse to Western readers, he summons the
expressive power of Hafez (located in the heart) through several centuries
and two different languages (Persian and German) in order to free himself
from his own critical constraints:

> "Loose the knot of the heart," says Hafiz. At the Opera I think
> I see the fine gates open which are at all times closed, and that
> tomorrow I shall find free & varied expression. But tomorrow I
> am mute as yesterday. Expression is all we want: Not knowledge,
> but vent: we know enough; but have not leaves & lungs enough
> for a healthy perspiration & growth. Hafiz has: Hafiz's good things,
> like those of all good poets, are the cheap blessings of water, air,
> & fire. The observation, analogies, & felicities which arise so
> profusely in writing a letter to a friend. (*JMN* 10:68)

Longing for inspiration over knowledge, Emerson returns to the source of
creativity for the poet whose voice and vision he covets, claiming, "such is
the only man I wish to see and to be" (*JMN* 10:165) Though he would con-
ceive of such inspired origins Platonically, from the Sufi tradition he engages
they extend back to his Persian poet's covenant with God based on love, as
opposed to Adam's agreement founded more on religious stricture. Devoted
through the heart as opposed to the mind, Hafez found himself destined for
divine intoxication that would manifest in enlightening lyric moments. This is
in part what Hafez means when speaking of "the inevitability of his being a

drunkard" (Avery xii). Emerson's pre-arrival at a displaced Mecca in America similarly subverts cerebral and legalistic limitations of an Adamic agreement with a Biblical or *Qur'anic* God. In "Experience," where he lays claim to the very origins of Islam, he makes a rather Hafez-type demonstration by reaching his own kind of divine intoxication, as if beyond reason: "I make! On no! I clap my hands in infantine joy and amazement" (*CW* 3:41). Though it remains contextually more justified to take Emerson's understanding of wine in the verse of Hafez as "intellectual freedom" (*TN 2:120*) in the sense that he remains free to think on his own terms, coming closer to the poet whose sensibility he covets, he once again approaches with his phrase something like the ambiguity of a Persian pun. His critical assessment of the Persian trope used by Hafez could just as well mean the freedom *from* intellectualizing, a transcendence over strict determinants of meaning through the "vent" of inspired poetry.

To better understand how far back Emerson attempts to travel to overcome even the fatalistic constraints of language that threaten to separate him from his Persian inheritors, consider Anvar's positioning of Hafez "among those privileged souls who have been singled out by destiny" to recollect the pre-eternal "through the vision in which they can only narrate in a language that cannot be the language of common reality which has built on the illusory truth of logical thinking." Such vision, continues Anvar,

> may account for his choice of "Ḥāfiẓ" as his *nom de plume* (*takhalluṣ*) —that is, "the one who remembers, who has preserved the memory" of what happened in pre-Eternity. "Remembering" here implies not only keeping in mind the dazzling experience of epiphany—but also bearing consciously, with all its weight, the momentous Trust of love, along with its knowledge and the heavy responsibility which being a trustee entails. (127)

Insofar as Hafez "relied upon the creation myth elaborated by the Sufi mystics," he could both rely upon "repeated allusions to verses and terms from the Qu'rān" while freeing himself more toward a "mystical" relation to the divine with "bacchanalian imagery of wine and erotic love" (Seyed-Gohrab 119). Hafez thus successfully used verse as well as Sufi philosophy to liberate his aesthetic from the daunting influence of his holy source text. The effects of such poetic transcendence would naturally prove attractive to Emerson, extending back to his own Platonic understanding.

Through the "vent" or divinely inspired expression of Persian poets, Emerson in his own way could approach a closer transrational connection to their comparable atemporal origins. For Sufis, as for Emerson, the question

of free will "could not be solved by efforts of reason." Stepaniants offers the
following summation for the means by which Sufi mystics best sought an
answer to the questions of the divine: "Since the disputation could not be
settled rationally, it should be transferred from the sphere of reason to a
sphere where the heart reigns" (74). Emerson's own balance between reason
and revelation can be seen in his Persian namesake Sa'di, whose "general
regard of intellectual knowledge is high" (Katouzian 80) even as he follows
"the great Sufi seeker" to "reach a point that is hidden from intellectual
knowledge" (Katouzian 86).

Emerson appears so close to this source of Sufi wisdom centered beyond
the intellect that his statements from the "Over-soul" seemingly describe it:
"Meanwhile within man is the soul of the whole; the wise silence; the universal
beauty, to which every part and particle is equally related, the eternal One"
(CW 2:160). Much like the Sufis channeling the revelation of divine power,
Emerson assesses the soul as "not the intellect or the will, but the master of
the intellect and the will" (CW 2:161). The "vent" of Hafez that he esteems
over knowledge also manifests in especially translingual moments, such as
the music of the opera in the aforementioned example where he captures
the spirit of the classical Persian poet. As he writes: "In times of passion, in
surprises, in the instructions of dreams . . . we shall catch many hints that
will broaden and lighten into knowledge of the secret of nature" (CW 2:161).
Keeping in mind the covenant between Hafez and the divine, as well as the
location of Sufi wisdom in the heart as opposed to the head, Emerson's writing
on fatalism begins to simultaneously speak both for and as Hafez: "Whoever
has had experience of the moral sentiment cannot choose but believe in
unlimited power. Each pulse from that heart is an oath from Most High" (CW
6:16). More than linguistic equivalence or poetic meter in English or Persian,
echoes of the pre-eternal "oath" or "covenant" for both Emerson and Hafez
unify seemingly disparate literary traditions. As Emerson writes, "one blood
rolls uninterruptedly, an endless circulation through all men, as the water of
the globe" (CW 2:173–174). The pulse of the universal heart can be felt in his
engagement with Sufi philosophy. In part through such union with the Persian
poets, Emerson "comes to the conclusion that the doctrine of fatalism may
be turned to a beneficent force, if it is properly understood" (Obediat 80).

At such an essential point of reconciliation to Hafez, Emerson confronts
language itself, the "Tongue" of the "Secret," as the ultimate veil to the pre-
eternal. Returning to the transparent eyeball, his gaze seemingly conflates with
the regressive glimpse of the divine as experienced by the fourteenth-century
classical master. For such Sufis, poetry becomes a means to access, and express,
fleeting yet significant mystic vision. As Anvar explains:

[W]here words fail—and they constantly do so when what is at stake is the "Invisible" or the realm of inner realities (*ʿālam-i bāṭin*)—poetry produces mirror images that reflect what usually cannot be imagined, vocalized or remembered. In the same way that the shimmering mirror like surface of the mirror/cup reflects the face of the beauteous Cup-bearer (*Sāqī*), each *ghazal* and each image, and line in it, reflects, as successive mirrors/monads, a whole world standing beyond the frontiers of consciousness. It could be argued that each line of the *Dīvān-i Ḥāfiẓ* is transfused with a beauty cast by this reflection of the Beloved (*Sāqī*) in the same way as, in mystical terms the microcosm reflects the macrocosm. Thus, his poetic images reflect both in their form and meaning an echo of the primordial beauty experienced by the human soul in pre-Eternity. . . (127)

Emerson assumes such a consciousness-transcending gaze in his translation of a Hafez poem, channeling his source poet's possession of a mythical Persian's king's wine cup through which he could view the entire universe: "Bring the wine of Jamschid's glass . . . I, as Jamschid, see through worlds" (*CW* 9:256). By translation as well as imitation, Emerson in English summons a comparable "echo of the primordial beauty experienced by the human soul in the "pre-Eternity . . ." However, like Hafez in his native Persian, he too must confront the limits of language, that which "cannot be . . . vocalized or remembered." Such limits extend all the way back to predestination for Hafez, where he paradoxically discovers freedom in fatality. Rather than resisting his predecessor's lyric confrontation with fatalism, Emerson embraces it, as evidenced by his affinity for the line "Woe to him who suffers to be betrayed by fate" (*CW* 6:16), which he calls, "the proudest speech that free-will ever made"[6] (*JMN* 10:55).

The rhetorical connection between Emerson's transparent eyeball and the Sufi's mystic vision, previously developed in chapter 2, thus returns as an even more essential point of comparative origin. Stating, "I am nothing" (*CW* 1:10) around his transformation best reflects just how close he finds himself at his own linguistic and visual limits. Though Bloom is correct in his assessment that "there is not much to say, nor anything original to say" ("Central Man" 30) about the transparent eyeball, for that very reason Emerson's reductive articulation of his formative vision as he attempts to arrive at his conception of pre-eternity begins to explain why Persian influence, as well as so many other critical discoveries in his writing, remain so elusive. As Emerson explains of his reckoning with pre-determination:

> But to see how fate slides into freedom, and freedom into fate,
> observe how far the roots of every creature run, or find, if you
> can, a point where there is no thread of connection. This knot
> of nature is so well tied, that nobody was ever cunning enough
> to find the two ends. (*CW* 6:20)

Such a description about the ineffability of discerning freedom from fate
extends to the functioning of language itself, wherein signified slides under
signifier. It accounts for Emerson's articulation of his self-negation, his ability
to both assert and disavow his presence by stating, "I am nothing." Insofar as
this "knot of nature" in the quote above tethers him to the fatalistic struggle
of the Persian poets, he finds himself better able to collapse the meaning of
his verse and even his very identity into their playfully frustrating attempt to
"find the two ends." In this respect the Persian mirror of Bloom's "revisionary
ratio" that positions Emerson against the influence of Hafez collapses and
confuses at a final, fatalistic breaking point. Emerson becomes Hafez, while
Hafez becomes Emerson.

The "transparent eyeball" as the most pre-eternal site imaginable for
Emerson, his figurative Mecca in America where even he has yet to arrive, thus
predicates vision on the indeterminacy of meaning. As previously cited in the
introduction, Pease finds Emerson's elusive trope attempting to out-metaphorize
metaphor itself "between the gaps" of "the child's prereflexive relation with
nature" and "idealist abstractions" (50). Identifying the transparent eyeball as
a "catachresis" (59), Pease's identification of a figurative breakdown that makes
possible spiritual vision both despite, as well as because of, linguistic impediments even more closely mirrors the rhetoric of Sufi poetry. Consequently, it
comes to reflect the Persian Sufi's divine gaze: ". . . the eyeball is trans-parent,
trans-individual, trans-objective . . . undefinable as either subject or object,
God or nature . . . like the living glance exchanged when God and nature
look face to face" (Pease 59). Consider the resurfacing of Emerson's "living
glance" in Anvar's comparable description of Hafez's vision:

> The importance of catachresis in the *ghazals* of Ḥāfiẓ in gen-
> eral . . . seems to be related to the violence of the experience of
> love. Actually, it is not just a way of putting things: the catachresis
> is here supposed to produce a vision and arouse a commotion
> that should provide a glimpse of what really happened on the
> day of *alast* and, thus, to liberate the memory of the soul. (135)

Much like Emerson can only keep reverting to literary figuration and self-
referencing in his attempt to capture his transparent origins, for Sufis, "Each

detail of beauty contributes to lift a veil, but, at the same time, the veil is never really lifted because the secret it conceals must not be told except by allusion" (Anvar 125). In this way Emerson begins to most look *like* the Persian poets by looking *as* them. Unable to appropriate their source language, he precedes it, subsuming their gaze that attempts to penetrate the limitations of their own rhetoric.

While Emerson's transparent eyeball seems like the perfect deconstructive trope for comparative analysis, its relatable application makes it impossible to truly separate him from his identification with his Persian poets. He seemingly draws too rhetorically close to his Persian influences for his critical tradition's own good. Around a site comparable to the American's description of his transformation into transparency, Hafez attempts to articulate a similar experience of mystery at the threshold of the symbolic, ultimately reverting to the same paradox of naming his attempted transcendence. Both Emerson and Hafez approach so near the meta-functioning of language itself that they seemingly become each other in the American/Persian mirror. To show the difficulty of distinguishing Emerson's origins from Sa'di and Hafez, consider the following description by Derrida in relation to the ninety-nine names for God in Islam, "all of which point to the comprehensive unity inherent in the all-embracing Greatest Name" (Schimmel *Numbers* 271). Such naming remains just as elusive as Western deconstructive theory:

> What we know, or what we would know if it were simply a question here of something to know, is that there has never been, never will be, a unique word, a master-name. This is why the thought of the letter a in différance is not the primary prescription or the prophetic annunciation of an imminent and as yet unheard-of nomination. There is nothing kerygmatic about this "word," provided that one perceives its decapita(liza)tion. And that one puts into question the name of the name. (Derrida 27)

Much like Emerson's search for the spirit of a divine source through the "knot of nature," Sufi mystics paradoxically seek comparable transcendence while relying on the negation of one ultimate signification.[7] However, while Sufi poetry written in Persian or Arabic indeed remains subjected to the same law of the symbolic as literature in any language, its foundation on Islam makes it distinct from Western literature. There is indeed something more "kerygmatic" and "prophetic" in the various appellations of Allah, even as the ninety-nine names paradoxically demonstrate similar indeterminacy introduced by Derrida. The aforementioned story about the villagers pulling one of their own back to their side after he ascends the wall of mystery suffices here as an example of the distinction between East and West. While both Sufi mysticism and secular deconstructive theory orient their figurative play of meaning around an inexplicable lacuna or gap on the other side of symbolic reasoning, the former pulls the native Easterner from the wall back into his or her tradition with a much different chain of signifiers, many of which remain linked to the *Qur'an*. Further reinforcing the difference, even prior to scaling the wall the Sufi, through passionate spiritual devotion, has caught glimpses of what lies beyond it. He passes on such divine wisdom, some of which transcends constraints of language, to a student able to receive it within a specific religious tradition.

That the Islamic influence Emerson included in both "Self-Reliance" and "Saadi" derives from words of Ali proves especially instructive of the connection between the American and Persian poets in relation to Islamic origins and the question of fate. Born in the Kaaba of Mecca, Ali is believed to have received esoteric knowledge from Muhammad. While the prophet relayed book knowledge known as *ilm-e-safina* in both the literal words of Allah through the *Qur'an* and in his recorded sayings and behaviors in the *Hadith*, he further was granted "knowledge of the heart" (*ilm-e-sina*), which he passed on to his son in law. Such spiritual insight—which resembles the "heart's native language" of Hawthorne's American Romanticism (*Scarlet Letter* 195)—subsequently gets shared among Sufis "'heart to heart'" (Khanam 10) by a comparable teacher-student relationship to that of Muhammad and Ali (Khanam 15). Predicated on the same spiritual practice required of all Muslims, Sufis follow a mystic path of intense spiritual devotion, attempting to manifest a relationship with the divine through invocations of God's many names, either "silently, loudly, with or without music, etc." (Khanam 18). Poetry for Persian Sufis like Sa'di and Hafez offer another such spiritual demonstration.

Given their rhetorical similarity, differentiating Emerson from his foreign predecessors requires a partial return to the latter's true origins of the Arabic source text from which much of their philosophy and verse derives. To counter Western theoretical assumptions that reinforce Emerson's appropriative translation practice so invested in figurative reinvention on his own terms, the *Qur'anic* influence of his Persian source poets needs to be taken more literally. Even as it considerably re-inscribes Emerson's aesthetic, which Platonically renders Persian verse so close to his that it negates all difference, the Arabic foundation of Islam subtly begins to expose the limits of his imagined equivalence. As Schimmel explains: "Learning the Arabic letters is incumbent upon everybody who embraces Islam, for they are the vessels of revelation; the divine names and attributes can be expressed only by means of these letters . . ." (*Mystical Dimensions* 411). If, as Schimmel continues, "It is scarcely possible to fully understand and enjoy the poetry of the Muslim world, mainly of Iran and the neighboring countries, without a thorough knowledge of the meaning given to those letters" (*Mystical Dimensions* 412), then Emerson's English renderings based on his illiteracy in Persian and Arabic as well as his uninformed imitations of such verse predicated at least in part on the *Qur'an* replace the barest semblance of meaning equivalence with his own mimetic fantasies of divine revelation. While he of course attempts to overcome the Persian masters in traditional ways that Bloom articulates in his theory of influence, his subversion of the Persian in which they write as well as the Arabic that constitutes their religion proves the most egregious and by far the least critically examined.

Emerson's tendency of assuming original meaning in translation at such an essential level as seen in Hafez's comparable relation to fatalism so successfully veils a profound difference between his own tradition and the Sufi poets that simply to expose it necessitates an almost absurdly reductive reading. Take the first letter of the Arabic alphabet, a simple *alef* (ا). Favoring an integral spiritual wisdom over intellectual knowledge, Sufi mystics have claimed that all of the world is found in this letter (Schimmel, *Mystical Dimensions* 18). "When God created the letters he incited them to obey. All letters were in the shape of alif, but only the alif kept its form and image after which it has been created" (*Mystical Dimensions* 417). Somewhat contrary to Derrida's explication of the letter "a" in *différance*, the alef does seem closer to "the prophetic annunciation of an imminent and as yet unheard-of nomination." There is indeed something "kerygmatic" about it. Though still subjected to the play of language insofar as it takes its position next to an endless combination of letters, the *alef* continues to embody at least a trace of the divine in classical Sufi poetry. Mystic poets' figural relation to this first letter in the Persian alphabet as "a slender vertical line often used as a comparison for the beloved," defines their close proximity to divinely scripted origins in their essential play of language: "What shall I do—?" asks Hafez in a couplet cited by Schimmel, "My teacher gave me no other letter to memorize!" (*Mystical Dimensions* 417). Though imbued with integral cultural and linguistic resonances associated with Islam, it simultaneously seems to capture Emerson's similar concern with the playful impossibility of "dragging together" the "poles of the universe" between fatalism and free will. Like the "stupendous antagonism" of this dichotomy for Emerson, an *alef* for Sufi mystics "is the letter of ahadiyya, unity and unicity, and at the same time the letter of transcendence" (*Mystical Dimensions* 418).

Despite Emerson's Persian and Arabic illiteracy, as well as because of it, the *alef* thus stands as the best introduction and conclusion to the comparative difference between him and the Sufi verse he attempts to appropriate.

Uniquely individuated yet unified to the whole, the foreign letter seems to
further define the spirit of Emerson's self-reliance, insofar as his individuated
self tries to encompass divine unity. Erroneously assuming an equivalence,
however, Emerson exposes the limits of his own as well as his subsequent
American translators' literary appropriation of verse underpinned by Islam
(which will be further examined in chapter 5).

One early Sufi circle founded in Shia' Islam, deriving from Ali and
especially concerned with the mystic science of interpreting letters associated
with Islam known as *jafar*, found that "the alif reflects Ali in the human face,
with the khatt-I equator dividing the nose" (*Mystical Dimensions* 412–413).
Though not specifically referenced by Hafez or Sa'di, such personification that
seems more integral to their literary, linguistic, and religious tradition suggests
how Ali as well as the Arabic and Persian "alef" radically changes in Emerson's
use of the English alphabet, which begins with a much different letter "a."

In this respect, the fatalistic quotes in Emerson's "Self-Reliance" essay
and "Saadi" poem, originating from the presumed founder of Sufism who
appears in German and English through a transformed "A," inverts Emerson's
gaze in the Persian mirror. As he follows Hafez and Sa'di by looking at Ali,
Ali looks back at him, insisting on a self informed by an Islamic tradition
defined by an alphabet originating with an *alef*. In this sense, Ali returns to
be taken more seriously and more literally, as if to tell Emerson in all of his
rhetorical evasiveness, which often reads as a kind of visually frustrated desire:
"Thy lot or portion of life . . . is seeking after thee; therefore be at rest from
seeking it" (*CW* 2:50).

Despite Emerson's best intentions toward a relentless insistence on self-
reliance, his "imitation" of Ali becomes a kind of linguistic "suicide." The *rend*
in this respect both reduces and subjects the ego to fatalism associated with
Islam, ironically "*rend*-ering" an English translation much more authentic to
the original underpinnings of verse that he attempts to completely accommodate as his own. While Derrida's "*Différance*" essay begins like the opening
of a Greek epic with an "a": "I will speak, therefore, of a letter" (3), Emerson's
"Self-Reliance" near the conclusion cites the words of a progenitor Sufi who
derives from an ultimate divine source scripted with an Arabic "ا." Though
seemingly mirror images of each other in the symbolic, the letters cross in
different directions, even at the most basic level of writing (right to left and
left to right). Consequently, they can be seen as marking the fundamental spot
of Emerson's Western transparency as it tries to subsume an entire literary
tradition founded on Islam.

The difference remains unrecognizable, however, since Emerson so
effectively preempts even his own brazen cooptation of Islam in a few key

ways. First, he consistently approaches the Persian tradition before the Arab conquest of Iran, citing as an authority the first Persian prophet Zoroaster throughout much of his oeuvre. Second, he follows his own pattern of anticipating the inherited Persian poets' religion with Western influences, as seen when he cites his own European spiritual influence as a source for the Islamic Prophet: "Mohamet seems to have borrowed by anticipation of several centuries a leaf from the mind of Swedenborg, when he wrote in the Koran . . ." (*CW* 8:53). Emerson personally continues to go even further back in time by establishing himself in the realm of the pre-eternal where beside Hafez he would receive a glimpse of divine. Finally, as seen throughout much of this chapter, he develops a theory of fatalism and free will so affined to the cosmology of the Sufi poets and their Islamic influence that it negates all difference by appealing to a universal "Law." Insofar as it "disdains words and passes understanding" (*CW* 6:27), it attempts to overcome language itself, despite its ultimate tethering to the symbolic.

Deciphering the difference between Emerson and his Persian predecessors becomes as impossible as finding the "point where there is no thread of connection" between fate and freedom, especially since such a thinly differential thread as the Arabic *alef* "ا" becomes critically indistinguishable in Emerson's English translation. As he says of his search, predicated on the negative relation of the symbolic order, the "knot of nature is so well tied, that nobody was ever cunning enough to find the two ends" (*CW* 6:20). At best the comparative critic can expose some threads of style and meaning extending from Emerson's aesthetic in his English language and American Romantic tradition that allow him to make such seamless appropriation. If, as Cervantes states, "translating from one language into another" is like looking at "tapestries from the wrong side" (877), then unraveling the meta-linguistic process through which Emerson develops his Orientalist gaze begins to reveal how he comes to transplant Mecca onto Boston Common. To this end, the following chapter attempts to locate Emerson's emerging theory of translation from his own ideas about writing, showing how his reflections on language and rhetoric allow him to roll out a Persian carpet for his own entry into the American tradition.

Chapter 4

The Subversion of Equivalence

Emerson's Translation Theory in Praxis

> Original power is usually accompanied
> with assimilating power . . .
>
> —*Ralph Waldo Emerson* (*CW* 8:100)

Though not specifically written to address translation, Emerson's theories of rhetoric in a few key essays on language, intertextuality, and Persian poetry offer a means by which to consider his approach to foreign verse, demonstrating how he reconciles imitation with an aesthetic predicated on originality. Examination of how he figures such ideas informed by Platonic philosophy into praxis begins to suggest an emerging translation theory, especially juxtaposed with his personal notes on Orientalist readings, wherein he introduces his view of ancient literature through the extended metaphor of a telescope capable of obviating temporal and linguistic difference. Insofar as his rhetorical attempts to subvert foreign equivalence directly influence Pound's intermediary source texts, which in turn come to shape much of modern poetics in the West, they prove surprisingly generative in mid-nineteenth-century America. Though Pound more overtly and self-consciously "came to think of translation as a model for the poetic act," what Kenner summarizes as "blood brought back to ghosts" (150), Emerson through his earlier individuated poetic vision begins to subtly preempt such a Romantic embodiment of foreign literary tradition and, seemingly by extension, the ultimate power of poetry.

First and foremost, by laying claim to an exaggerated intertextual rhetorical strategy, Emerson legitimizes his appropriation of Persian poets, allowing himself to adopt Saʿdi's name and even his voice. His essay "Quotation and Originality" justifies his copying of foreign masters as well as his reworking of their verse into his own. On closer study, the essay displays his best attempt to reconcile the inherent contradiction of self-reliance identified by Buell, wherein "we are to trust what is true" provided it remain "universal" (59). To introduce how current writing depends on textual predecessors, he begins his discussion by citing "innumerable parasites" in nature that survive by "suction" (*CW* 8:93). Asserting that "originals are not original" (*CW* 8:94), he encodes his writerly intentions into his rhetorical theory, wherein past influence depends on present creation. Demonstrating such an argument in his own writing, his essay "The Poet" takes his idea of poetry as first "language" from Giamattisa Vico (Jung 131), an argument he then begins to refashion as his own. As he says of "the old and the new" in "Quotation and Originality," when offering a broad survey of literature, "there is no thread that is not a twist of these two strands" (*CW* 8:94). By implication, his agency as poet-translator comes to revivify a work of literature much like Benjamin sees a text undergoing an afterlife in translation (254). Further imitating the Persian *ghazal*, his aesthetic foregrounds comparable interweaving of disparate allusions with the poet's own lines in a series of contained couplets, which Hafez compares to the threading of pearls.

On one level, of course, Emerson reiterates the Platonism seen throughout his oeuvre. "All minds quote" (*CW* 8:94), he writes, which essentially casts humanity in the realm of imitative forms. The world itself for him is comprised of quotations: "We quote not only books and proverbs, but arts, sciences, religion, customs and laws; nay, we quote temples and houses, tables and chairs by imitation" (*CW* 8:94). Ending such a catalog on chairs calls significant attention to Plato's classic example of imitative form and its conceptual recreation by the human intellect, wherein a chair is mere representation of the ideal object. Emerson extending such Platonic conception to "All minds" effectively renders his theory of quotation universal and entirely inclusive of the phenomenological world. Language itself thus offers a symbolic means to reify through reiteration, presumably irrespective of origin.

His deeper interest in the fundamental sources of literature, wherein "The originals are not original" and "The first book tyrannizes the second" (*CW* 8:94) further substantiates his reckoning with predecessors. Anticipating Bloom's theory of poetic influence, Emerson again reprises his own central problem in *Nature* with building "the sepulchres of the father." Throughout much of "Quotation and Originality" he indeed reiterates, which is to say copies, versions of this recurring argument. The same kind of Fall from originality articulated in "Experience" resurfaces here as he laments, "People go out to look at sunsets that are not their own . . ." Just as with books, "they *quote* the sunset and star and do not make them theirs." Even worse, Emerson argues that quotation makes people "foreigners in the world of thought" (*CW* 8:99). Yet he too keeps citing the very problem of reliance upon quotation, as though on a recurring loop around his own de-centering and all-encompassing transparent eyeball imbued with the fantasy of originating Platonic conceptualization.

He begins to reconcile lack of originality through his notion of "Genius," which he states "borrows nobly" (*CW* 8:100). A paragraph earlier, he offers the aforementioned statement: "Original power is usually accompanied by assimilating power." Later in the essay, he posits a kind of ironic equivalence between both sources, relating that "it is as difficult to appropriate the thoughts of others, as it is to invent" (*CW* 8:101). Positioning himself into his theory as seminal American poet, critic, philosopher, and translator, he further privileges the one previously quoting the esteemed work: "Next to the originator of a good sentence is the first quoter of it" (*CW* 8:100). In this respect it becomes especially relevant that he first introduces Persian verse to mid-nineteenth-century readers in his nation. While the translator Sir William Jones predates his Persian renderings into English, Emerson importantly claims having presciently anticipated his own discovery of Sa'di's biography, envisioning himself as the first to arrive in Iran, as well as in America, at his own poetic ideal. In this sense he replaces Plato's chair with his own self-chosen Persian poet. As exemplified in his "Experience" essay, addressed in the second chapter of this study, he himself arrives in a figuratively transplanted "Mecca" as Romantic infant, "ready to die out of nature, and be born again into this new yet unapproachable America . . ." (*CW* 3:41).

To this end, through quotation he conceives of the Persian predecessor's effect on his own English Romantic inheritors, concerned more with a creative interpretation of their influence than an equivalence of meaning in the verse, as if justifying his own approach to translation and imitation: "Hafiz furnished Burns with the 'Song of John Barleycorn,' and furnished Moore with the original of the piece 'When in death I shall recline /Oh, bear my heart to my mistress, dear, etc.'" (*CW* 8:98). Though literally "carrying over" something from the original source text, the spirit of originality for Emerson prevails in his and others' contemporary reworking. As he explains: "The divine resides in the new" (*CW* 8:105). In "Poetry and Imagination," he offers yet another telling example of his revivified engagement with the classical Persian verse tradition:

> Every correspondence we observe in mind and matter suggests a substance older and deeper than either of these old nobilities. We see the law gleaming through, like the sense of a half-translated ode of Hafiz. The poet who plays with it with most boldness best justifies himself . . . (*CW* 8:5)

Addressing this passage, Einboden offers a keen distinction between mere imitation and the transformative process of influence at the crux of Emerson's rhetoric: "Rather than Hafiz himself, it is Hafizean rendition that Emerson endows with revelatory import." In this respect, continues Einboden, the passage offers "a fit description of his own hybrid practices" wherein he "privileges acts of poetic 'transition' rather than settled poetic products . . ." (*Islamic Lineage* 151).

By frequent and rather original juxtaposition of brilliant writers like Shakespeare and Hafez against his own writing, Emerson strategically makes paratactic claims upon their respective genius. If "All minds quote," then as frequently as possible he ensures that they do so on his own universal terms. Herein lies the process by which Emerson through close rhetorical association comes to call himself "Sa'di," ultimately claiming his predecessor's identity by channeling his words into his own lyric voice. Ironically, he achieves a kind of radical equivalence to both source text and author identity by subverting the very concept of literary inheritance from a specific discourse, tradition, etc. Emerson's all-encompassing transparent eyeball, like Sa'di's "speech" where "suns rise and set" (*CW* 9:247), continues to indiscriminately cover both Western and Eastern horizons of influence, especially when considering how the difference between authentic quotation and something like mere plagiarism remains predicated on experiential vision.

Further relating quotation to Emerson's perception of nature, Ralph LaRosa argues that he shapes his "radical aesthetics and ethics" from a "revolutionary reevaluation of experience not simply '*with* the eye' but '*through* it.'" Only by this standard can "the unity of past, present, and future be understood" (14). Through the quoter's acknowledgment of the natural world in the source text, he "reveals the perpetuation of God in the work," thereby expressing "oldest thoughts in a fresh, compelling style." Emerson's Platonic assessment of outward forms in nature that substantiates his criteria for invention as summarized by LaRosa closely parallels Sufi verse that would reveal divine mystery: "Man must perceive that nature is a sentence writ large, a universal quotation; his means to realizing this unity is through 'invention' which *re-discovers* preexisting truth" (15). In this respect, Emerson's *Nature* "bears personal witness to core truths about the self and the world, or consciousness and nature" (Richardson 226) much like the Sufi's heart. As he writes in his essay: "All science has one aim, namely, to find a theory of nature" (*CW* 1:8).

On closer inspection, his theory proves further applicable to the verse of his source poet Hafez in his own language and country. As if further anticipating his understanding of quotation and originality, poets following Hafez have attempted to "insert their own verses" into a collection attributed to the classical master "for the sake of gaining fame under his name." To this day, some scholars thus remain unsure as to what officially belongs to the original Persian master (Schimmel, "Critics" 262), which might help account for Kane's observation that there is no agreed upon scholarly edition of the *divan* or "collected works" of Hafez (115). Though Emerson most likely had no knowledge of this practice, he uncannily mirrors it in both his own translation and rhetorical approaches. As translator as well as editor of Persian verse in English, he supports an approach to the literary tradition of Hafez even as he subverts it through his own imitative renderings. That he calls himself Sa'di egregiously strays from the poet's original verse, even as he simultaneously can be seen as building on it.

Just as Emerson retroactively anticipated such textual interventions of Eastern poetry, he also appears to have presciently articulated a key concept in Western deconstructionism. When compared to relatively recent literary theory, "Quotation and Originality" remains especially contemporary. "Intertexuality," a term Julia Kristeva significantly invented in her translation of Mikail Baktin (Martinez Alfaro 268) can be taken as a truism in the understanding of literature today. Emerson's Romantic times, however, seem to have more heavily favored the genius of the individual. Two of his poetic contemporaries, Walt Whitman and Emily Dickinson, retroactively have become critically established as American poetry's grandfather and grandmother by their eccentrically distinct voices. Emerson by contrast positioned his aesthetic toward even more of an accommodation of what Kristeva calls the "literary," defined as "an intersection of textual surfaces rather than a point (a fixed meaning) . . ." Insofar as his representative texts, and his own typifying of them, renders his rhetoric "the equivalent of quoting" (Pease 67), it constitutes what Kristeva deems "a dialog among several writings" (65).

Such a theoretical approach further authorizes Emerson's copy-and-paste approach to translation. With his conception of the literary, he effectively nullifies the difference between his original and translated texts from Persian through German sources. As in Borges's poem quoted in the introduction to this study, "Emerson" stands as an amalgamation of writers he reveres, much like Hafez and Sa'di embody their precursors. Returning to Emerson's own intertextual metaphor, he threads together the old and the new as he refashions himself as "Sa'di," projecting his own self-reliant ideal onto the thirteenth-century Persian poet. Imitation and translation for him fail to adhere to strict categorization, transcended by a spirit of the "divine" manifesting in his concept of literary "Genius."

Since for Emerson "there is no originality," equivalence of meaning from source to target text therefore becomes relatively insignificant. "Christian

dogmas" are found in Plato, while sacred books "from India or Arabia" correspond to the Bible (*CW* 8:95). The sacred for Emerson thus holds no textual
boundaries, further enabling him to link religious traditions as he moves
toward an ultimate Platonic equivalence. As he writes in his essay on Persian
verse, "The Persian poetry rests on a mythology whose legends are connected
with the Jewish history, and the anterior traditions of the Pentateuch" (*CW*
8:125–126). Engaging the fatalistic influence of the *Qur'an* through the filter
of Persian verse informed by Sufism, he can further accommodate and even
to some extent elide such integral influence in the poetry he translates. He
thus justifies his aforementioned comment on the integrity of the most ancient
Persian sources he accesses, where he dismisses "the question whether the
Zend-Avesta or the Desatir are genuine antiques, or modern counterfeits,"
declaring that he remains "concerned with the good sentences; and it is indif-
ferent how old a truth is, whether an hour or five centuries" (*JMN* 16:265).
Such refutation of temporality extends to an outright disregard for literal
authenticity. The aesthetic itself for Emerson legitimizes a work of literature,
transcending boundaries of religion, language, and culture.

Emerson's attempts to overcome inherent differences between languages
and poetic traditions by meta-reflection of his all-seeing and all-overcoming
transparent eyeball dramatizes the critical tendency of figuratively rendering
the inexplicable loss of the source text in a new language. Insofar as translation
resists a unified theory, comments on it tend to revert to metaphor, paradoxically attempting to overcome rhetorical limitation while also foregrounding the
impossibility of such an endeavor. Robert Frost's ubiquitous statement that
"poetry is what gets lost in translation" (Brooks 8), for example, refutes the
idea of rendering verse into another language through the subtle irony of a
poetic epigram. Similarly, Cervantes's aforementioned comment through his
character Don Quixote on how translating a text is like looking at the wrong
side of a tapestry (837) offers a problematic rendering in relation to the viewer's
subjectivity while privileging the vision of the source author. By addressing the
rhetorical makeup of all literature in "Quotation and Originality," Emerson more
radically subsumes the loss of the foreign text. His conflation of classical and
contemporary authors, through inclusion of different languages and traditions,
naturally accommodates translation. To this end his comment that any literary
"thread" is comprised of "two strands," both "the old and the new," provides the
figurative fabric of Cervantes's inverted "tapestries." Emerson, however, sees it
from both sides, conflating Persian source and translated "text(iles)" or Persian
carpets, so to speak, to the point where they become seamlessly interchangeable.

Of course, much can be said structurally about the distinction of one
language or work of literature from another. That Emerson so frequently

opts instead for broad literary conceptions of translation as opposed to specific comments on linguistic difference exemplifies his greater concern with influence and his assertion of creative inspiration that can overcome it. Less focused on semantic variance between Persian and English, or what happens when bringing the source text of the former through German into the latter, he develops a theoretical perspective that helps him understand and justify his appropriative approach to foreign renderings. More than merely getting "lost in translation," his rhetorical theory in praxis dislocates any point of origination whatsoever, hence the invariable re-turning of verse around the site of his elusive transparent eyeball.

The meta-reflections that Emerson further offers on his sustained reading of foreign renderings as well as scholarship on the Persian verse tradition especially help him to better justify and envision his own translation practices. As if seeking to extend the reach of his gaze to the Persian Sufi's mirror that so perfectly appears to reflect it, at the beginning of his essay "Persian Poetry" he introduces his own extended metaphor applicable to translation. Such a trope proves particularly apt for his sustained interest in emulating the coveted mystic vision of Hafez, who he tellingly says "sees too far":

> Many qualities go to make a good telescope,—as the largeness of the field, facility of sweeping the meridian, achromatic purity of lenses, and so forth; but the one eminent value is the space-penetrating power; and there are many virtues in books, but the essential value is the adding of knowledge to our stock by the record of new facts, and, better, by the record of intuitions which distribute facts, and are the formulas which supersede all histories. (*CW* 8:124)

More than specific details that might better render an equivalence of meaning into English, for Emerson it is ultimately "intuitions which distributes facts." Here again he reinforces his claims on "divine truth" and the concept of "Genius" that transcend literal origins in "Quotation and Originality." Insofar as it easily enables him to view and understand the deep past of a foreign tradition like Persian poetry, this central metaphor subsumes multifaceted aspects of verse translation that typically warrant careful negotiation. Despite the importance of the "purity of lens" and considerations of "the largeness of the field," the "essential value" of literature resides within "intuitions which distribute facts." Such creative vision enables the reader/viewer to "supersede all histories." Einboden tellingly sees Emerson's telescope as "Collapsing distance" and "translating spatial transcendence into temporal" (*Islamic Lineage*

142). By foregrounding the atemporality of literature via his "formulas which supersede all histories," Emerson further anticipates Pound's modernist claim that "all literature is contemporaneous." As Pound argues: "Provincialism of time is as damned as provincialism of place" (*Contributions* 235). Emerson before Pound attempts to disregard such local distinctions as impediments to a grander aesthetic effect. Important for the American tradition, and similar to Pound, above all Emerson also continues to make metaphorical, which is to say creatively original, claims on foreign renderings. For Emerson, translation gets rediscovered in poetry, just as it does for Robert Frost as his inheritor, who paradoxically writes a one-line epigram about losing poetry in translation. Pound too figuratively re-creates a process of translation through his own verse that proves comparably able to "supersede" the history of Asian poetics.

Despite language or religious difference between American Romanticism and Persian Sufism, the greater "truth," which in his "Quotation and Originality" essay is revealed through contemporary inspiration, still gets both relocated and re-created. Herein lies the center of Emerson's paradoxical de-centering rhetoric in relation to translation, wherein he can manifest self-reliant vision in the context of so much mimicry. Following the logic of his influence theory, he positions himself on the other side of the same Persian mirror in which he sees the classical masters, concerned with an aesthetic of self-rendering in the writing of his own sentences. In this comparatively critical light, it becomes rather clear how he anticipates the portrait of Sa'di before his reading of the poet's actual biography, as well as how he so easily assimilates the Persian predecessor into his own identity.

Extending the trope of the mirror used for this study to Emerson's telescope—an object made of mirrors—further reveals the mimetic functioning of a theory predicated on quotation as it surfaces in relation to his foreign source texts. In Persian poetry, "parrots appear frequently with mirrors." The Sufi poets would teach the birds language by holding up a mirror before them and speaking behind it (Schimmel, *Brocade* 182). In the American tradition, such a metaphor appears particularly apt for Emerson, who Kane has called "our most consistent ventriloquist" (134). Seeing himself in his Persian predecessor, whose infinite vision he covets, Emerson describes Hafez as "a poet for poets, whether he writes . . . with a parrot's, or, as at other times, an eagle's quill" (*CW* 8:133). In his *Notebook Orientalist*, he translates these words of Hafez that reinforce his own reversion to Platonic origins: "I am a kind a parrot, the mirror is holden to me/ What the Eternal says, I stammering say again" (*TN* 2:114). Like Emerson before him, the two different birds' quills, respectively from the mimetic parrot and the original eagle, follow the "two strands" of the "old and the new," scripting quotation as well as originality. Also like

Emerson, Hafez ultimately defers to the "Eternal" as a kind of "Over-Soul" behind the Sufi mirror that manifests a renewing authenticity regardless of textual temporality in nation, language, or literary tradition.

Far from a flippantly Romantic claim on the spirit of a transcendent "truth," Emerson grounds such a divinely informed approach capable of overcoming influence through reasoned linguistic theory. His essay "Language" states how "Words are signs of natural facts," etymologically derived "from some material appearance" (CW 1:17). Like the "Fall" described in "Experience," which theoretically initiates separation of signified from signifier while presuming ultimate Platonic unification similar to the Sufi's quest for the divine, the origins of language now "remain hidden from us in the remote time when language was framed" (CW 1:18). Predicated on "a belief that language is, from the first, radically metaphoric," for Emerson it "becomes our only means of access to the immaterial world" (CW 9:liv–lv). This meta-relation proves radically extensive, able to reflect on rhetoric from the most transcendent vantage point. Emerson's attempt to telescopically extend the tracing of language back to its origins importantly ends in poetic image, eventually reaching linguistically universal symbols akin to his Platonic ideal:

> As we go back in history, language becomes more picturesque, until its infancy, when it is all poetry; or all spiritual facts are represented by natural symbols. The same symbols are found to make the original elements of all languages. It has moreover been observed, that the idioms of all languages approach each other in passages of the greatest eloquence and power. And as this is the first language, so it is the last. (CW 1:19–20)

In the "Poet" he makes even broader claims, such as, "poetry was all written before time was," leaving contemporary poets to capture through inspiration such "cadences" that then become "the songs of nations." (CW 1:5–6). Herein lies the ultimate "sepulchres of the fathers" that begin Nature, resurrected in "The Poet" as "a sort of tomb of the muses." In this essay too, after stating that "language is fossil poetry," Emerson predicates essential origins on the visual: "The etymologist finds the deadest word to have been once a brilliant picture (CW 3:13). In addition to recurring mention of an all-encompassing stylistic and meaningful expression, a "divine truth" that remains "new" in "Quotation and Originality," he continues to locate such reversion to sight in his most essential reading of language. In this respect, Hafez and Sa'di remain especially accessible despite his illiteracy in their Persian language, insofar as according to him they work primarily with the "image addressed to the eye" (CW 8:127).

Robert Kern's assessment of Emerson's rhetoric tellingly identifies the American poet-translator's own stylistic criteria that privilege "a good sentence" over the veracity of content in the collection of Persian spiritual writing: "Emerson's importance of a theorist of language, in fact, lies not so much within the originality or profundity of his thinking as in the expressive power of some of his formulations of ideas about language as 'fossil poetry'" (36). By looking as far back in history as possible, surface appearances of integral symbols in nature gloss over most, if not all, symbolic differentiation. Such "expressive power" essentially reinforces an aesthetic concern of creative style over authentic meaning. Emerson's translation theory thus begins to emerge along with his literary tracking of an ideally primal and translingual poetry demonstrated by his own rhetorical practices. If he considers language so closely linked to nature that it becomes the ultimate "sepulchre" in the form of a poetic fossil, he attempts to transcend its inherently dichotomous signifying tension by translating its origins into an essential image. Such a reading, or rather viewing, naturally obviates linguistic difference, thereby supporting his Platonically universal ideal of language origin. Through his linguistic theory, he thus effectively begins to invent, or rather reinvent, an American approach to literary translation capable of subverting equivalence.

Early in the next century, Pound—who like Emerson before him saw the poet and even the scholar's purpose as "much more to dig up the fine things forgotten than to write huge tomes 'about' this, that and the other" (*Contributions* 115)—will use interpretative trots of Chinese ideograms provided by the American Orientalist and art historian Ernest Fenollosa to creatively render ancient Eastern poetry. In addition to mimicking Emerson's theory, Fenollosa curiously began his academic career copying his predecessor's life. At Harvard, he studied under the Emersonian Charles Eliot Norton. Upon graduation, he attended Harvard Unitarian Divinity School, Emerson's significant alma mater. With Western erudition inclusive of Eastern spirituality, Fenollosa, like Emerson, developed an interest in Asian poetic traditions. Returning Eastern influence on the American tradition, he went on to teach Emerson's writing to his students at Tokyo Higher Normal School (Nute 74). Coming full circle in imitating Emerson's relation to transnational influence, he introduced a way of reading Chinese poetry informed by his predecessor's theory to the seminal modern American poet.

"Following Emerson," explains Jung, "Fenollosa regards Chinese characters as the medium for poetry because they are a kind of shorthand way of converting 'material images' into 'immaterial relations' (132). Following Fenollosa in turn, Pound came to view the Chinese ideogram "not as a picture of a sound" but "a picture of a thing" (134). Fenollosa's *The Chinese Written*

Language as a Medium for Poetry, completed and edited by Pound, reprises much of Emerson's perspective on language and image. Like Emerson before him, he elevates poetry in an attempt to interrogate "universal elements" of language origin predicated on universal image:

> My subject . . . is poetry, not language, yet it is in the soil of a language that one has carefully to uncover the delicate roots of poetry . . . the roots of poetry are in language. [In] a language so alien to ours . . . it is necessary to inquire how those universal elements of form that constitute Poetics can . . . derive appropriate nutriment. (79)

Fenollosa then likens poetry written in "visible hieroglyphics" to the aesthetically transcendent form of music with its comparably accessible "verbal medium of semi-pictorial appeals to the eye" (79).

Despite comparably stressing how Persian poets "affect short poems and epigrams" with an "image addressed to the eye" (*CW* 8:127), Emerson accessed Persian poetry through von Hammer-Purgstall's German on the basis of linguistic interpretation. None of the three languages involved in his translations operate pictorially as Chinese and Japanese do for Fenollosa and Pound. Even so, Emerson's meta-view of his foreign renderings insist on an ultimate regression to universal meaning realized through transcendent vision. As Ira Nadel explains: "Chinese for Pound partly meant the recovery or reinvention of the innocent speech of Adam, returning to a world that Emerson idealized" (13). Emerson's telescopic view of the literary past manifesting "intuitions" through which Hafez "sees too far" and "sees throughout" would seemingly overcome all textual limitations, subverting strictures of equivalence. Such "divine truth" foregrounded in "Quotations and Originality" factors into "the formulas that supersede all histories." In this respect, Emerson at least to some extent anticipates the approach to translation by Pound who, "aims neither at dim ritual nor at lexicographic lockstep, but at seeming transparency" to capture "the vigor of the great original" (Kenner 554).

Though beyond Emerson's intentional reach, the Sufi mysticism underpinned by the primal Arabic *alef* explained in the previous chapter proves especially representative in such a comparable formula. The American poet-translator's presumption in rendering verse informed by sacred texts of which he had little knowledge corresponds to the brazen image-based creative interpretation of Asian literatures by both Pound and Fenollosa after him. In his own way, Emerson overtly tends toward containing the essence of Persian source texts by focusing on visual representations of what proves most characteristic of the foreign verse. In the same "Introduction to Persian Poetry" where he references the predication of images on the eye, he catalogs "the staple imagery of the Persian Odes," an Orientalist summation of the "nightingale" and "tulip" as well as an extended blazon of beauty with "the down of the lip, the mole on the cheek, the eyelash, etc." (*CW* 8:127). Esteeming the excessive vision of Hafez, who "sees too far," Emerson anticipates, which is to say sees before seeing, Sa'di's "portrait." Partly slighting the meaning of the *alef* from Arabic and Persian, understood as an all-determining representative letter from the ultimate source text of the *Qur'an*, Emerson further glosses over images from the Persian tradition through von Hammer-Purgstall's renderings much like Pound superficially interprets the characters of Chinese and Japanese through Fenollosa's trots. Much of his ability to subvert an equivalence of meaning derives from his "mis-seeing," to revise Bloom's frequently used term of "misprision" associated with "mistaking" (*Anxiety* xiii). Anticipating Pound, his literary inheritor who will erroneously assume visual authority over Chinese ideograms, Emerson here too can be understood as projecting himself, seminal American Romantic figure, as a visual pun on comparative letters from two disparate lyric traditions: an English "I" upon the Arabic "ﺍ."

Regardless of such appropriation that overlooks significant differences, he often gets relatively close to source texts, as previously shown in his location of fatalism in Persian verse. Lest his rather creative interpretation of Sufi poetry that achieves such a transcendent comparison leave the impression that he always takes at best a superficial approach to foreign verse, it's worth considering his disciplined study of Orientalist literatures. Tracking his examination of both primary and secondary sources in relation to his translation practice begins to reveal the significance of his especially informed misunderstanding of Persian verse. This is to say that despite his illiteracy in the source languages, he gets much right about the original poetry, enabling him to make what he "mis-sees" such an integral part of his own aesthetic. Such close misrecognition in turn proves as generative for the American poetic tradition as Pound's more egregious misreading of his respective foreign sources. For over twenty years, from the mid-1850s through the 1870s, Emerson maintained what editor Ronald Bosco calls "a working repository for his translations of Persian poetry and prose" in his *Notebook Orientalist*. Comprised of translation drafts, paraphrases, and quotations from Orientalist scholars such as Max Muller, as well as original lines of verse that will surface in publications such as *May Day* (*TN* 2:37), the entries read much like an extended translator's notes often included with a published rendering. Insofar as it reflects broad thinking about the literary framework of the Persian tradition, this exhaustive compendium offers substantial evidence that Emerson took quite seriously the verse he translated and imitated.

Supporting Bosco's reading of this text as one of Emerson's "working notebooks," wherein he revises his thoughts about poetry and renders poems from the German (*TN* 2:5), a closer consideration of the notebook reveals recurring concepts from his rhetorical theory laid out in other essays while showing how applicable they remain to his approach to translation. Early on in the collection, for example, Emerson through quotations of Max Muller juxtaposes his telescopic view of Persian literary history with his tendency toward a translingual unification of poetry informed by Platonism: "There was a time when the ancestors of the Celts, the Germans, the Slovanians, the Greeks and Italians, the Persians and Hindus were living together within the same fences . . ." (*TN* 2:41). On the same page, Emerson excerpts Muller's reiteration of his own thoughts on language: "The terms for *God*, for *house*, for *father, son, mother, daughter*, for *dog & cow*, for *heart & tears*, for *axe & tree*, identical in all the Indo-European idioms." Citations from a German Orientalist and comparable European scholar next to Emerson's ideas, as well as his translations from German source texts and original poetry, further reinforce his aesthetic laid out in "Quotation and Originality." Inserts within the manuscript, including a letter to Emerson regarding a specific translation, newspaper clippings, and an advertisement for books about the East (*TN* 2:38) tangibly dramatize outside influence on Emerson's private record. Such critical ekphrasis embodies the process of Emerson's reading and translating foreign literature, rendering his notebook into what Bosco describes, in a telling reapplication of the American poet-translator's own words, as a radical "kind of quotation, a resorting to other men's cisterns . . ." (*TN* 2:12).[1] Following Emerson's theory and rhetoric, the editor of *Notebook Orientalist* expresses the difficulty of differentiating the original "lustres" among Hafez, von Hammer-Purgstall, and previous translators. Ultimately, says Bosco, Emerson achieves an "ideal of poetic syncretism" (*TN* 2:12). Here again Emerson's elusive transparency in his all-inclusive "eyeball" becomes so hard to locate because it so vastly subsumes European scholarship, original Persian sources, and comparative readings from the Western tradition.

In addition to exemplifying Emerson's intertextual approach to Persian poetry, the physical manuscript containing English renderings, imitations, and quotations also tangibly reflects his approach to literary translation as an ongoing process. As Bosco describes the original notebook: "Emerson wrote in ink over unrelated pencil passages, usually the earlier passage is printed first, followed by the later one." To make order of poetry sections in the notebook, the editor must number "various layers." Throughout Emerson's notebook, he further has to make sense of "pencil erasings" as well as unreadable "mutilations" such as torn-out pages (*TN* 2:5). Pagination, often out of sequence in the spirit of what Emerson read as the "inconsecutiveness" of the Persian poets *(CW* 8:127), gets erased, then correctively inked over. Even if Emerson's telescopic gaze at Iran were inverted, wherein a Persian poet like Hafez with no knowledge of English looks back at the notebook's translations and scholarly musings on his verse, the somewhat translingual materiality of the marked and erased text itself would in part begin to reflect the critical and theoretical underpinnings of Emerson's approach to translation.

Extending the inversion of Emerson's appropriative approach to a poet like Hafez further exemplifies the American poet-translator's decentering rhetoric that attempts to transcend linguistic limitations to achieve an original voice. If Westerners were to read Emerson's *Notebook Orientalist* as Persian readers continue to approach Hafez's *Divan,* opening a page at random like the American Methodists for divine revelation, what would they discover? When conducting this unconventional critical experiment, the scholar's index finger first landed on the lines of Hafez, translated by Emerson from von Hammer-Purgstall's German: "The sepulchre has overmuch / Unprofitable time" *(TN* 2:47). These sound much like Emerson's own concern with "sepulchres of the fathers" at the beginning of *Nature.* The next attempt, twenty pages later, marks the well-known line in English surfacing in an abridged poem from Attar's famous *Conference of the Birds,* wherein the flock of "thirty" ("si" in Persian) manifest as one collective "bird" ("morgh"): "They saw themselves all as Simorg / Themselves <as> in the eternal Simorg" *(TN* 2:67). Though an accurately rendered line from the original poem, such unity within the context of so much seeming fragmentation both thematically and stylistically speaks for the writing in Emerson's notebook as well as his relation to the many authors, as well as disparate texts, it contains. Regardless of what quote might fatalistically arrive in the next attempt at such a method of critical selection, following Emerson's approach it will, like the individual bird, invariably join his more comprehensive and all unifying aesthetic.

Failing to land upon the previously discussed poem about Sa'di's loss of his son, considering that it reappears in various forms, chance favors its eventual selection. That Emerson's biography connects to a poem he opts to keep re-translating suggests both considerable foregrounding of his own life in his editorial selection that informs his translation practice, along with his tendency to sublimate it within a foreign tradition. Fatalistically, like the Islam underpinning Sufi poetry to which he found himself drawn, Emerson himself puts his own index finger on Sa'di's poem out of so many by this poet and several others.

In this respect, Emerson pursues an additional rhetorical strategy as anthologist, wherein he excerpts lines from complete poems as well as entire books. Assuming critical authority over a foreign tradition, he dictates the representation of lines by Persian poets with the same rhetorical strategy established in "Quotation and Originality." "Hoard Knowledge," for example, a twenty-three-line poem by Hafez translated in the *Notebook Orientalist* (*TN* 2:26), gets taken out of context and reduced elsewhere to a single quatrain (*CW* 8:136–137). The famous mole for which Hafez would trade an empire with Tamerlane also gets taken from a longer poem, surfacing as one among many other comparably extracted couplets. Defining Persian verse as mostly "short poems and epigrams" with an "image addressed to the eye" (*CW* 8:127), Emerson justifies his own metonymic reduction of an entire *ghazal* to a mere couplet: "Take my heart in thy hand, O beautiful boy of Schiraz! / I would give for the mole on thy cheek Samarcand and Buchara!" (*CW* 8:134). In a grander sense, his entire notebook through a series of quotations follows such an approach, allowing him to re-create his own extended American *ghazal*, which he titles *Notebook Orientalist*.

Ironically, his dismissive summary of Firdousi, tenth-century poet of the national epic *Shahnameh* (*Book of Kings*), which in over 60,000 couplets preserved the Persian culture and language through Arab conquest and the spread of Islam, copies Hafez's figurative treatment of literal empire in the couplet wherein he bargains away politically significant territory for beauty. "Persians have epics," concedes Emerson, after which he more greatly esteems their "epigrams" (*CW* 8:127). Calling Firdousi "the Persian Homer" and deftly offering the reader a good paragraph synopsis of his tome in his "Introduction to Persian Poetry" (*CW* 8:126), Emerson proves himself a Western poet ahead of his time by at least referencing a text so historically important to Iran. Even so, as American Hafez he trades such a nationally definitive text that preserved the Persian culture and language from Arab invasion and consequent imposition of the Arabic language for a mere fragmented couplet isolated, like a mole on the beloved's face, from the massive body of classical verse. Though unfair to severely critique his ethics for favoring short lyrical excerpts of other poets, insofar as he remained perhaps the most forward-thinking scholar and poet of his English-reading nineteenth century interested in the verse of other traditions, considering such practices helps provide a more comprehensive view of his approach to translation.

In addition to choosing individual poems and even parts of poems to translate and arrange, Emerson's rhetorical theory allows him to coopt foreign verse on his own more creative spectrum of equivalence. Curiously, however, such seemingly brazen reinterpretation again paradoxically captures some greater sense of the Persian verse. Though Emerson may at times disregard integral meaning, he better translates a sense of the inherent intertextuality found in the writing of Hafez. Perhaps without knowing or fully appreciating this aspect of his source poet, he nevertheless reinforces something of the original Persian verse, much like he has previously been shown to locate his struggle with fatalism in the lines of Hafez and Sa'di. Enamored with the verse of Rumi, his predecessor, Hafez memorized much of it. As an avid quoter and assimilator of multiple influences, Hafez like Emerson imitated and appropriated various texts, making them his own with comparable and lyrically timeless "divine truth." Of course this is not to disregard the importance of fidelity in translation to American poetry. However, such intertextuality in a foreign tradition to which Emerson felt himself deeply attracted can be seen to a certain extent as justifying, if not somewhat mirroring, his own approach.

The extent to which Emerson at times stylistically intervenes in his literary translations reveals how radically he can respond to his Persian counterparts, and how such creative interpretation often leads him to take further poetic possession of the source texts he engages. Explicating Emerson's "informal process of creative translation" in lines of his *Notebook Orientalist* that eventually get published in his essay "Persian Poetry," Einboden reveals how "from a simple translation of his source" Emerson "elects to replace material" to the point of attempting to "superimpose poetry" by "effecting rhyme" upon an original paraphrase of prose. "First rewriting these lines," Emerson then undergoes a process of "redacting his own revision" (*Islamic Lineage* 146). Consider first the lines from "Persian Poetry" as quoted by Einboden: "Fit for the Pleiads' azure chord/The songs I sung, the pearls I bored." The earlier version from Emerson's *Notebook Orientalist*, also quoted by Einboden, demonstrates the active drafting process of literary translation: "Songs ~~hast thou~~ he sung, pearls ~~hast thou~~ he bored / ~~Worthy~~ Fit to strings against the Pleiads azure chord ~~of Heaven~~ (*Islamic Lineage* 145).[2] Einboden then cites another version from Emerson's notebook: "Fit for ~~Strung on~~ the Pleads azure ~~cord~~ chord / The songs he sung, the pearls he bored" (146). Such lines begin to show how significantly Emerson makes claims on the Persian poets in his English renderings. Even such seemingly passive observations of grammar made by Einboden of Emerson's simple switch of pronouns in his creative rendering prove especially relevant to Persian verse translation:

> Instead of intimately addressing a "thou," Emerson's lines now account for a "he," shifting the subject of this Persian poem, advancing from second person to third person with pencil adjustments. (*Islamic Lineage* 146)

Ironically, in making the original poem more his own, Emerson here too more faithfully captures a ubiquitous translation problem of rendering ambiguous

pronouns from the Persian language. While the previous chapter cited Einboden's finding of Emerson changing pronouns to make his revision of lines
from the *Qur'an* more personal, here Emerson is shown to make the personal
more objective. That the mirrored relation of his own approach surfaces in
a grammatical trait indigenous to the Persian language continues to draw
Emerson even closer to an equivalence with his foreign source text, even
while he attempts to move more creatively further away from it.

The Platonic gaze that ultimately defines how Emerson views appropriative translation becomes especially visible in *Notebook Orientalist*. In his
typical fashion, he begins the manuscript on the East with an epigraph from
the West: "Ex oriente lux" (*TN* 2:39). Antithetical and fragmented in relation
to the entries translated from Persian that will follow, this single line poem
again reinforces Kane's observation of the American translator's tendency
toward the Persian *ghazal*. More than carrying over poems from one language
into another, Emerson from his inception of this notebook brings disparate
literary traditions together. This line effectively mirrors the terseness of the
epigrams Emerson cites as typifying Persian poetry (*CW* 8:127), making it an
apt choice for an epigraph. Quite tellingly, it remains one of a very few completely foreign phrases necessitating translation in the entire notebook about
foreign literature. Its Latin origin sets up the entire manuscript as especially
Orientalist. "Light from the East" promises to illuminate his metaphorical
"telescope" and reveal all that Emerson deems important about Persia, which
elsewhere he considers an "all or nothing life" centered in exotic sounding
(e.g., "hazardous") "extremes" (*CW* 8:124).

Beginning his epigram with a kind of reverse translation by using
the quintessential classical language from his own tradition to comment on
the ancient East begins to signal Emerson's project of mirroring the Persian
tradition on his Western terms. Latin, a so-called "dead language," embodies
Emerson's concept of "fossil poetry," with the aforementioned origins ultimately
extending back to visual transcendence as a once "brilliant picture" (*CW*
3:13). Here lies the "sepulchres of the fathers" as represented by the vestiges
of authors from the Roman literary tradition such as Virgil, Ovid, and Horace
that Emerson so esteems. The shell of these three foreign yet Western words
of the epigraph that frame a notebook about Orientalist literature mirrors
Emerson's deep reach toward classical writers from East and West. What
follows from the Latin—an amalgamation of various notes, scholarly quotes,
and translations—extends the significance of Kane's analysis of Emerson stylistically reflecting the *ghazal* while further dramatizing the intertextual and
interlingual conflation of Emerson's own writing and translation. Insofar as
the Platonic underpinnings of Emerson's theory would obviate all rhetorical

differences, the Latin epigraph embryonically contains the promise of a new
revelation, the kind of "divine truth" that Emerson sees as transcending all
temporality. As he becomes the first American to significantly break open
the Eastern tradition, he extends as poet-translator a living application of his
theory to a now lifeless Western language by repositioning it among varied
quotations derived from Persian sources.

In a notebook recording his sustained telescopic gaze toward the East
illuminated with inspiring verse of Persian poets, Emerson thus attempts
to reprise the "brilliant picture" of a foreign tradition on his own terms.
Like the epigraph connecting East and West through Latin, he goes on to
re-create Persian poetry within the American tradition in English. Using
source material to inspire original poems like "Bacchus" and "Merlin" that
by the definition of translation studies since Dryden constitutes "imitation"
(Schulte 17), Emerson re-creates through translation lines and poetic identities that he considers representative of his own living image. "Half himself"
according to his own constitutive requirements of a man, he completes his
"other half" through translated "expression" (*CW* 3:4). In such a disparate
catalog of Persian poems, notes from scholars, and original observations, a
personal portrait continues to emerge throughout this notebook connecting
to his overall Orientalist aesthetic. Having based his self-invention on Sa'di,
whose portrait he claims to have anticipated before his reading of the poet's
Gulistan, he channels in translation the aforementioned advice of the deceased
Persian son addressing the father beyond the grave: " 'If my dark house thy
heart affright / Saadi strive upwards to the light' " (*TN* 2:97). "Light from
the east," which also radiates the transcendent vision of Hafez, thus revivifies
Emerson's personal themes as well as the kind of divine truth embedded in
the transnational sepulchre of "fossil poetry." The "once brilliant picture" of
"a deadest word" (*CW* 3:13) resurfaces in such light, ultimately illuminating
Emerson's own Romantic self-image

To look, therefore, at the effect of the Eastern gaze on Emerson in his
notebook offers a kind of Rorschach test of his rhetorical identify formation.
The Latin epigraph itself begins to exemplify his fusion of hybrid influence
in the aforementioned attribution of the Greco-Roman god Apollo to his
namesake in his poem "Saadi." When the poem is read in the context of
domestic and foreign allusions, the divine truth that temporally and linguistically transcends the source text in Emerson's conceptualization sanctions
Sa'di's inspiration from both Western and Eastern "muses" (*CW* 3:243–248).
Despite carrying over such inspiration, the accretion of various observation
notes and scholarly quotations in *Notebook Orientalist* holistically fail to

unify as a work of literature, much like Pound bemoaned his inability of his *Cantos* to cohere. Both poet-translators, in part through their appropriation of Eastern poetry, eventually achieve a kind of individuated American lyric identity, yet by far-different means. Whereas Pound begins to emerge more as himself in his *Pisan Cantos* through personal containment following his detention in Italy during World War II, Emerson becomes increasingly more self-evasive and expansive through his reliance on Eastern literature in his notebook. He significantly finds much of his voice through even greater displacement in a foreign poetics. Mourning his own "retrospective" age, Emerson looks telescopically deep into Persian tradition. Multitudinous facts, scholarly citations, and poetic voices fill his notebook, a vast compendium written over several years that can be seen in part as a search for his lyric identity. In his close tracking of Emerson's rather radical changes of original sources in translation, Einboden offers a substantial corrective to Yohannan's earlier accounting of roughly 700 lines, revealing instead up to 2,000 that he then goes on to itemize in an exhaustive appendix (*Islamic Lineage* 159–165). Emerson's greater investment in the Persian tradition by structural analysis alone suggests significant (and somewhat latent) formative influence. Einboden best summarizes his own findings on how Emerson transforms the Persian verse, and by implication how the verse begins to transform him, through an examination of various versions of translations in his notebooks:

> Emerson's mature campaign of Muslim translation remains elusive due to its intimate identity and environs, his versions of Persian poetry . . . infused by his own personality, with Sufi lines increasingly reflecting the American's subjectivity through repeated rendition. (*Islamic Lineage* 145)

Consequently, Emerson's subversion of equivalence through translation and imitation, as understood through his *Notebook Orientalist* as well as through other writings about Persian poetry, manifest in his own original verse. According to Bloom, two representative poems, "Bacchus" and "Merlin," establish a seminal dialectic for American verse, with the former introducing a complete "poetic incarnation" and the latter a "merging with necessity" akin to "subsuming" the Freudian "Reality Principle" ("Bacchus and Merlin" 301). Insofar as Bloom sees their influence extending to such obviously foundational poets as Whitman and Dickinson ("Bacchus and Merlin" 305), both poems by implication can be understood as foregrounding the generative effect of Persian translation and imitation on the American tradition. That "Bacchus" derives from Emerson's appropriative reading of Hafez and "Merlin" from his attempt to become Sa'di suggests that Emerson locates much of his influential dialectic in his attempt to become by turns his two favorite Persian poets.

Deemed foundational to American poetry by Bloom, who calls it "Emerson's finest" for its theme of complete "renovation" ("Bacchus and Merlin" 301), "Bacchus" reflects the same "light from the east" that Emerson sought in his foreign reading and translation. In his own voice, Emerson renews the verse through his foreign predecessors, again clearing the way for visionary transcendence by looking to the Persian mirror. For the American tradition, Persian poetry thus enables him as quintessential literary forefather to "free man from his own ruins, and restore him as the being Blake called Tharmas, instinctual innocence triumphantly at home in his own place" ("Bacchus and Merlin" 301). If this particular poem proves as relevant to the American tradition as Bloom claims, Emerson's effectively predicates his greatest verse achievement that so effectively renews Romantic innocence on Persian poetry. In "Bacchus" he creates, or rather re-creates through imitation, the "sunbright Mecca of the desert" of "Experience," finding himself "born again into this new yet unapproachable America" (*CW* 3:41), which arrives as almost a paraphrase of Bloom's critical assessment.

The title itself exemplifies how Emerson incorporates his rhetorical theories related to translation, as well as his imitation of original foreign verse, into his own poetry. "Bacchus," the Roman god, is a translation of Dionysus, the Greek god of wine. Categorizing the ecstasy-producing power of wine, which plays on a central trope of classical Persian verse under the Greek god in the title, follows Bloom's Western tendencies of theorizing literary predecessors under Greek names. Like the Latin epigraph heading his *Notebook Orientalist*, Emerson relocates foreign influence into an ancient Western tradition, paradoxically domesticating translation by rendering it familiarly foreign. The "nocturnal root" of the vine extends in this poem to the depths of Greco-Roman myth, wherein "acrid juice / Of Styx and Erebus" transforms into an eternal "everlasting dew." Encountering this wine, Emerson, having "by the draught assimilated" various traditions across "Atlantic streams," transcends like the Sufi mystics "through all natures" via representative tropes of a Persian "bird language . . . which roses know so well" (*CW* 9:232–233).

Such intertexuality embodies the kind of Platonic unity of languages explained by scholars like Muller that Emerson read and recorded in his notebook. With disparate influences framed by direct address to a Roman god, the poem further represents Emerson's belief in a "divine truth" manifesting through various sources, languages, and traditions. Through the wine, "winds of remembering / of the ancient being blow," seemingly able to recollect

the loss of integral spiritual meaning after the Fall laid out in "Experience."
Emerson pleads: "Retrieve the loss of me and mine," desiring to belong to
the fundamental originating song of poetry at the basis of his understanding
of all language if only "the grape requite the lote" (*CW* 9:233).

Such an attempt at spiritual recollection further mirrors Emerson's
telescopic gaze toward Hafez, a Persian poet whose vision he covets as he
longed to see "too far" and see "throughout," adding "such is the only man I
wish to see and to be" (*JMN* 10:165). Diverging from a long Hafez poem that
Emerson previously translated, "Bacchus" ironically attempts the recreation
of a Persian predecessor by repositioning him within comparable Platonic
origins. The imperative voice in the very first line directly imitates innumerable appeals by Hafez and others in *ghazal* couplets: "Bring me wine" (*CW*
9:232). Sufi poets, however, typically request it from a "*saki*" (wine server)
who additionally serves as the beloved, or object of desire (Yarshater 975).
He who brings the wine eternally provides spiritual essence to those thirsty
enough to receive it in a wine cup, which in turn represents purity akin to
Christ's admonition of the blessed that remain empty until ultimately finding
spiritual fulfillment. The first line of the very first *ghazal* by Hafez reads in
English: "Hey wine boy, keep giving us more to drink" (Sedarat, "Hafez" 35).
In his own Hafez translation on which he bases much of "Bacchus," Emerson
changes "*saki*" to "Butler" when asking him to "fetch the ruby wine" (*CW*
9:255), domesticating him within a Western class system. Rather than appealing to a *saki* in his own poem, Emerson twice makes his address directly to
"Bacchus," cutting out the middle man, so to speak, much like he seemingly
obviates the intermediary German renderings in his own translations. A
page later in the poem, he names him a second time: "Pour, Bacchus! the
remembering wine;" (*CW* 9:234). Subverting the equivalence of the physical
representation of a wine server in the material world, Emerson in his imitation
goes directly to the divine source, an impetus seemingly sanctioned by his
"Over-Soul" that surfaces in the poem's Platonic underpinnings of his theories
regarding rhetorical inheritance. In the place of the beloved as ubiquitous
intermediary in the physical world by which Persian poets attempt to reach
the divine, Emerson again uses the intertextuality of Greco-Roman myth to
reflect on verse far more foreign. Repositioning himself between traditions
substantially helps him in the formative renewal of his poetic voice.

"Bacchus" further demonstrates Emerson's aforementioned projection
on the use of wine by Hafez, wherein the American finds a Persian counterpart to his famous rejection of what he considered an excessively stale and
formal communion in the Unitarian church. He appeals to the Roman god
for "Food which needs no transmuting" because it "is already man" (*CW*

9:233). Juxtaposed with his familiar critique of the Christian church, reduced to "ashes for bread" and "diluted wine," Emerson would further find himself "by the draft assimilated" to a Sufi poet's comparable unification "through all natures" (*CW* 9:232–233). Reading elsewhere the figuration of wine by Hafez as "intellectual freedom" (*TN* 2:120), the ubiquitous Persian trope in an imitation of the poet further links him to the aesthetic transcendence of music: "Music and wine are one,—That I, drinking this, / Shall hear far chaos talk with me" (*CW* 9:233). Without the aforementioned signifiers of "roses" and "bird language," which Emerson himself cites as other representative tropes of Persian verse, the theme could simply be summarized as an expression of the "Over-Soul." Positioning his own poetry in Persian context thus effectively dramatizes the connection of his aesthetic theory—informed by linguistic and literary unification—with his belief in spiritual transcendence.

Imitating Hafez by rewriting the original that he read in German to make the poem his own, it becomes impossible to fully explicate what Emerson takes from his Persian predecessor as opposed to the German intermediary rendering, which supports a Bloomian reading of the American Sublime. Emerson follows both Goethe and Hafez in calling for a wine that is more than mere wine to reach insightful vision (Buell 152). Yet Emerson's more officially translated version out of which this poem emerged,[3] the original of which von Hammer-Purgstall as editor of the German source cited as one of the verses that earned Hafez the title of "Tongue of the Secret" (*CW* 9:255), references "Jamschid's glass" (256). This too could be considered a mere carry over from the German version, were it not for Emerson's grander claim on its metaphorical import in his own poem. Paradoxically, the art of literary translation again justifies Emerson's subversion of meaning as he moves beyond mere literal naming to better capture the deeper and more transcendent spirit of the original source. Insofar as "man is only half himself, the other half is his expression" (*CW* 3:4) Emerson imaginatively polishes the Sufi mystic mirror in the Persian allusion to the reflection in Jamschid's cup, interjecting his appropriative practice into his own self-expression. Considered a locus of all-knowing power held by various kings in Persian mythology, the cup of Jamschid is said to reflect the whole world and reveal the seven heavens of the universe. "Lo," translates Emerson, "this mirror shows me all!" (*CW* 9:257).

A frequent allusion in the poetry of Hafez—one of the many rhetorical reasons that the Persian poet comes to claim the "Tongue of the Secret"—wine as metaphor carries Emerson's "Bacchus" to the throne of an atemporal palace where the American makes claims on an ancient future yet to materialize: "Kings unborn shall walk with me . . ." (*CW* 9:233). Emerson's own history that will get written as if for the first time, much like his essay "Experience" displaces Mecca to the new world, in turn links human eternity to the seven heavenly sisters of Western antiquity. The essence of Western Romantic free expression through Goethe, whose translations and adaptations he read in German, surface in the same intersecting circle of influence wherein latently appropriated vision originates with the "first circle" of his own transparent eyeball.

The speaker's appeal in a Persian rhyming couplet to "Pour . . . the remembering wine" and so "Retrieve the loss of me and mine," ultimately comes down to reviving his own original "dazzling memory" (*CW* 9:234). Going so far back in an ancient intertextual recollection, he longs to find himself born again, capturing the transcendent "divine truth" at the crux of his ideal rhetorical understanding. In his own translation, Hafez requests, "Give me wine to wash me clean" (*CW* 9:257) a plea for complete renewal supportive of Bloom's "Bacchus" reading. Again a return to the ancient Middle East comes to mean a return to a primal *tabula rasa* in the new world. In asking Bacchus to fill his cup, Emerson really asks him to

> write my old adventures with the pen
> Which on the first day drew
> Upon the tablets blue,
> The dancing Pleiads and eternal men. (*CW* 9:234)

Emerson concludes his imitation of an Eastern poem he translates by writing over it with the convention of Western elegy. The eternal renewal itself gets preserved in a cosmos back to a beginning before all origins. Foregrounding innumerable divisions of East and West as if to overcome them, he ultimately appears to subvert translating equivalences in a return to the all-unifying Platonism on which his rhetorical theory remains predicated, thereby transcending his own intertextuality. He arrives at the fantasy of an empty blue sky, a figurative renewal as clear as the first day of *Genesis* before dichotomies predicated on the symbolic (sky and sea, vegetation and animals, etc.). Extending his perspective beyond the limitations of comparative meaning, he "sees throughout" and "sees too far." Returning to his Hafez translation, "A cup of wine imparts the sight / Of the five heaven-domes with nine steps . . ." (*CW* 9:258) much like the ideally renewed vision in "Bacchus" is able to "Refresh the faded tints" (*CW* 9:234). Emerson finds a way of seeing in own poem, then, by further reflection on his visionary predecessor.

That "Bacchus" proves so closely tied to Emerson's coveting the vision of Hafez, which he metaphorically reads as both potentially transformative as well as ideally unreachable, closely aligns his Persian predecessor with his

seminal American poem. In his Hafez translation that informs "Bacchus,"
Emerson aptly calls the wine cup a "toy of Daemons" (*CW* 9:259). Such a
reading of both poem and imitation in relation to Hafez offers further sub-
stantiation of Persian influence on the progenitor American poet-translator. "If
a single American has incarnated our *daimon*," argues Bloom, "it is Emerson"
("Bacchus and Merlin" 297). His inspired play, which would return poetry
beyond the usual sensibility of Romantic childhood to the very infancy of all
of creation, very much involves him toying around with the verse of Hafez.

Counterpointing "Bacchus," "Merlin" lacks comparable Persian signifiers.
It reads as if it has "subsumed" them along with Bloom's understanding of "the
reality principal." Paradoxically, this further exemplifies Emerson's approach to
foreign influence, inviting greater critical speculation as to how it might even
more significantly figure in this poem. At best, the early Emerson critic Joel
Benton has intuited "an almost playful Persian touch" (26) in the following:

> He shall not his brain encumber
> With the coil of rhythm and number;
> But, leaving rule and pale forethought,
> He shall aye climb
> For his rhyme.
> "Pass in, pass in," the angels say,
> "In to the upper doors,
> Nor count compartments of the floors,
> But mount to paradise
> By the stairway of surprise." (*CW* 9:224)

Benton reads these lines "as if Hafiz or Firdousi himself were speaking" (26).
Even so, he too critically reiterates Emerson's intertextual aesthetic informing
his approach to translation, noting how his "sensitive harp" seems to capture "the air many tones," including "echoes of Marlowe, Chapman, Milton,
Marvell, Herbert, Herrick, and Donne, and of all schools . . ." (27). Further
re-inscribing such an appropriative approach to translation, as if dictated
by the writer whose work he critically assesses, he repositions Emerson in
Goethe's transnational relation of Hafez: "What Goethe says of the Spanish
poet Calderon . . . serves equally well if you substitute for his name Emerson's:

> Many a light the Orient throws,
> O er the midland waters brought;
> He alone who Hafiz knows
> Knows what Calderon has thought. (27–28)

More than merely identifying a "Persian touch" in "Merlin," Benton seems to contextualize Emerson's intertextual translating aesthetic, which accesses Hafez through comparable displacement of German rendering. Ironically, what makes Benton's reading most Persian according to Emerson's rhetorical theory is that poets and poetry from all traditions become so easily interchangeable. To understand Hafez is to understand an interchange between Calderon, Emerson, and Goethe. Rewriting the last line, Benton uses the "midland waters" to interpose a mirror, much like an intermediary translation, between his American poet and the Persian tradition. Following Emerson's lead, he thus gives the German Romantic's stanza, as well as the displaced quote by the Spaniard, an American touch.

Direct analysis of "Merlin"—a poem heavily influenced by Welsh poetry, Emerson's childhood love of Ossian, as well as his interest in the romance *Morte D'Arthur* (Edward Emerson 440)—fails to detect sufficient Persian influence for this very reason. Emerson again dislocates traditions by his Romantic self-evasion. Much like the return of repressed grief from "Experience" in his translation drafts of the poem, wherein Sa'di mourns the loss of his son in *Notebook Orientalist*, a Persian influence that informs "Merlin" surfaces beyond the specific text. In "Poetry and Imagination," while a displaced Merlin gets credited as the source of poetic inspiration, Emerson defines his Platonic conception of poetry by citing the oldest Persian prophet:

> Our best definition of poetry is one of the oldest sentences, and claims to come down to us from the Chaldáan Zoroaster, who wrote it thus: "Poets are standing transporters, whose employment consists in speaking to the Father and to matter; in producing apparent imitations of unapparent natures, and inscribing things unapparent in the apparent fabrication of the world;" in other words, the world exists for thought: it is to make appear things which hide: mountains, crystals, plants, animals, are seen; that which makes them is not seen: these, then, are "apparent copies of unapparent natures." (*CW* 8:10)

Returning to his translingual origins, he further writes how the inspirational poetic "power is in the image because this power is in nature" (*CW* 8:10).

Emerson also again in this essay uses a panoply of varied influences to embody an aesthetic that attempts to transcend meaning itself, much like his own transformation into a transparent eyeball. Consider the positioning of his Persian poet among ancient as well as more contemporary Western greats:

> Homer, Milton, Hafiz, Herbert, Swedenborg, Wordsworth, are
> heartily enamored of their sweet thoughts. Moreover, they know
> that this correspondence of things to thoughts is far deeper than
> they can penetrate,—defying adequate expression[.] (*CW* 8:15)

Such an inability to access this correspondence without his concept of inspired
"Genius" places this grouping of writers, and Emerson along with them, in the
realm of metaphorical mystery. Though of course this fails to qualify as Sufi
mysticism, in Emerson's appropriative Persian mirror it nevertheless comes
to resemble it. Later in "Poetry and Imagination," juxtaposing "Zoroaster
and Plato" as essential examples from East and West, Emerson argues that
the poet must "use nature as his hieroglyphic" (*CW* 8:37) again reinforcing
a return to image beyond received language (figuratively placed in Ancient
Egypt) that can only be translated through inspiration.

   Around distinct Persian signifiers in the essay, such an ineffable correspondence gets related to Merlin, whose absence significantly accounts for
poetic insight. Nothing in Emerson's estimation proves as memorable in the
poem "Morte d'Arthur" than "Sir Gawain's parley with Merlin in his Wonderful
prison" (Edward Emerson 8:88). Responding to Gawain's plea to appear before
him, Merlin replies, "you will never see me more, and that grieves me, but I
cannot remedy it, and when you shall have departed from this place, I shall
nevermore speak to you . . ." Emerson quoting this passage from Thomas
Bulfinch's *The Age of Chivalry* (30) quoting Gawain quoting Merlin attempts
to "penetrate" layers of textuality, as if to get from "thoughts" to the very
origination of "things." Though considered by his interlocutor "the wisest
man in the world," Merlin has made himself inaccessible, explaining, "I have
been fool enough to love another more than myself, for I taught my mistress
that whereby she hath imprisoned me in such a manner that none can set
me free'" (*CW* 8:35). Merlin then seals his own fate, telling Gawain, "neither
will any one speak with me again after you, it would be vain to attempt it;
for you yourself, when you have turned away, will never be able to find the
place . . ." In this sense, Merlin in Emerson's favorite poetic passage embodies the separation between the "correspondence of things to thoughts." The
resulting tension, however, paradoxically leads to the very lyric revelation
that overcomes such division. Before his muse ends up "defying adequate
expression," he foretells Gawain's fate (*CW* 8:35).

   Following Emerson's influence on Benton, wherein the American poet
seemingly inserts himself in his criticism (similar to how Benton inserts
Emerson into the verse of Calderon), Merlin's inspiration by separation can be
seen as reflecting the Sufi poet's relation to his beloved. Voluntarily imprisoned

by the woman he adores, he reaches Gawain through a mysterious relation beyond the intellect. Consider how Hafez in Emerson's translation similarly channels his verse from painfully accepting, if not willing, comparably contained desire: "Ah, could I hide me in my song, / To kiss thy lips from which it flows!" (*CW* 8:142). To a certain extent, the lyrical separation allegorizes Jalaluddin Rumi losing his beloved teacher Shams, which effectively broke his heart open from the limitations of reason and into the realm of divinely inspired verse. Emerson's translation aesthetic, in theory and praxis, seems to invite such idealized parallels. Associated with ubiquitous allusions to Persian literature, his Merlin thus begins to tell a comparable backstory.

Though informed by a variety of influences, a closer reading of "Merlin" suggests Emerson's further identification with Sa'di, a poet on the other side of Hafez in his personal Persian dialectic. The same revelation by a prophetic intermediary at a remove from his audience seen in "Poetry and Imagination" surfaces in "Uriel," a precursor to "Merlin." When "SAID" eavesdrops on "the young gods talking" (*CW* 9:33), he sounds much like how in the essay esteeming Merlin the angels overhear Allah praising the Persian poet. Though Uriel surfaces as the "devilish prophet," explains Kane, Sa'di remains his privileged witness (134). At its best, poetry for Emerson in this essay that uses Merlin as its strongest example achieves an ideal Platonic "correspondence" through the "verse of Saadi, which the angels testified met the approbation of Allah in Heaven" (*CW* 8:36).

If "Bacchus" seems somewhat based on Emerson's translation of the more foreign and elusive Hafez, then "Merlin" tends to reflect the self-portrait of his more realistic ideal who he sought to domestically imitate. While Zoroaster in "Poetry and Imagination" corresponds to Merlin's prophetic nature, Sa'di's inspiration in the poem titled with his name, able to "seek the living among the dead" (*CW* 9:246), exemplifies similar power to the Persian poet's verse in the essay that remains "capable of restoring the dead to life" (*CW* 8:36). Also like Merlin, Sa'di in Emerson's depiction "dwells alone" (*CW* 9:243), separated from others even while inspiring them with "each transparent word" (*CW* 9:245) as if his audience were a greater reflection of his beloved. The muse advises Emerson's ideal poet to self-reliantly resist outside esteem, telling him "Gentle Saadi, mind thy rhyme;/ Heed not what the bawlers say, Heed thou only Saadi's lay" (*CW* 9:245–246). Similarly, Merlin creates verse from a place of individuated integrity, safely aloof from worldly distraction: "He shall not seek to weave, / In weak, unhappy times, / Efficacious rhymes" (*CW* 9:225).

Though Benton finds that Emerson "takes an Oriental freedom in his own measures" (27), it remains hard to say how he substantiates such a

finding, as he cites very little about the metrical difference between traditions. Most likely, the beginning and middle of "Merlin I," which asserts an
exotic, mystic disruption of Western musical norms, leads him to such an
exotic conclusion. Here too there are strong correspondences with Emerson's
"SAADI":

> The trivial harp will never please
> Or fill my craving ear;
> Its chords should ring as blows the breeze,
> Free, peremptory, clear.
> No jingling serenader's art,
> Nor tinkle of piano strings,
> Can make the wild blood start
> In its mystic springs.
> The kingly bard
> Must smite the chords rudely and hard,
> As with hammer or with mace;
> That they may render back
> Artful thunder, which conveys
> Secrets of the solar track . . . (CW 9:223)

The measured music of the "trivial harp" fails to summon the "mystic springs,"
reminiscent of how when others beside Sa'di attempt to play, "Shall the harp
be dumb" (CW 9:243). The Platonic echo of the "artful thunder," able to relay
originating "secrets," further resembles, in an essay that uses Merlin for its
most poetic example, the seeming inability to penetrate "the correspondence
of things to thoughts" (CW 8:15). Disregarding intellect, just as "Uriel" ignores
linear reason, "He shall not his brain encumber / With the coil of rhythm and
number." Instead, he will "mount to paradise / By the stairway of surprise'"
(CW 9:224), achieving revelation as if beyond linear Western logic.

As Benton continues to argue, like "the Asiatic bards," Emerson uses
"the machinery of subtle, unexpected and fantastic conceit" (26). Overcoming
the banality of mere "Efficacious rhymes," as if spiritually challenging stylistic
structure like the Sufi mystics in their *ghazals*, the muse goes beyond the
trajectory of an especially enlightened

> Bird, that from the nadir's floor
> To the zenith's top can soar,
> The soaring orbit of the muse exceed that journey's length.
>   (CW 9:225)

Though not specifically Persian, the birds known as "houris"—spiritual com-
panions[4] representative of divine perfection in Islam—lead Hafez to heavenly
transcendence at the conclusion of Emerson's translation.

> Call of Houris to my sense:—
> 'O lovely bird, delicious soul,
> Spread thy pinions, break thy cage;
> Sit on the roof of seven domes,
> Where the spirits take their rest. (*CW* 8:258)

Unlike Bacchus, however, where music along with wine completely overcomes
earthly limitation beyond "the belly of the grape" (*CW* 9:232) to enable the
poet to transcend time and walk with "Kings unborn" (*CW* 9:233), "Merlin"
limits the harp to strikes from "The kingly bard" (*CW* 9:223). In this way, like
Emerson and similar to Sa'di relative to Hafez, Merlin embodies the reality
principle. "Merlin II" further achieves a perfect structural balance in the world
for "The rhyme of the poet" that "Modulates the king's affairs . . ." wherein
"two married sides / In every mortal meets" (*CW* 9:228).

Ultimately "Merlin," argues Bloom, "becomes one with the spirit that
'finishes the song'" ("Bacchus and Merlin" 304), a "merging with necessity"
(305) he sees as originating with Emerson and further extending through
the American poetic tradition. Insofar as "Balance-loving Nature / Made
all things in pairs" (*CW* 9:228), as recorded in "Merlin II," Emerson finds a
Persian counterpart reflective of his aesthetic. While such direct influence in
this particular poem must of course remain speculative, Emerson circumstan-
tially inhabits so much of the Persian tradition that critics like Benton seem
to hear it "Murmur" in Merlin's "house of life" (*CW* 9:229).

At the conclusion of "Merlin II," rhymes counter each other to both create
and disassemble: "In perfect time and measure they / Build and unbuild our
echoing clay . . ." (*CW* 9:229). These lines can be read as analogous to Emerson's
relationship to the Persian tradition, wherein he encounters a playfulness in
his identification as Sa'di much like Benton sees him expressing an "Oriental
freedom in his measures." Such freedom remains contingent upon a certain
constraint, much like Gawain encounters Merlin imprisoned by love in the
essay that so esteems Sa'di. "Justice is the rhyme of things," writes Emerson
in the poem, wherein "even matches odd" until it finally "finishes the song"
(*CW* 9:229). His namesake in the imitative poem "SAADI" of course also
sings, but in an insistence on self-reliance, he does so "alone." "Many may
come," writes Emerson about his ideal poet, "But one shall sing" (*CW* 9:243).
However, Emerson in the latter poem is both American *and* Persian poet, a

balance of West and East, even and odd. Exemplifying an attempt to reconcile
"the Reality Principle only by subsuming it," Emerson's "Merlin" becomes for
Bloom "the archetypal American poem that our best poets keep writing, once
they have passed through their crises of individuation, have found their true
limit, and then fail to accept any limit as their own" ("Bacchus and Merlin"
301). Bloom goes on to declare that "Merlin, who can no more be defeated
than Nemesis can be thwarted, becomes one with the spirit that 'finishes the
song'" (304).

Yet ironically, when considering Emerson's relation to Persian influence as defined by his rhetorical theory and exemplified in "Merlin," despite
a perceived American self-reliance against the Sufi's attempt to "dissipate
it into ecstasies" (Packer 101), he seems to reconcile much of his seminal
"crisis of individuation" by becoming Sa'di, who models for him in the essay
referencing Merlin how to write verse that meets "the approbation of Allah
in Heaven" (*CW* 8:36). Emerson in this respect complicates Bloom's assessment of "Merlin" as an archetype for American poets, the subsuming of the
Reality Principle, but on another's terms. Though beyond the scope of this
study, it warrants mentioning for further consideration how Whitman and
Dickinson, the two respective ancestors of the American tradition that Bloom
cites as inheriting Emerson's dialectic between "Bacchus" and "Merlin," sought
comparable evasion of rhetorical limitation through persona. "When I state
myself, as the Representative of the Verse—," writes Dickinson, "it does not
mean—me—but a supposed person" (*Letters* 176). Whitman invented his
own untitled image on the cover of *Leaves of Grass*, identifying many pages
later in "Song of Myself" through distanced third person self-objectification:
"Walt Whitman: a kosmos, of Manhattan the son" (46). The latter goes on, of
course, to morph into a multitude of foreign and domestic signifiers, embodying much like Emerson a diverse array of voices in his oeuvre.

Bloom is no doubt correct in proclaiming, "Emerson our father . . . the
presiding genius of the American version of poetic influence, the anxiety of
originality he hoped to dispel . . ." However, much of his "oscillation between
poetic incarnation" (Bacchus) and the "merging with Necessity" (Merlin),
which is crucial to his "emergence and individuation" ("Bacchus and Merlin"
305), involves the appropriation of translated precursors. Emptying verse from
the distant past, as if coming as close as possible to the Platonic origins of
"fossil poetry," he attempts to empty the "sepulchres of the Fathers" and insert
himself in their place. "Subsuming the Reality Principle," as Bloom describes,
also involves the sublimation of a Persian precursor. This is to say that, for
Emerson, much of "the American version of poetic influence" surfaces in the
verse of Persian poets, among other displaced, foreign traditions.

Chapter 5

Americanizing Rumi and Hafez
The Return of Emerson's Verse Translation

> I have come to understand that really,
> honestly, there is no such thing as the
> poem translated from one language into
> the next. There can't be. What happens,
> rather than a translation, is that we get
> something like it, but written by the new
> person, the translator. There's just no way
> around it.
>
> —Matthew Rohrer ("Translations" 152)

While Emerson's influence on the American poetic tradition has become a critical given, the effect of his appropriative contribution on literary translation remains relatively unrecognized. Thus far this study has argued how his imitative modeling of foreign source texts in English as well as his introduction of a linguistic theory that Fenollosa followed as an Asian language informant anticipates Pound's modern approach to translation. Having broadly established Emerson as predecessor, more specific consideration of contemporary American trends in English renderings of classical Persian verse can now be seen as further revealing the extraordinary extent to which he continues to make his translating presence visible. As Elena Furlanetto argues, the popularity of Rumi's verse in the twentieth century, especially with Coleman Barks, "should be seen as the culmination of a much older dialogue between American literature and Sufi poetry" (202). It's worth noting how Schmidt, in his assessment of Barks's translations, returns to Emerson's own foundational Orientalist text: "If one wants to fathom how the writer Coleman Barks has managed to turn Rumi into a best-selling poet in contemporary America, one

143

would do well to place Alger's *Poetry of the East* alongside Barks's *The Soul of Rumi* and see their common wellsprings" (25). Much of this interchange significantly begins with Emerson's translating and writing in the voice of classical poets from Iran.

Closer analysis of English renderings by the two most popular American contemporary translators of Persian poetry, Daniel Ladinsky and Coleman Barks—along with the well-known contemporary poet Matthew Rohrer's recently published versions of Hafez—demonstrate surprisingly extreme examples of Emerson's translation tendencies covered in preceding chapters: a seemingly Platonic fantasy ultimately unifying languages and traditions while obviating all temporal difference between ancient source text and modern translation, radical self-sanctioning claims upon foreign predecessors that allow American translators to imitatively become their respective Persian poets, and the relative dismissal of Islamic influence. Also like Emerson, they remain illiterate in the language from which they translate, relying on previous versions for their poetic interpretations while further privileging what they consider the spirit, as opposed to the literal meaning, of the text.

Because Ladinsky exaggeratedly extends Emerson's fantasy of an American identification with a classical Persian poet, he warrants first and especially close comparative consideration. A best-selling translator of Hafez's poetry, he continues to mass produce his renderings based on his own conception of the Persian poet and his verse. As Murat Nemet-Nejat observes in a review of one of Ladinsky's Hafez collections, "there is not a single poem (*gazel*) of Hafiz of which any one of the poems . . . is a translation or adaptation or extrapolation or deconstruction" ("Review"). Emerson of course projected much of his own understanding upon the Persian poets, previously shown in his extremely self-reliant imitation of his namesake in the poet Sa'di as well as such authoritative interventions in his English translation practice as excerpting fragments and anthologizing them according to his own preferences. Even so, his renderings of Persian poems ultimately derive from corresponding German versions, and he distinguishes translation from his own imitations in publication. In what Ladinsky calls translations of Hafez, he tends to radically expand Emerson's identification with a poet like Sa'di, projecting an idea of the Romantic self that displaces linguistically determined meaning to reinforce the fantasy of transcendent affinity with the foreign poet irrespective of originating differences. Consider how he claims his Persian predecessor visited him in a prophetic dream to sanction his verse renderings:

> I feel like my relationship to Hafiz defies all reason and is really
> an attempt to do the impossible: to translate Light into words—to
> make the luminous resonance of God tangible to our finite senses.

> About six months into this work I had an astounding dream in
> which I saw Hafiz as an Infinite Fountaining Sun, who sang hun-
> dreds of lines of his poetry to me in English, asking me to give
> that message to "my artists and seekers." (*Gift* 5–6)

Returning to Emerson's incomparable esteem of Hafez for his ability to
"see too far," (which Ladinsky cites on page 1 of his introduction to his book), as
well as his extended metaphor of the temporally and linguistically transcending
telescope for Persian verse, the contemporary American intends to reach the
master by translating "light" itself—as opposed to equivalent Persian meaning—
"in words." It is as though he inherits, if not borrows or even outright steals,
Emerson's aforementioned epigraph for his own *Notebook Orientalist*: "Light from
the East." His claim of Hafez coming to him in a dream also revisits Emerson's
fantasy of encountering an Eastern "pundit to whom he gave the name Osman,"
able to present to him as a kind of spiritual teacher "the world flowing out as
emanation" (Richardson 349). Insofar as his relationship with the classical Sufi
poet he translates "defies all reason," he enables himself to expand on Emerson's visual identification with Hafez to the point of transcending any source
text whatsoever. Filling the "transparent eye/I" with the fantasy of "Hafiz as an
Infinite Fountaining Sun," he therefore attempts to outshine even Emerson by
mirroring the all-seeing Persian Sufi who originates verse mysteriously capable
of reaching beyond the threshold of specific language difference.

While Emerson has been shown to identify with his source poet through
a comparable figurative relation to wine, wherein the early American's disavowal
of the sacrament in the Christian tradition corresponds to his reading of the
Persian Sufi using the forbidden trope to represent "intellectual freedom,"
Ladinsky imagines himself as actually drinking from the cup of Hafez. Here
again he exaggerates Emerson's previous Platonic union that attempts to obviate all temporal and linguistic difference. Reviving his relationship with his
foreign poet on equal terms, he too offers a corrective to Emerson's lament
of his nineteenth-century culture's tendency to "buy ashes for bread" as well
as "diluted wine" (*CW* 9:232). Claiming like Emerson a transcendent communion, Ladinsky, in an Amazon review of his own translation titled "My
Portrait of Hafiz" (which by title alone resembles Emerson's anticipating Saʿdi's
"portrait"), self-authorizes his brazen appropriative approach to his Persian
predecessor's poetry:

> I think this old great Persian Master and I once shared some
> bread together, and some magnificent wine he poured into me,
> that is still there and fermenting . . . and caused all my words,
> vision, and (hopefully) sacred needed mischief.

Completely breaking from any kind of linguistic equivalence between source and translated poem, Ladinsky equates himself to his own idea of the fourteenth-century Persian poet. In this respect, the telescope and the mirror used by Emerson as critical tropes to comparatively analyze an American engagement with the tradition of Sufi poetry gets turned narcissistically back upon the original "eye" as "first circle." Separating wine from its basis in both Christian as well as Islamic traditions, Ladinsky extends Emerson's allegorizing of wine in Sufi poetry by further claiming an actual communion with Hafez. To quote further from Nejat's review, "As God talked to Moses in Hebrew, to Mohammad in Arabic, Hafez spoke to Daniel Ladinsky in English. Mr. Ladinsky is translating a dream, not a 14th century Persian text." Reconsidering Benton's assessment of Emerson's maintaining a "balance" between interjecting his own influence on his Hafez translations by dipping his "own original quatrains in a little tincture of the wine and spirit of Oriental thought," Ladinsky by comparison signs his own name on the original Persian bottle (or wine cup, to better place the metaphor in fourteenth-century context).

Though an especially egregious example of creatively transgressing source text equivalence far beyond Emerson and Pound, Ladinsky also effectively, albeit too radically, dramatizes the American tendency to privilege the spirit of the original foreign poet over literal meaning. As he himself argues, "scholarship in Hafiz can, it seems to me, greatly compromise his spirit and make him appear far less than I have seen and know he is" (*A Year* xii). To this end, Ladinsky includes a foreword in one of his books titled, "Releasing the Spirit of Hafez," seeing himself as liberator of a primal and transcendent energy from the original Persian that becomes tragically repressed by the usual approaches to translation. As he explains, "No holds barred, to me, is rule number one in poetry . . ." (*A Year* xi). Though Emerson did rely on relatively accurate German renderings of Hafez's verse, in referring to the translations of ancient spiritual writings attributed to Zoroaster he dismissed a need for strict authenticity. In disregarding even the semblance of any kind of equivalence to the original poems, Ladinsky takes Emerson's intertextuality much further, to the extent that scholars must question whether to cite his original poetry as source author or attribute the poems to him as American imitator (this study has opted for the latter). The book jacket of his best-selling translation collection states: "Ladinsky has succeeded brilliantly in translating the essence of one of Islam's greatest poetic and spiritual voices" (*The Gift*). Considering that he has completely disavowed even the slightest connection to the original source poetry, exactly what essential connection to Hafez does his publisher claim has been made?

Reiterating his argument that his source poet lacks a firm "scholarly foundation," Ladinsky concludes that "all we truly have of Hafiz in ANY language is a version" ("Portrait"), thereby justifying his own interpretation. In his introduction to another collection of translations, he argues that "careful efforts to honor the *form* of the poetry can sometimes ignore or violate the *spirit* of Hafiz." As if to further justify his own interpretative approach, he appeals to an irreconcilable ambiguity in the source text: "A single couplet can be translated many different ways, and each one would be 'right' (*God Laughing* x). Having so qualified his approach, which includes citing Wilberforce Clarke's nineteenth-century translations as his English source, he admits that though his versions "are not intended to be literal or scholarly or even 'accurate,'" he nevertheless aspires to make them "True—faithful to the living spirit of this divine poet" (*God Laughing* xi).

Citing Emerson's statement, "Hafiz is a poet for poets," Ladinsky goes on to impose his own critical standard, which seems further reminiscent of Emerson's transcendent aesthetic insofar as authentic verse from the Persian master must "flirt with the sublime" or "lift the corners of your mouth with delightful humor" ("Portrait"). Also following Emerson's transplanting "Mecca" in the "new and unapproachable desert" that he figuratively discovers as the first to arrive "in the West," Ladinsky even more freely displaces the origins of a Persian poet who predicated his verse on words revealed to Mohammad at Mecca. Much like Emerson attempts to subvert what he perceives as Islamic constraints impinging upon Sufi verse to figuratively align his self-reliant spirit underpinned by Transcendentalism with Persian poets whom he admired, Ladinsky interposes his own spiritual relation in his translation process, commenting, "I have prayed hundreds of times for help to try and reveal something of Hafiz's soul and beauty" ("My Portrait").

In this respect fidelity to source text for Ladinsky resembles Emerson esteeming the integrity of any predecessors' writing based on a conception of timeless "genius." Following Emerson, he favors the spirit of originality that surfaces as if for the first time in endless quotation, wherein "The divine resides in the new" (*CW* 8:105). On the title page of a translated collection, Ladinsky offers this transcendent prayer: "May these poems help reveal the Truth / Of God's Divine Playfulness and Light / And his Sublime Intimacy with Us" (*I Heard God Laughing*). The spirit of revelation comes upon Ladinsky following an explanation from his great Indian teacher that no one has yet to properly translate Hafez. As Ladinsky explains: "That night, though I did not (and do not) know the Persian language, I wrote my first version of a Hafiz poem, working from a literal English translation" (*I Heard God Laughing* x–xi). Such inspired self-sanctioned claims upon the spirit of a predecessor's work reflect Emerson's intertextual theory, where timeless inspiration of one author can get renewed elsewhere, regardless of linguistic, cultural, or temporal variance.

Along with Emerson before him, Ladinsky intuits the spirit of the Persian masters, though with the pretense of even greater mystery, more akin to illiterate Muhammad transcribing the revealed words of Allah. An epigraph attributed to the "Hadith of the Prophet Muhammad" in his book of daily Hafez mediations reinforces his claim upon divine agency: "God has treasuries beneath the Throne, / the keys to which are the tongues of poets." Such quotations that assume the poet's authority further reflect Emerson's many epigraphs, and specific mention of the poets' tongues sublimated under God's kingdom reiterates Emerson's intertextual note in an introduction to a specific Hafez translation: "His German editor, von Hammer, remarks on the following poem that 'though in appearance anacreontic, it may be regarded as one of the best of those compositions which earned for Hafiz the honorable title of 'Tongue of the Secret' " (*CW* 9:255).

More than inferring such seeming correspondence with his American predecessor's Persian renderings, Ladinsky explicitly references his direct response to Emerson's translations. In his introduction to *A Year with Hafiz: Daily Contemplations*, a meditation book offering one Hafez translation for each day of the year, he states: "I have freely collaborated on Emerson's Hafiz poems, often trying to complete fragments of translations he left" (xiii). Dedicating April to his reworking of Emerson's renderings (because, as he cites, Emerson died in this month), he sees himself as part of a "unique lineage" in an ongoing process through original and intermediary languages of bringing his source poet into English, calling his own versions "Hafiz-Hammer-Emerson-Ladinsky poems" (xiii). Some entries merely reword, or slightly alter, his predecessor's versions. For April 1st, Ladinsky takes Emerson's, "The glass with wine is like the Lord Jesus / It wakes the dead to life" (*TN* 2:94), and changes it to "Wine is like the Lord Jesus; it can bring the dead to life" (*A Year* 103). Titling the poem with the first line, however, Ladinsky has excerpted the couplet from Emerson's thirteen-line poem, which appears in a much longer series by Hafez translated in his American predecessor's notebook. His abridged couplet misses the greater context of a bound heart, the need to love as purely as gold, as well as risking the daunting waves of the sea to retrieve pearls (*TN* 2:94). Ironically, claiming to complete previous fragmented translations, Ladinsky adopts Emerson's editorial authority to excerpt a mere few lines for his own anthologizing purposes. In this respect he bests Emerson, who made comparable moves with the Persian poets, at his own appropriative game.

Were this an aberration in Ladinsky's approach, it might not warrant much comment. His later entries that further revise Emerson, and, consequently, Hafez, become much more egregious. The verse he titles "Your Scent I Know," appearing on April 27, which he cites as the date of Emerson's death, again reworks just two lines, but then goes on to invent an entirely new poem seemingly based on the last two lines of Emerson's translation. Consider first Emerson's rather equivalent rendering from Hafez:

> Drink wine, and the heaven
> New lustre diffuses,
> And doubt not that sinning
> Has also its uses.
>
> The builder of Heaven
> Has sundered the earth,
> So that no footway
> Leads out of it forth:
>
> On turnpikes of wonder
> Wine leads the mind forth,
> Straight, sidewise & upward
> Southward and north.
>
> Stands the vault adamantine
> Until the last day;
> The wine-cup shall ferry
> Thee o'er it away. (*TN* 2:73–74)

Compare this to Ladinsky's version:

YOUR SCENT I KNOW

> The ferry to any shore, to any land, to
> any realm, it is the wine cup, the heart.
> An unseen vessel it is though to most,
> love, but so capable of travel, via a prayer
> or a soul's deep wish.
>
> And your spirit's arms, they can reach
> out and really touch anything you want
> to hold.

It should be that way, and it is. For you,
dear, all within time, are right before me.
Your scent I know; your ways I shape. (129)

Aside from the verb "ferry" with "wine cup" as subject, a construction that
Emerson uses only once in his Hafez translations, the relation of this poem
to Ladinsky's version seems quite tenuous. Reworking the last two lines in
a much different context, Ladinsky essentially writes a new poem, just as
throughout his translations he completely rewrites Hafez, at best retaining a
random Persian signifier like a wine cup. Through this process of abandoning
a previous text as authentic source, he claims to "complete" both a fragmented
Emerson and Hafez. He further extends what he considers a tradition of verse
translation by developing his own "Hafiz-Hammer-Emerson-Ladinsky" lineage.
Ironically, he ends up exposing the translator's ideal "invisibility" by replacing
his source poet's "Tongue of the Secret" with his own voice. In this respect, he
fills in Emerson's all-accommodating and subsuming "transparent eyeball"
with his egregiously visible intervention as poetic imitator.

   Ladinsky's more radical subversion, and at times complete opposition,
to original source poems of Hafez and translations by his predecessor comparatively reveal a much better appreciation for how much closer Emerson
comes to the original Persian versions. For a couplet he titles "Wine is like
the Lord Jesus," he only slightly changes Emerson's "It wakes the dead to life"
(TN 2:94) to "it can bring the dead to life" (A Year 103). Even when honoring basic meaning, however, he still makes greater adulterations. Working
backward through what he considers a "lineage" of Hafez translators, the
radical break from the source text really occurs with Ladinsky, as evidenced
from another one of his attempted "completions" of Emerson:

WRITTEN ON THE GATE OF HEAVEN

   It is written on the gate of heaven:
   Nothing in existence is more powerful than destiny.
   And destiny brought you here, to this page,
   which is part of your ticket—as all things
   are—to return to God. (A Year 123)

The first two lines read much like Emerson's previously quoted translation,
which surfaces in his "Fate" essay: " 'Tis written on the gate of Heaven, 'Wo
unto him who suffers himself to be betrayed by Fate!' " (CW 6:16). As revealed
in chapter 3, Emerson uses the couplet by Hafez to advocate for a courageous

challenge against a pre-determined universe that actually reinforces the Sufi's own relation to fatalism informed by Islam. In this respect he achieves greater fidelity to the source text by locating a correspondence between his own American philosophy and a much different foreign poetics. Consequently, he accommodates Persian verse to his own lyrically playful freedom against the idea of predestination. As he explains in the same paragraph after his translated quote, "Does the reading of history make us fatalists? What courage does not the opposite opinion show! A little whim of will to be free gallantly contending against the universe of chemistry" (CW 6:16).

Claiming an attempt to "complete" Emerson's Hafez renderings, Ladinsky too revises Hafez, but by redirecting destiny much further toward his own translation project. He therefore more egregiously appropriates his predecessor's appropriation. "Render" according to Ladinsky in the introduction to another Hafez collection, means " 'surrendering' and 'yielding'—in this case, opening to the guidance of the spirit contained within the poetry" (I Heard God x–xi). Following this definition, he implicates the reader in his own "surrendering" to such "spirit." Assuming in the first two lines the voice of Emerson and, by extension, Hafez, he switches to the second person to connect the experience of his imitation to "destiny." The page of poetry itself becomes a metaphorical "ticket" to the divine. Rather than wrestle with mystery and fatalism along with Hafez in his original poetry, Ladinsky simply promises "a return to God" via his verse. Positioned in a poetic "lineage" of "Hafiz-Hammer-Emerson-Ladinsky," he thus audaciously claims the final word as Persian poet-translator, asserting himself, however imitatively, at the end of a long intertextual signifying chain.

Despite some invention on Ladinsky's part, relative to poetic influence, Emerson with his closer and better informed misreadings of Hafez belongs more to Bloom's "figures of capable imagination," categorized as those who "wrestle with their strong precursors, even to death" (Anxiety 5). As "unsurpassable prophet of the American sublime," Emerson claims with first-person Adamic authority to "make my own circumstance" (Anxiety 103). In addition to better rendering the relation of Hafez to fate, the two lines in the couplet quoted above further show Emerson's attempt to capture the ubiquitous monosyllabic end rhyme of the Persian ghazal tradition. The complexity of such a recreated translation invested in a struggle between freedom and fate paradoxically bridges his own definitive self-reliant aesthetic with Persian poetry, producing a generatively reconfigured hybrid voice in the "third space" of his American tradition. The dialectic he establishes between "Merlin" and "Bacchus," which has been read as extending back to the respective influences of Sa'di and Hafez, exemplifies such wrestling with Persian precursors. Emerson further complicates and justifies his predecessor relations with a rhetorical theory that effectively authorizes his positioning himself within the origins of classical Persian poets.

Ladinsky, by contrast, in his contemporary address to the reader, wherein he metaphorically transforms the page on which his poem is written into a "ticket" to God, perhaps imitates some of the self-adulation of Hafez, but fails to develop verse with any significant literary response to his so-called source poet. Consequently, according to Bloom's model he belongs more to those "weaker talents" who merely "idealize" (*Anxiety* 5). Much like Wilde's *The Ballad of Reading Gaol* becomes for Bloom "an embarrassment to read" because "every lustre it exhibits is reflected from *The Rime of the Ancient Mariner*" (*Anxiety* 6), Ladinsky's translations even in their extreme creative divergences surface as relatively failed mimetic attempts of Hafez's better English translators such as Emerson, Wilberforce Clarke, and Elizabeth Gray.

Nevertheless, Ladinsky's project continues to reflect Emerson's previous attempt to mirror the Persian masters. Citing Hafez as Emerson's "personification of a human being and poet," Ladinsky—through redundant misuse of the literary term "personification"—reveals his attempt to closely follow Emerson in esteeming the Persian poet. Tracing the trajectory of his predecessor's visual approach, he further cites Emerson coveting Hafez's mystic sight: "He sees too far, he sees throughout; such is the only man I wish to see or be" (*A Year* xiii). For all of Emerson's appropriative translation practices, he nevertheless continues to play on such unreachable vision that tends to approximate his source poet's spiritual aspiration, figuratively rendering a translated telescopic power for momentary glimpses of inspired "genius." Such attempts to realize Platonic unification with his Persian predecessor tend toward relatively faithful English renderings. Similarly, much of the lyric tension informing Emerson's assumed identification with Sa'di and Hafez, which derives from his theoretically informed attempts to interpose a rhetorical mirror between disparate languages and traditions, bring him rather close to his Persian predecessors. Ladinsky seemingly parallels such an approach by extending Emerson's telescopic reach. However, by attempting to "complete" Emerson, and, by implication, Hafez, he goes too far toward forcing a correspondence. Rather than Emerson's informed tension between self and other in the aforementioned Lacanian mirror stage, Ladinsky posits himself as the ultimate fantasy of presumed completion or wholeness. Such theoretical comparison begins to account for why his Hafez translations often read as insultingly simple and didactic. What begins in an originally fragmented lyric tradition and extends as generative poetry through German and into English traditions degenerates with Ladinsky proclaiming complete authoritative possession of his predecessor through creative imitation.

Ironically, despite Ladinsky's explicit claim of continuing the translation work of Emerson, his supposed worldly aesthetic that attempts to "liberate" Hafez in translation from constraining forms as well as scholarly deconstruction re-imposes a Western inclination toward unity far more than his American predecessor who explicitly favored Persian verse for its "incompleteness." Though only twelve lines long, the following representative poem approximates a coherent form more aligned with the English tradition, the antithesis of the Persian *ghazal*. Consequently, like most of Ladinsky's other poems claimed to be written by Hafez, this "Persian sonnet" revisits early appropriative English translators' misunderstanding of a verse form that helps define an over one-thousand-year foreign poetic tradition:

Keeping Watch

In the morning
When I began to wake,
It happened again—

That feeling
That You, Beloved,
Had stood over me all night
Keeping watch,

That feeling
That as soon as I began to stir

You put Your lips on my forehead
And lit a Holy Lamp
Inside my heart. (*I Heard God Laughing* 47)

Besides the fact that this poem has no original source among the Persian poems of Hafez, its imposition of a title, disregard of fragmented *ghazal* couplets that cohere only through rhyme, and omission of the poet's self-naming in the final couplet fail to honor any conventions of the form in which his source poet actually wrote. Unlike Emerson's own "Bacchus," which has sufficient referential sources in his Hafez translations even as he redefines them on his own terms, Ladinsky's poems can't even sufficiently qualify as imitation.

Yet in giving appropriative permission to the American tradition, Emerson as *a priori* poet-translator so conflated the lyric "I" to the transcendence of predecessor source poems that such reductive imitation seemingly becomes inevitable. It is as though his own all-encompassing transparency ("I see all") figuratively leaves little or no room for his inheritors in his formative third space. Though Ladinsky's brazen pretention warrants the ethical and aesthetic disparagement it receives, much of his translation practices retroactively appear to have been sanctioned by Emerson's seminal attempts. The influence ranges from assuming editorial authority over what to excerpt for English representation from the vast oeuvre of Hafez to more brazen creative interpretations as assuming the vision and identity of the classical Sufi poet. Prescribing daily mediations of verse that he attributes in one of his books to Hafez, Ladinsky goes so far as to copy the process by which Iranian readers randomly select a poem from the master's *divan* to tell their fortune. Reclaiming the temporal order as well as the language in which to present a classical foreign poet thus extends, if not radically perverts, Emerson's ubiquitous reversions to Platonic unity of all traditions.

In a sense, Ladinsky does come much closer to Emerson when attempting to adopt a similar Platonic justification for equating languages and literary traditions. In addition to having Hafez visit him in a dream and instruct him to translate his poems into English, he like Emerson before him appeals to Orientalist scholars. Similar to Emerson's citing of Muller and others in his *Notebook Orientalist* on the originating unity of languages, an essay at the back of Ladinsky's collection *I Heard God Laughing* by consulting editor Henry Mindlin (referenced as an authority) groups all Sufis irrespective of particular schools or regions into one spiritual category. Further paralleling Emerson's Platonic conflation of East and West while ignoring the integral Islamic foundation of Persian Sufi poets, he notes how Sufis in ancient Greek get "identified with the wisdom (*sophia*) schools of Pythagoras and Plato." Mindlin continues to explain how, "At the time of Jesus," the Sufis were known as "Essenes or Gnostics" (78).

Reinforcing a transnational approach, in addition to accessing Persian sources through Emerson and in turn Emerson's German intermediary renderings by von Hammer-Purgstall, Ladinsky claims an introduction to Hafez through the "great spiritual master Avatar Meher Baba" during his time in India. Curiously, he seems to mimic the Sufis by working under the instruction of a *murshid* like Hafez before him, who, as explained by Mindlin, was a spiritual disciple apprenticing under a master (*I Heard God Laughing* 78). A student of world literature, albeit with Orientalist views, Emerson with limited knowledge of the Persian language and literary tradition nevertheless committed to making Sa'di and Hafez his great teachers. Modeling their vision, he tries to reconcile his voice with his predecessors through close attention to scholarly context as well as application of his rhetorical theory and varied imitative attempts. Contrasting such an approach, Ladinsky disavows literary

interrogation of source poems from his *murshid*, seeking instead the introduction to a "remarkable atmosphere of love." In place of Persian references
about Hafez's classical Sufism, he cites his spiritual teacher's translated books
as most helpful to his own project. Above all, the greatest assistance he seems
to have received in his translation, as evidenced by the aforementioned quote
stating his constant prayers for guidance, comes directly from the divine.
Though somewhat reflective of Emerson's privileging an elusive spirit over
literal equivalence, here again he attempts it in a much more simplified,
reductive manner.

While at profoundly greater variance from the authentic source poems,
Ladinsky's versions comparably reflect Emerson's imposition of his own
American sensibility upon Persian verse, especially insofar as he too attempts
to reach the transcendent "law" of spiritual inspiration that his predecessor
poet-translator found in Hafez. However, while Emerson figuratively attempts
to reach the infinite vision of Hafez through informed philosophy and his
own layers of literary theory, Ladinsky simply claims an equal relation. Like
Hafez, he too "Heard God Laughing" in the title of one translated collection.
Asking a psychiatrist friend to select the best of his translated poems that
might help readers, Ladinsky explains that she responded with her selection
in a mere five minutes, having just returned from a meditative retreat in the
mountains where she quite possibly found herself "zapped by a satori or two
and had a new radar system installed" (*A Year* xiv). This parallels the aforementioned visit Hafez paid to Ladinsky in a dream, wherein the Persian poet
told his chosen American translator to bring his verse into English. Emerson's
momentary "genius" connecting contemporary and ancient authors thus gets
reduced to rather untenable, if not absurdist, claims. Even so, such a predecessor concept nevertheless seems to authorize his inheritor's translation project.

Often in addition to attempting to sound like Hafez, Ladinsky in his
translation seems to channel Emerson's transcendentally affirming and posi-
tive tone. Understanding the reader's depression in his Hafez daily mediation
book, much like his predecessor establishes himself as a reassuring spokesman
of America's nineteenth-century social ailments, Ladinsky advises that "you
are with the Friend now and look / so much stronger" able to "stay that way
and even bloom!" (*A Year* 338). Consider elsewhere individual lines such as
"I am happy even before I have a reason" (*I Heard* 63) and "That the saint
is now continually / Tripping over joy" (*I Heard* 66). Often Ladinsky's voice
comes rather close to Emerson's transcendent Over-Soul. "I hear the voice
/ Of every creature and plant" (*I Heard* 72) reads much like the passage in
Nature following his predecessor's transformation into a transparent eyeball:
"The greatest delight which the fields and woods minister, is the suggestion

of an occult relation between man and the vegetable" (*CW* 1:10). Imposing titles on poems that never had them in the original versions, he further renders them contemporary on his own terms, which at times sound vaguely similar to Emerson's imperative pleas: "Set This Dry, Boring Place on Fire!" and "Let Me Near You Tonight" (*I Heard* vi–vii), as well as his matter-of-fact self-reliant statements like "I Am Determined" (*I Heard 44*). Such imitations are reflective of an a-religious all-encompassing "feel good" American spirituality that can be seen as beginning with Emerson. Though more relevant in the context of nineteenth-century Romanticism, this tone with scarcely any basis in original Sufi mystic philosophy still resonates in the United States, as evidenced by the popularity of Ladinsky's translations and much more by his contemporary Coleman Barks's English renderings of Rumi. From a literary perspective, especially following the movement in American poetics, this spiritual voice often seems overly affirming, retroactively calling for Melville's criticism of his own contemporary's attitude by assessing him as "cracked across the brow" (34).

On closer examination, however, Emerson actually proves more cynically disparaging of American positivism in the form of established religious authority as well as greater self-effacement of his own poetic agency than such twentieth- and twenty-first-century inheritors as Ladinsky. He undoubtedly tempers, at least in part, his effusive attitude by adhering closer to the intermediary translation of von Hammer-Purgstall, and therefore to the original Persian verse. More important, he also seems to correspond with the Sufi mystic's foregrounding of a rhetorical self that fails to cohere. His own authorial agency, which he simultaneously asserts and disavows in a transparent eyeball invested in overcoming the "sepulchres of the fathers," reflects a comparable interrogation by Hafez of patriarchal religious structure. Ladinsky may presume to position himself outside formal religion, yet his very strict and unquestionable reliance on his new age spirituality ironically reestablishes comparable hegemonic ideologies of nineteenth-century Christianity as well as fourteenth-century Islam that Emerson and Hafez respectively challenge. Nowhere does Ladinsky, who constantly reaffirms the self's individuated spiritual connection to the universe, significantly oppose the religious hypocrisy with which Emerson rightfully acknowledges as integral to the verse of his source poet:

> The other merit of Hafiz is his intellectual liberty, which is a certificate of profound thought. We accept the religions and politics into which we fall, and it is only a few delicate spirits who are sufficient to see that the whole web of convention is the imbecility

of those whom it entangles,—that the mind suffers no religion and no empire but its own. It indicates this respect to absolute truth by the use it makes of the symbols that are most stable and reverend, and therefore is always provoking the accusation of irreligion. Hypocrisy is the perpetual butt of his arrows: "Let us draw the cowl through the brook of wine" (*CW* 8:132).

Elsewhere, Emerson translates such lines as, "Hafez thou art from Eternity / By God created for a man / Who abhors hypocrisy . . ." (*CW* 8:132). Even Emerson's imitation of Sa'di opposes his ideal poet to what the "sad-eyed Fakirs preach" (*CW* 9:244). Ladinsky presents no comparable opposition to established religious hypocrisy, which figures as one of his Persian poet's most ubiquitous themes. He relies instead on an affirmation of surface-level spiritualty: "We should try to make all spiritual talk / Simple today:" (*I Heard* 7). While Emerson might have the advantage of being born in a time wherein he happened to undergo a struggle comparable to Hafez against religious forms, such biographical explanations go only so far in explaining the difference.

Surprisingly, for a poet criticized in the nineteenth century for an overreaching optimistic sensibility who may at times read too much intellectual freedom into his predecessor, Emerson nevertheless frequently captures the darker underpinnings of fate in Hafez and others, as seen in the following couplet: "Loose the knots of the heart; never think on thy fate: / No Euclid has yet disentangled that snarl" (*CW* 8:130). As previously revealed in an extended comparative analysis, Emerson locates much of the philosophic tension of his "freedom vs. fate" argument within Sufi verse subtly informed by Islam. Ladinsky by contrast, intent on using his own translation gospel to "liberate" the spirit of Hafez, interprets his source poet as free from any kind of contrasting, deterministic force whatsoever. He therefore asserts his usual all-affirming and transcending American voice:

I rarely let the word "No" escape
From my mouth
Because it is so plain to my soul
That God has shouted, "Yes! Yes! Yes!"
To every luminous movement in Existence. (*I Heard God Laughing* 33)

Overall, Ladinsky insists on an especially surface-level aesthetic, rendering his translations into his own superficial inventions. What context he provides in his translator notes for his source poet reads like something out of

contemporary American trans-spiritual movements found in the self-help and
spirituality section of the bookstore:

> Hafiz describes some of the preparations required for the inner
> "Journey of Love." He urges us to let go of habitual attitudes and
> unnecessary attachments, which only weigh us down. To make
> this Journey, we must be light, happy and free to go dancing! (*I
> Heard God Laughing* 2)

To further demonstrate his naïve levity relative to his American predecessor, in his proclaimed continuation of Emerson's initial translation of
Hafez, consider how Ladinsky especially demonstrates just how far he strays
from any kind of referential authenticity to the original text. In his notes,
Emerson renders this single line within a longer translated *ghazal*: "The
earth is a host who murders <kills> his guests> (*TN* 2:64). Elsewhere, in
publication, he excerpts a similar couplet from the same poem: "The world
is a bride superbly dressed;—/Who weds her for dowry must pay his soul"
(*CW* 8:130). By contrast, Ladinsky uses the original first line from Hafez (and
Emerson) to render his own second line, ultimately transforming both the
entire couplet and poem:

> The earth is a host that murders its guests.
> But what can die?
>
> All dying just removes more of the husk
> over the soul's vision.
>
> All dying thins the veil over a wondrous
> world within. (*A Year* 122)

Unlike Emerson's pithy translated excerpt, Ladinsky's version starting with
the second line has no relation to the original poem of Hafez. The following
rather accurate translation of the couplet after Emerson's quoted line by Julie
Scott Meisami shows just how creatively liberating Ladinsky has become:
"The last resting-place of everyone is a handful of earth; / say what need
then to raise a palace to the skies?" (138). In his refutation of an equivalent
rend that validates Kane's reading of Emerson's self-reduction as similar to
the Sufi's *malamatti*, Ladinsky insists on the endurance of the self without
comparable humility.

Paradoxically, Ladinsky's forced insistence on his own Romantic ideal in his approach to Persian verse translation tends to exemplify Emerson's intertextual theory of quotation and originality, even as it egregiously perverts it. In his "Portrait of Hafiz," he explains that while he first offered his renderings to Penguin as "VERSIONS," the "minds of the very literate" at his press recontextualized them under what he considers a broader definition of translation: " 'A written and spoken rendering, an interpretation of the significance of a work in another language . . .' " He adds that the closer one gets to Hafez, it becomes less clear, and by implication less relevant, "what he may or may not have said." Quick to qualify that he is not a Persian scholar ("Portrait"), his calling the very authenticity of source texts into question justifies his own translation project, subtly making himself a greater stylistic authority. This Orientalist stance resembles Emerson's early explanation that he didn't care if "the Zend-Avesta or the Desatir are genuine antiques, or modern counterfeits," concerned only with "good sentences" (*JMN* 16:265). Working with what he considers possibly spurious source poems and a spiritually informed aesthetic that esteems style and inspiration over equivalence of meaning and textual authority, Ladinsky thus establishes an approach allowing himself relative free creative reign. Extending Emerson's transnational juxtaposition of foreign texts within a previously defined American "third space," he inserts in his translations such animals and insects as "elephants" and "ants," which never appear in the actual verse of Hafez (Nemat-Nejat). Even more creatively egregious, he includes an aberrant narrative from Indian folklore in his English rendering that never appears in any Hafez poem (Nemat-Nejat). Just the presence of this narrative proves stylistically antithetical to the disparate couplets of the *ghazal,* a form predicated on fragmentation. Here again by attempting to "complete" both Emerson and, by implication, Hafez, Ladinsky re-imposes his own aesthetic agenda onto his translation process.

Overall, such a comparative reading strongly suggests that Emerson as seminal American appropriator of Persian verse initiates such a tendency toward the radical breaking from the original verse of the foreign poet in his translation approach. Ladinsky as creative inheritor strays much further than his predecessor, to the point of rendering himself equivalent to his source poet as opposed to his poetry, both of whom then seem to reach the status of Platonic *a priori* origination where all becomes equated. Despite such an extreme exaggeration of some of Emerson's translation tendencies, however, Ladinsky's appropriative approach to Hafez continues to suggest considerable generative influence from his American progenitor poet-translator's earlier creative example.

Publication of Hafez translations by the acclaimed contemporary American poet Matthew Rohrer, who like Ladinsky knows no Persian, further supports a pattern of Emerson's early appropriative influence. His relatively recent collection *Surrounded by Friends* includes especially loose imitations and translations of Western writers such as Dante, Marcus Aurelius, Hungarian poet Attila Jozsef, Romanian poet Virgil Banescu, as well as ancient Japanese poets Issa, Buson, and Basho. Following Emerson, who also translated writers from various languages, the majority of Rohrer's English renderings from foreign sources are his "Translations from Hafiz," featured in his book's last section.

Such a brazen transnational claim upon so many traditions without knowledge of the languages in which the original literature was written mirrors Emerson's cosmopolitan aesthetic underpinned by Platonic unity. The subjectively lyrical "I" at the center of Rohrer's book proves empty or at least transparent enough to accommodate so many diverse poetic voices. Consequently, he conflates the strict dichotomy between translated and imitated voices. As evidenced by such titles as "Poem Written with Basho," Rohrer also juxtaposes his own writing with his esteemed predecessors. Disregarding temporal and linguistic distance while mining the integral "spirit" of various texts, he too follows Emerson's "Quotation and Originality." His justification for translating Persian poetry despite illiteracy in the source language further resembles Emerson's claim upon an elusive genius beyond ownership by any one writer. This becomes especially clear in the epigraph to this chapter.

Having discovered Wilberforce Clarke's early versions of Hafez, Rohrer finds them "terrible English poems" with "faux-Victorian verbs ending in –eth" and "diction twisted until it was unreadable" (*American Poetry* 25). In actuality, the offensively florid constructions of these rather faithful versions to the original verse merely speak to the nineteenth-century English poetic tradition into which Clarke translated. Debunking retrospectively antiquated grammatical constructions, Rohrer can better replace them with his own contemporary versions. By doing so, however, much like Emerson he further gives himself stylistic permission to opt out of fidelity to Clarke's renderings. Claiming familiarity with other versions (that remain uncited), Rohrer deftly summarizes what he considers Hafez's central themes, followed by his own translating process:

He was talking about getting drunk. He was talking about love, longing, walking around the city at night with his head in the stars. He was talking about what it feels like to be alive. It made me so mad I hardly even thought about what I was doing. I wrote out in bald, direct language what one of the poems was actually about. And then another one. And I kind of liked this sort of game of wading, late at night, through the writing to find what he was really saying. I did ten of them, and then I went to sleep. (*American Poetry* 25)

Though without the need of Ladinsky's visitation from Hafez in a dream, Rohrer similarly intuits what the Persian poet "was really saying" through other English versions. Brazen Romantic claims of spiritual proximity to the original Persian poet, despite profound linguistic and cultural differences, further link both translators to Emerson. As Rohrer explains to justify his own appropriation like Emerson before him, channeling the inspiration of Hafez defies all limitations:

He is describing here a moment felt often by readers of translations and even poetry in its original language: the moment the reader can see past or through the limits of language, history and culture to the unbridled and boundless "movements" of human perceptions. If you are reading a poem in an original language (often one you yourself have written) that seems limited in its music or perception, you might well attempt to rewrite it . . . (*American Poetry* 25)

Rohrer's rewritings especially adhere to an aesthetic of rendering the voice of Hafez with contemporary tone, diction, style, and even radically displaced cultural context. Outraged at Wilberforce Clarke's previous Victorian translations, he seemingly wants to bring out a lost spirit of the text. To this end, his versions begin to move toward very loose imitations, rewriting the fourteenth-century Persian poet like a kind of Brooklyn hipster, with such lines as, " 'O heart be joyful' I read / on a restroom wall" (85) and "I'm still looking for someone / who thinks I'm cool" (86). Retaining some conventional images of Sufi poetry that have been previously cataloged by Emerson, Rohrer most profoundly strays from the original source text in his subjective interpretation. While much closer to the original poet than Ladinsky, insofar as his versions do correspond to previous renderings by Clarke, he too makes creatively appropriative claims upon the Persian poet's verse rather than attempting to surrender his own lyric "I" to better foreground his predecessor's couplets

in equivalent translation. Returning to the alternative space identified by
Barnstone where the poet-translator cathects a new voice in which to bring
the foreign verse into English, Rohrer even more than Emerson before him
attempts to insist upon himself:

> In the morning
> when I went into my garden
> to pick a rose
> a nightingale started to freak out
>
> which
> the more I thought about it
> freaked me out (*Surrounded* 91)

Rohrer's comparable recreation of the Persian poet in his own American
self-image reflects Emerson's previous imitative modeling of Saʾdi in other
stylistic and thematic approaches. Like Emerson, he disregards the Islamic
underpinnings of the poems he translates, transforming the Sufi metaphor of
wine even more toward his own purposes. Wine for him means little more
than what it might to the average New Yorker in the twenty-first century:

> All I want to do
> is get drunk with my wife
>
> An endless glass of wine
> both of us on the floor. (*Surrounded* 89)

Ironically, the very temporal distance Rohrer cites in his critique of florid
nineteenth-century renderings ensures that Emerson remains truer to the
original *ghazals* of Hafez. This difference can be seen in Emerson's aforementioned reckoning with communion in his inheritance of his Christian
tradition, as well as in simple stylistic considerations. Unlike Rohrer in the
postmodern twenty-first century, Emerson in his day, schooled in rhyme and
meter, could formally adapt couplets from the German while still seeming,
to use one of Rohrer's adjectives, "cool." Unlike Emerson's deft rhymes that
often approximate a Persian sensibility, the closest Rohrer comes to a sense
of formal reiteration is anaphora between short stanzas: "May you never have
to sit. . . . May everything blow over . . . May you move unmolested" and
so on (*Surrounded* 88) Adhering relatively close to the German, Emerson

unlike Rohrer can further foreground conventions such as the self-referential Persian poet in the final couplet. Similar to Ladinsky's even greater variance from Emerson by arranging the supposed verse of Hafez according to his own Western chronology in a daily mediation, Rohrer takes the liberty of renumbering Hafez's *ghazals*, which as in Shakespeare's English sonnets remain consistent with numeric identification in the original Persian. Having first obviated a temporally linear relation to his Persian predecessors, Emerson again seems to have set a precedent for such rearrangements based on the Western calendar among his American inheritors.

Further recalling the seminal all-encompassing transparency, Rohrer becomes most egregiously Emersonian in what Kazim Ali describes as his attempt to "see *past* or *through* the limits of language, history, and culture to the unbridled and boundless 'movements' of human perceptions" (152). While Rohrer imitates Hafez with the same kind of claim upon aesthetic transcendence, however, Emerson adhered much closer to intermediary German renderings in what he accurately termed translations, differentiating them from other more creatively mimetic attempts such as "Bacchus" that he identified as original poems. Lacking Emerson's theoretical basis of an originating unity of language and traditions, Rohrer conflates both translation and imitation into his voice with the rationale that he knew what the poems, sullied by florid Victorian English renderings, originally intended. Considering that he has no Persian knowledge, he therefore further exaggerates Emerson's appropriative approach to the foreign poetry.

Like Ladinsky's and Rohrer's tendencies to radically extend Emerson's earlier and rather substantial claim on foreign traditions on his own creative terms, Coleman Barks freely appropriates the verse of Jalauddin Rumi as American translator. He receives the gift of Arberry's more authentic Persian translation by his American mentor, the spiritually inclined poet Robert Bly, who advises him to "free these from their cages" ("Rumi's Poetry"). Such formal liberation again extends to Emerson's claims upon editorial authority, wherein Barks chooses what to anthologize that will comprise *The Essential Rumi* as well as his own arrangements on a specific theme like *Rumi, the Book of Love: Poetry of Ecstasy and Longing*. Like Ladinsky, who seems to claim permission to translate from Emerson's rendering classical Persian literature into the realm of atemporality, Barks also chronologically reorders his source poet into the Western calendar with his own meditation book: *A Year with Rumi: Daily Readings*. Imposing both his own titles as well as dates like "*January 1: A Just-Finishing Candle*" (13) upon poems of his choosing, which he has further adulterated in translation, Barks recreates Rumi's verse in style and theme while also recontextualizing them in his own American tradition. Barks at times also renumbers some poems that Rumi himself had previously sequenced. Lewis, for example, locates an error in a translated "ode" numbered "3,748," pointing out how Rumi only went up to 3,500 in his specific collection of such poems (590).

Emerson's fantasy of identification with the Persian masters to the point of actually becoming them in the case of Sa'di extends to Barks in yet another uncanny influential dream, much like his contemporary Ladinsky. Barks reports dreaming of a mysterious Sufi teacher advising him to continue with the work of translating Rumi (Kalyani). Thereafter, he came to meet this spiritual mentor in real life, much like Emerson first envisioned a portrait of Sa'di before encountering the poet's actual biographical description. Considering Bawa Muhaiyaddeen, the Sri Lankan mystic, on an equal spiritual level as Rumi's teacher, and consequently as well as Rumi himself, Barks receives the same imperative order to translate in his dream that he does from Bly when awake. Like Ladinsky with his own model for a *murshid* who came from outside Iran, Barks credits this student-mentor dynamic as re-creating the love and mentoring relationship between Rumi and his great teacher, Shams-y-Tabriz, which helps him meet in "that mysterious place we call the heart" (Lawler 4). Again like Ladinsky, spiritual introduction for the one who renders lines of the Sufi mystic supersedes any pedagogy in literary translation as well as in the source language of Persian. Using literal English trots from John Moyne—as well as previously published translations by Reynold Nicholson, Arberry, and others—Barks, like Ladinsky, follows Emerson in privileging the spiritually timeless "genius" (which he identifies as "heart") of a text that transcends even language difference.

By practicing Sufism with his own spiritual teacher who he anticipated in a mystic dream that defies Western rationality, Barks further self-authors an allegorical back story to his Persian source poet. By far the best parable from the Sufi tradition to demonstrate both the *murshid/murid* relationship as well as to contrast inner wisdom versus acquired academic knowledge involves various versions of the story about the learned Jalauddin Rumi first meeting his enlightened teacher, Shams of Tabriz. A man of great erudition at midlife, Rumi sat beside a stack of books he'd been reading when he first encountered the man who would become his *murshid*. "'What are those?'" asks Shams. "'Something you do not understand,'" replied Rumi. Upon hearing this response, Shams took the books of his chosen student and put them in the fire. He then retrieved the texts, miraculously unburned. "What have you done?" asked Rumi. "'Something you do not understand,'" replied his master (Mojaddedi xx–xxi). The story demonstrates a level of consciousness beyond received knowledge, comparable to Barks's qualification that his Rumi translations remain "outside of academia." Like Emerson's "Self-Reliance" essay that paradoxically relies on outside sources to transcend influence, it attempts to overcome predecessors, even overcome all book learning, through the interposition of texts. In the story, books obviously fail to teach some vital lesson, implying outside erudition can take one only so far, much like Emerson favoring inspiration and even youthful intransigence over static knowledge. Barks's intimate experience with his teacher attempts to mimic how Shams surfaces as an "outside" mentor, opposing his enlightened wisdom to the metaphor of books as a lesson that will in turn come to be retold both as poetry and scholarship.

Barks seems to appropriate the lesson behind such a spiritual student-teacher context by performing his own biographical transformation, which in turn legitimizes his position as Rumi's translator. Differentiating Barks's superficial relation to his teacher with no real grounding from his source poet's relation to Shams, Majid Naficy says of the latter:

> Rumi's slavish obedience of sufi to his "morshed," that is, master[,] is a fundamental concept in Rumi's mysticism and the main reason that after 700 years his Mevlevi Order is still run by the hereditary line of the male offsprings of Rumi's son, Sultan Veled in Turkey. (Naficy)

Citing the beginning of Barks's rendering from Rumi's chapter 12 entitled, "The Sheik: I have Such a Teacher," Naficy explains how for Barks as appropriative translator "this cultish and authoritarian relationship" with a firmly established and revered hierarchy "is portrayed as an egalitarian and ideal one." Attempting to further mystify the relation of his own portrait to Rumi as if insisting on his equation to him, Barks writes: ". . . Coleman to Bawa, Rumi to Shams . . ." thereby "suggesting an affinity between Rumi's master, Shams of Tabriz, and his own unlettered guru, Muhammad Raheem Bawa Muhaiyaddeen, a Qadiri Sufi sheik who came to the US from Sri Lanka in 1971 and died in Philadelphia in 1986" (Naficy). Here again an American poet-translator turns an imagined portrait of a Persian predecessor into his own mirrored reflection, while also like Ladinsky positioning himself as the last in a signifying chain of Persian source poets' renderings.

Again tending to model Emerson's approach to classical Persian verse translation even while beginning to excessively stray from it, Barks ignores the underpinnings of religion that vitally inform Rumi's verse. As has been shown, Emerson through his close reading of Sufi poetry actually accesses the philosophy of fatalism found in Islamic writing. Barks by contrast deliberately elides religious influence to better produce an accessible and more universal translation. As he himself admits, "I took the Islam out of it" (Seelarbokus 279). In the place of Islamic symbols, he substitutes "values and ideals that appeal to American popular culture" (Seelarbokus 272). More than merely omitting Islamic references, he interposes his own more Western inventions in his translations. His positioning of Jesus next to the original allusion to the Prophet Muhammad (Seelarbokus 279) calls to mind Emerson's Greek gods as well as a cosmos more informed by a Judeo-Christian tradition in his Persian translations (Seelarbokus 278). Without growing up in Iran, it remains especially difficult to fully grasp how integral Islam proves to the country's culture and its literature. Even assuming a decent command of the religious text, relaying how ideas within it inform recurring themes and allusions to a Western audience within the literature itself would become an especially daunting task. In this respect, Emerson with his awareness of Islam indeed proves well ahead of his own time, as well as the contemporary American poetic tradition that he continues to influence.

Though Barks like Ladinsky deviates much further from equivalence in their translations and imitations than Emerson, their general approach nevertheless tends to reinforce his earlier example. Barks's blatant disregard of Islam insists upon favoring style over integral meaning, again much as Emerson expressed little concern whether words attributed to the founder of Zoroastrianism were spurious, concerned above all with "good sentences." His deliberately taking the Islam out of the Sufi poetry it informs displays an Emersonian impulse in the American tradition to accommodate literary as well as spiritual difference by creative appropriation. Assuming personal authority over a source text based on the words of the divine revealed to Muhammad, the all-consuming "I" of the translator seemingly operates like Emerson's transparent eyeball with an ideal invisibility between Persian source and English target poems. This aesthetic effectively domesticates a foreign poetics based on the especially misunderstood literal-religion of Islam and the culture it informs. Consequently, Barks achieves his predecessor's ideal of literary unification through spiritual understanding that obviates difference, even while retaining an exotic Orientalism through rhetorical reconfiguration. As if returning to a version of Emerson's early American approach to Persian translation, Barks links such spiritual manifestation from the foreign text to his predecessor's comparably Platonic transnational and even translingual humanistic underpinnings:

> Just now, I feel there is a strong global movement, an impulse that wants to dissolve the boundaries that religions have put up and end the sectarian violence. It is said that people of all religions came to Rumi's funeral in 1273. Because, they said, he deepens

our faith wherever we are. This is a powerful element in his appeal now. (Ciabattari)

Barks's further backstory as translator as recounted in one of his books reinforces Emerson's intertextuality. Ironically "called" in his youth to "Emily Dickinson's churchlessness," he also begins memorizing what he terms "soul-books," which include *Les Misérables* and *The Return of the Native*. Seeking to pass such influences onto his daughter, he adds Shakespeare, Blake, Mary Oliver, and others to his list (*A Year with Rumi* 4). He then summarizes his own literary tradition into which he translates Rumi by radically freeing it from any kind of categorical principle, further imitating Emerson's all-encompassing intertextuality that included the Persian poets. Under what Barks considers "openness and inspiration," which reads much like Emerson's "genius," he includes "Whitman" along with "Basho, Cervantes, Homer, and Allen Ginsberg." His assessment of Eastern and Western literary traditions retroactively furthers the case for Emerson's aesthetic informed by translation of global literatures as both transformational and generative: "We are lucky to have so many luminous figures in this country," explains Barks, "but this lineage is not *American*. It comes down through such varied innumerable strands that it cannot be called a lineage at all" (*A Year* 5). His debunking of literary lineage, which juxtaposes Thoreau, Hemingway, Whitman, and even Michael Stipe of the American band REM with Homer and other classical foreign poets, follows Emerson's literary displacement in "Quotation and Originality." He too re-inscribes "the old and the new" wherein, "there is no thread that is not a twist of these two strands" (*CW* 8:94). Such "strands" further reinforce the previously mentioned textile metaphor of translation used by Cervantes, a writer Barks also includes in his list of go-to foreign sources (*A Year* 5). Like Emerson, Barks attempts to conflate both foreign and translated texts, negating linguistic difference as much as possible and therefore seeing the poetry from both sides of the tapestry.

While this ecumenical recontextualization of Rumi helps explain the accessibility of Barks's translations, it also continues to invite harsh criticism for their egregious transgressions more so than Emerson, who could at least gain insights from his source poets' perspective through German intermediary renderings and rather thorough Orientalist scholarly interrogation. Connecting the domestication of Rumi to his popular translator's ignorance of the source text and his source poet's Iranian origins, Lahouti argues:

Coleman Barks . . . draw(s) an American picture of our Iranian Molavi more in tune with the lack of restraint and dissoluteness of American culture than with Molana Jalaleddin's Islamic knowledge

and Iranian culture. Even though [the] translations have increased
[his] fame in the West, they have unfortunately no coloring of
Islamic and Iranian Sufism—it is as if Molavi were American,
born in New York, and trained in the schools of Dr. Barks, Dr.
Chopra, and their ilk. (50)

If viewed from the perspective of the appropriated literary culture,
such critical outrage becomes understandable. It is difficult if not impossible to offer a comparatively inverse (Persian to English) example of such
textual adulteration, insofar as the *Qur'an* simply by allusions alone proves
substantially more informative of Iranian poetry than the Bible of American literature. The closest possible approximation would be writings of the
early Puritans, like the journals of William Bradford or the poetry of Ann
Bradstreet. Though worthy of study and even great appreciation, these texts
remain far from as comparable in literary significance to America than Sufi
poets from the thirteenth and fourteenth centuries to their native Iran.
Imagining poetry from Emily Dickinson or a novelist like Herman Melville
without their Christian associations begins to suggest just how egregious
Barks's omission of Islamic influence in his Rumi renderings can become.
That the comparison still falls short can be ascribed in part to Emerson's
effect on American literature. A seminal influence on his contemporaries as
well as his inheritors, he especially divorces both his own biography as well
as his writing from strict religious associations. Anticipating the advice given
to both Ladinsky and Barks, he became the first translator as well as originator of American literature to significantly "liberate" foreign and domestic
writing from their Christian "cages."

In a review of Barks's translations, Robbins cites an especially well-known
passage that has been stripped of its original Islamic premise: "Out beyond
ideas of wrongdoing and rightdoing, / there is a field. I'll meet you there." This
reads very much like an inspiring Emerson quote so frequently extracted (if
not adulterated, or even invented) from a longer piece of writing, edited down
to fit on a bumper sticker. A comparative version that Robert Darr offers in
a review of Rumi's *Ruba 'iyat-é Jalaluddin Muhammad Balkhi-Rumi* translated
by Ibrahim Gamard (a Sufi scholar, Muslim, and active member of Rumi's
Sufi Mevlevi order) along with his co-translator Rawan Farhadi, proves much
more faithful to the original Persian: "Beyond Islam and unbelief there is a
'desert plain.' / For us, there is a yearning in that expanse" (144). A kind of
revelation beyond both Islam as well as the refutation of that comprehensive
religion means something very different than merely overcoming of right and
wrong ideas. Despite moving beyond religion, like challenges to comparable

strictures in Hafez the lines orient a seeming transcendence from the specific locality of Islam. Barks's version instead follows Emerson in transplanting Mecca as a very real and specific site of Allah's revelation to a figurative "American desert" devoid of origins. As if to justify his comparable relocation of Eastern revelation, Barks reports that as a student in college, prior to his prophetic dream, he first experienced a calling to "sublime beauty" in the Arizona desert (Lawler 6).

In the place of Islam, Barks in his English renderings makes compensatory interventions by an overdetermined Western relation to Jesus. While Rumi indeed draws on the way Islam esteems Jesus as a prophet, as Naficy observes, "the ratio of these allusions compared to Rumi's references is very low." Here again Barks, like Ladinsky, offers a rather exaggerated version of Emerson's appropriation through the anthologizing of certain Persian poems. With such commanding authoritative control over representing Rumi in English, he tends to dictate how a Western audience reads him as literature. Naficy further locates Biblical allusions of Rumi that get divorced from their spiritual referents in Sufi mysticism through English rendering. Citing Barks, he observes in the translation of a poem titled "Solomon Poems: The Far Mosque" how the translator "fails to understand that the allegory of King Solomon and Queen Sheba in which the former represents 'divine wisdom' and the latter 'Bodily soul' is really based on debasement of both 'body' and 'woman.'" Elsewhere, when Barks renders Jesus and his donkey, he also fails to note the spiritual and religious significance in interpretation.

When confronted with comments made by the Persian critic Franklin Lewis about separating Rumi too far from the Sufi culture informed by Islam in which he wrote, Barks in his defense offers a rather familiar response:

> Oh, I think Franklin needs to loosen up a bit. This exclusivity bit that this was the last prophet, and that the Jews are the chosen people, and that Jesus is the only begotten son of God, that exclusivity and each of those religions is dangerous to the health of the planet. I am more in favor of the health of the planet than I am of placing Rumi back in the thirteenth century. (Young)

Such an appeal to an aesthetic of transcendent humanism used to justify a deliberate choice to separate Rumi from his cultural and textual origins again rather closely resembles Emerson's early reliance upon an all-unifying Platonism.

As if taking the next step after his forced separation of Rumi's verse from Islam beyond the original poet's intention, Barks further divorces the sacred from the source text by reinterpreting the mysticism that emerges from it as simple eroticism. As Parsinejad explains,

> Instead of presenting the non-sexual concept of love in the Masnavi as it is, Barks distorts it . . . he pretends that in the sufi tradition satisfying the desires of nafs, particularly sexual gratification, is one of the stages of achieving divine love. ("Nicholson to Barks" 22)

Azadibougar and Patton offer an especially compelling critique of how, in Barks's abridged translation of Rumi's "Donkey Poem" from the *Masnavi*, a mistress, failing to understand her maid's sex trick with the donkey, dies while having intercourse with the animal. Tracking the translation in relation to the source text, the co-authors reveal how Barks's version greatly heightens the sexual tension at the expense of the poem's original didactic intentions, deliberately leaving the reader in suspense for a revealing narrative climax that never occurs in Rumi's poem. As they show, this again extricates Rumi from his esoteric Sufi teachings so foundational to his aesthetic (182–183). With little knowledge of the source text or Sufi culture in which it is positioned, Barks further misses "a network of literary, philosophical, and religious allusions" (180). Summarizing Barks's approach, they conclude that he

> has capitalized on the sexual content in the popular element, realizing that this—and the tension it creates with the established image of a spiritual Rumi—is capable of exerting a powerful pull on an American readership attuned to the scandalous and sensational. (185)

Despite such a deliberately erotic rendering, it warrants mentioning how Barks's translation project nevertheless attempts to antiseptically rid the Persian source text of anything potentially upsetting to Western readers, such as misogynistic or homosexual references. Following an examination of such tendencies, Lohouti concludes how "instead of conveying the misogynistic and antisexual concept of love in the *Mathnavi* as it is in the Persian text," Barks "distorts and misrepresents the letter and spirit of Rumi's work" (50).

Like Ladinsky with Hafez, much of Barks's process of coopting Rumi as agency thus involves the foregrounding of the aforementioned aesthetic that "liberates" the source poem from the free-play of poetic target language. As Barks explains in the foreword to his introduction for his *Essential Rumi*:

> . . . these poems are not monumental in the Western sense of memorializing moments; they are not discrete entities but a fluid,

continually self-revising, self-interrupting *medium*. They are not
so much *about* anything as spoken from *within* something. (i–ii)

His appeal to an embedded spirituality beyond literal content exaggeratedly
extends and even distorts Emerson's focus on poetic spirit or "genius." While
Barks never calls himself Rumi the way Emerson adopts the persona of Saʻdi,
his famously staged musical performances of his source poet arguably take
creative possession of the Sufi mystic. Translation itself becomes a performance
similar to how Emerson poetically performed the voices of both Saʻdi and Hafez
in his own American rhyme and meter, giving the former a Greek lyre to
render his song connecting East to West. Though admirable, Barks's addition
of literal musicians as a kind of compensation strategy for the musicality lost
in translation after Emerson's nineteenth century that still could favor formal
verse further adulterates the experience of the original text. As the most
transaesthetic of art forms, music naturally overcomes linguistic differences.
Consequently, Barks positions himself further as the kind of fluid "medium"
of spirit that he considers more central to Rumi's verse than actual words.
By so blurring the boundaries between source text and translation, original
poet and translator, and even music and poetry, he continues his attempt to
become Rumi through his inspired expression of his verse.

Such an attempt to lose himself in Rumi, however, paradoxically leads
him to assert his presence even more into his translations. Emerson's early
comment that the Persian poets have "the best copyright" built into their
poetics with the convention of self-naming at the end of the *ghazal* has real
relevance here. In a publishing age of fierce copyright protection, Barks's self-
conflation with Rumi's name, representative of a poet whose verse remains
safely in the public domain, astronomically breaks record earnings for both
American translators as well as poets. Undoubtedly he makes more on one collection than most English translators or poets earn through publication in their
lifetimes, having sold over two million copies worldwide. His English versions
have in turn been further retranslated into over twenty languages (Ciabattari).
What the Sufi calls the self-centered *nafs* that can impede divine connection,
roughly translated in the Western tradition as an especially egocentric relation
to the world, ironically allows Barks to materially prosper. His translation of
a Sufi poet who so inhabited the spiritual realm through self-forgetfulness
ironically makes Barks a "name" in Western poetry. Considering his status
as the go-to translator of his source poet as well as his seemingly trademark
musical performances of the verse, he transforms himself into Rumi perhaps
almost as much as he makes Rumi transform into him.

A contemporary American audience obviously proves receptive for
Rumi's message. Briefly surveying some of Barks's translations suggests why

they remain so popular. The rather tangible images and metaphors tend to relate an accessible spirituality: "I have a thirsty fish in me / that can never find enough / of what it's thirsty for!" (*Essential Rumi* 19). Citing Emerson's early translations of Persian poetry, which include Rumi's verse, Azadibougar and Patton reference "a persistent connection in America between spiritual movements and translators of oriental poetry" (175). Barks's personal spiritual backstory with his own Sufi teacher, as well as his intertextual accommodation of inspiration predicating the American tradition upon global literatures, surely helps to capitalize on such a connection in the late twentieth and early twenty-first centuries. Also inherent in Barks's quoted translation, as throughout much of Rumi's original verse, is accessible imagery and a didactic tone tempered with simple wisdom (Ciabattari). This aesthetic in part helps Barks, like Emerson before him, assimilate the Persian verse into English literary renderings.

Though such qualities can be located in many of the Persian source poems, making it somewhat unfair to criticize translations that attempt to foreground them in English, Barks overall tends to subvert the integrity of the original verse for his readers, as evidenced by this brief survey. Summing up the transformation of Rumi's poems into especially simplified versions accessible for mass consumption by a Western audience, Azadibougar and Patton argue,

> Barks' versions tend to transform Rumi's work from a "high culture" product into a "popular culture one." This means we must treat the new version as part of what it has become, i.e. popular culture. In other words, the "translated" version is not merely high culture with higher sales figures, but is a new entity . . . If the original Rumi has appeal on account of its spiritual or philosophical values, the popular Rumi may not necessarily have appeal for the same reasons. (176)

Concluding their rather exhaustive study of Barks's appropriation of Rumi's verse, Azadibougar and Patton quote their own translation, based on a previous scholar's rendering (Nicholson 189 n7) of the closely analyzed donkey poem's final couplet: "You heard the appearance and translated it / Unaware of what you said like a parrot." While expressing on one level Rumi's "frustration with language" in rendering spiritual insight with words, they add that such lines further "differentiate between the fake Sufi—who, without authentic spiritual understanding, wears the clothes of a Sufi—and the genuine sufi." Applying the parroting metaphor to Barks's grand Rumi project, they continue:

In the absence of knowledge, the act of translation becomes a form of parroting, the repetition of something without really understanding it. In the same way, Barks' rendition . . . parrots the most superficial and populist elements in the source while subtracting its spiritual significance and hence its coherence. (189)

Parroting—which has previously been cited as surfacing in Sufi poetry among mirrors, wherein the mystics believing the birds learned language in their reflection as poets spoke behind the reflective glass (Schimmel, *Brocade* 182)—serves in turn to conclude this brief study of contemporary Persian verse translators in America. Like Emerson before them, Ladinsky, Rohrer, and Barks do indeed attempt to capture something of the ineffable spirit beyond mere text. Ultimately, however, they revert to uninformed mimicry of their source poems, and at times of the Persian poets who wrote them. Compared with Emerson, who at least attempted to imitate through an intermediary echo of German translations as he tried to capture poets like Hafez writing "with a parrot's . . . quill" (*CW* 8:133), the attempts by translators criticized in this chapter egregiously begin to look (if not fly) away from integral Persian origins. Even so, though often far exceeding the appropriative gaze of Emerson, who began rendering the Sufi poets in his own voice, they nevertheless tend to parrot the example of their American predecessor.

Chapter 6

The Other Side of the Persian Mirror

Emerson's Gaze as Necessary Corrective

> Oft have I said, I say it once more,
> I, a wanderer, do not stray from myself.
> I am a kind of parrot. The mirror is holden to me;
> What the Eternal says, I stammering say again.
>
> —Hafez (translated by Emerson [*CW* 8:137])

While influencing such egregious variance from the foreign text in later English renderings, Emerson's early approach to translation also can be seen as extending to a contemporary view of Persian poetry that at times closely reflects original sources. Both in theory and praxis, his example appears to show a couple of comparably informed as well as creatively adept contemporary poet-translators how to achieve greater stylistic and tonal correspondence with source poems in their translations and imitations. Brief consideration of criticism, translation, and imitations of the Persian verse tradition by esteemed scholar, poet, and translator Dick Davis as well as by Kashmiri-American poet Agha Shahid Ali reveal much of Emerson's adherence to the original verse of Hafez and Sa'di. Davis's essay "On Not Translating Hafez," along with his own attempt at formally capturing the spirit of this Persian poet in his renderings, tend to mirror Emerson's successful mimicry of the foreign tradition. Shahid Ali's twentieth-century introduction of the Persian *ghazal* to America, both in his critical writing as well as in his English imitations, further demonstrates the example of his predecessor. Paradoxically, Emerson's all-accommodating approach to translation that leads faux translators such as Ladinsky into producing blatantly fraudulent English versions alternatively invites more authentic interpretations.

175

Though a British neoformalist and scholar of Iranian literature, Davis publishes his own poetry and translations with American presses and also taught for several years at The Ohio State University. While he undoubtedly absorbs considerable influence from writers in his native England, to some extent like many other immigrant poets in the United States he too must "go through" Emerson in a Bloomian sense. Among the best living translators of classical Persian verse, at the very least he emerges out of a tradition of rendering Persian poetry into English that first began with Sir William Jones in England and expanded in the nineteenth century with Emerson in America. On closer examination, much like Emerson before him, his approach to Persian poetry at times proves subtly ambiguous in theory and praxis, even to the point of violating his own ethical intentions. By attempting to offer a necessary corrective to egregious violations of his translating contemporaries with his knowledge of the Persian language and the literary tradition of Iran, he tends to establish a translating aesthetic that in key ways appears to circle back to Emerson's early example.

Davis's essay "On Not Translating Hafez" offers an astute catalogue of what proves difficult, if not impossible, to render from the fourteenth-century poet's verse. Exposing the vast temporal and cultural differences between ancient Iran and a contemporary English audience with categorical aphorisms that read as formal prohibitions against erroneous translation, it seemingly challenges the kind of excessively creative imitations that first originate with Emerson. However, like a Persian pun with multiple meanings, Emerson's rhetoric around his own Persian translations retroactively attempts to both violate as well as sanction Davis's strictures. Also like a pun in the foreign source text, such interventions in English translations prove hard to critically identify and explicate in English, meaning Emerson's effect continues to remain rather elusive. Returning to the early trope of the eyeball, in Davis's essay it remains marked by transparency, subjected to the lyric "I" that would seemingly disavow its presence to accommodate outside influence, including foreign traditions. In this respect, the origins of American translation lie at the center of Emerson's lyric vision, which reflects in part his Western telescopic gaze toward the Persian verse tradition.

Having closely tracked Emerson's translation aesthetic in theory and praxis, a comparative analysis begins to expose it in Davis's argument. Emerson's contradictory impulses that insist on translation despite irreconcilable languages and literary traditions begin to surface in the resistance of "Not Translating Hafez." As if subjected to his predecessor's paradoxical rhetoric, refuting the possibility of authentically translating Hafez comes to make translation possible for Davis. Consider how in his essay he first accounts for the irreconcilability of the Persian panegyric tone in English:

Here then we come to a major problem, which is that the appearance of a set of strategies considered intrinsically poetic in Persian—the inferiority of the speaker, praise of the addressee . . . is
relatively rare in English poetry, is not considered intrinsically
poetic, and can be seen as unnatural or absurd. ("Not Translating" 314)

As previously shown, Ladinsky and Barks invert the problem, making themselves the kind of grandiose subjects to whom the classical Persian poets
addressed in their verse. There is something especially Emersonian about
such astronomically bold claims upon the foreign poet. Like the American
poet-translator before them, these contemporary translators emerge with an
authoritative presence that commands an all-encompassing vision. Emerson,
however, predicated such perspective upon his own invisibility ("I am nothing
/ I see all."), often interposing an inherently abased relation toward the Persian
masters. As Davis importantly qualifies, "the ghazal was for praise . . . never
equivalence between speaker and addressee." Despite rejecting textual equivalence in an attempt to equate himself to his Persian predecessors, Emerson
nevertheless greatly retains a sense of the panegyric tone toward these source
poets. As has been shown, he makes Sa'di his poetic ideal and deems Hafez
beyond his visual reach. By contrast, Ladinsky attempts outright displacement of the poet he purports to translate, problematically seeing himself as
an authentic version of Hafez.

Exemplifying both Ladinsky and Davis, Emerson complicates his relation to the Persian poets, by turns seeking equal status then, as Kane has
revealed, reducing himself to the Persian Sufi's *malámati*. His previously cited
translation of Hafez returning to the dust from which he derives begins to
demonstrate the other side of his self-aggrandizement in the Persian mirror,
an awareness of and identification with such abasement in the original source
text. As opposed to his extreme appropriating inheritors such as Barks and
Ladinsky, he seems just as apt to "become nothing" as he does to "see all."
In his greatest praise of Hafez, he even tempers his visionary identification
with qualifying humility in the panegyric mode identified by Davis, noting
how his Persian predecessor "sees too far."

Unlike Ladinsky, Barks, or Rohrer, Emerson also anticipates Davis by
attempting to critically contextualize the panegyric. As if following his own
theory of intertextuality, in his preface to Sa'di's *Gulistan* he works the original
verse into his poetic praise of the Persian poet:

The superlative, so distasteful in the temper-ate region, has vivacity
in the Eastern speech . . . In his compliments to the Shah, [Saadi]

says: "The incurvated back of the sky became straight with joy
at thy birth." (vi)

Following his own ambivalent relation to his Romantic identity, Emerson
both elevates and reduces his adopted Persian namesake. Compared to Hafez,
who he places beyond reach, at times he seems to identify more with humble
Sa'di so as to better equate himself to his ideal predecessor: "Saadi, though
he has not the lyric flights of Hafiz, has wit, practical sense, and just moral
sentiments" (*Gulistan* vii–viii). Having reduced his ideal poet's status to more
of an earthly plane, Emerson then positions him among the timeless Western
greats, extracting him from his specific tradition to reach his literary ideal of
atemporality through another kind of intertextual panegyric:

> But the commanding reason of his wider popularity is his deeper
> sense, which, in his treatment, expands the local forms and tints
> to a cosmopolitan breadth. Through his Persian dialect he speaks
> to all nations, and, like Homer, Shakespeare, Cervantes, and Mon-
> taigne, is perpetually modern. (*Gulistan* viii)

In this respect, as if following his own model, Emerson both reduces and
aggrandizes the poet to whom he found himself most affined. Having critically
established his Persian namesake as a more realistic, down-to-earth literary
figure, Emerson in his imitation of Sa'di credits him with "Wisdom of the gods"
(*CW* 9:244), unrivaled critical praise in his own tradition that originates with
Greco-Roman deities. In this respect, according to Davis's assessment that "the
more extreme the praise, the more poetic the poem is considered to be in
Persian" ("Not Translating" 315), Emerson begins to transform his imitations
as well as his translations into more authentic versions of the Persian poets
he so reveres. Figuratively originating at the site of the transparent eyeball, he
makes himself and the American tradition ready for such a rhetorical stance
by becoming as "nothing" as figuratively possible, even as he paradoxically
inhabits the very Persian panegyric tone by seeing "all" to approximate what
Davis considers an "absurdity and distasteful flattery" in English verse.

Another characteristic of Persian poetry that Davis determines impossible
to adequately render in the Western tradition is the trope of wine. Pointing
out that even during prohibition in the 1920s wine has never been comparably
forbidden in the United States, he convincingly argues that Western English
readers can't intuitively grasp the spiritual connotations of wine opposed
to religious strictures of Islam. As Davis states, "It would never occur to a
western poet to explain the forbidden intoxications of mysticism . . ." ("Not

Translating" 312). In attempting to relay what gets lost in translation, he aptly compares an English translator trying to foreground the meaning of wine in Iran to "explaining a joke" ("Not Translating" 312). Such a problem surfaces most egregiously in the aforementioned Hafez renderings by Rohrer, who turns his Persian poet into a guy just wanting to go for casual drinks with his wife, as well as by Ladinsky, whose versions of Hafez would glory in an all-permissive state of drunken wonder without the distractions of religious tension that essentially inform if not determine the very culture from which the source poems derive.

While obviously not in complete understanding of the significance of wine in the Persian tradition, Emerson comes much closer than popular contemporary translators to the implications of the trope. His academic interrogations may tend to gloss wine in Persian verse as mere "intellectual freedom" (*TN* 2:120), yet he still locates the Sufi poets' mystical opposition to religious prohibitions. His own relation to the metaphor of wine in his era further exemplifies the temporal contingency of translation in source as well as receiving literary traditions. His personal reckoning with the Christian church discussed in chapter 2, which led to his self-reliant refusal of communion, creatively inverts the Sufi's intoxication of wine. To use Davis's metaphor for untranslatability, though far from telling the same joke in English, Emerson sees himself in a reflection of the wine cup poured by Hafez and others in their *ghazals*. Consequently, his Western gaze begins to demonstrate in English a more dynamic and authentic corrective to such a ubiquitous Persian metaphor. Returning to Benton's early assessment of his relation to the foreign poetry, Emerson captures a certain "tincture" of the Persian spirit, much like a critical aftertaste, or the effect of a joke.

Though somewhat disregarding religious influence on Persian translation, Emerson's Transcendental reckoning with the tradition of Christianity in his time also positions him closer than many contemporary translators to what Davis cites as the missing influence of Islam in classical Persian verse translation. Despite Davis's correct assessment about a dearth of mystical poets in English like those in Persian ("Not Translating" 311), Emerson's own struggle with the influence of Christianity that continues to inform his culture and even his own writing offers a rendering that at least approximates something analogous in the source tradition. The crux of his Platonic aesthetic problematically attempts to obviate all temporal and even linguistic difference, yet his specific resistance to his inherited religion reproduces a similar kind of tension found in Sufi poets like Hafez relative to the hypocritical followers of Islam who the Persian poet critiques. This proves an early and especially integral feat of relative equivalence, considering how the *Qur'an* remains

missing altogether in Ladinsky's new age, ethereal spirituality untethered to
any religious foundation whatsoever.

Simply by being true to himself and his aesthetics in nineteenth-century
New England, Emerson further seems to embody much of the greater literary
spirit of Hafez's fourteenth-century Iran. As explained by the one-paragraph
advertisement for a collection of translations by Davis in which Hafez's verse
prominently appears, "14th Century Shiraz was one of the most remarkable
literary flowerings of any period" (*Faces of Love*). Arguably Emerson's literary
setting, which F.O. Matthiessen famously named the "New England Renaissance" and Van Wyck Brooks titled in his early twentieth-century study *The
Flowering of New England*, comes comparatively closest among American
periods to when Hafez wrote his poems in Iran. While of course reasons
for the proliferation of significant national literature vary for each tradition,
conditions proved ideal for Emerson to reflect on his "retrospective" age
as well as on domestic and global influence, much like Hafez, according to
Davis, previously looked back to his own progenitors, especially Sa'di (*Faces
of Love* lvi). Most praising Hafez for "seeing too far" and "seeing throughout,"
Emerson locates in the Persian master an ability to look all the way back to
what he envisions as unifying Platonic origins and recollect, if not renew, a
figuratively charged intoxicating spirit that can negate all differences. Though
responding to many influences, as has been shown Emerson personally experiences a figurative rebirth by a comparable look back to Sa'di in his translation
of the Persian poet elegizing the death of his son. Such localized influence
exemplifies his more comprehensive development as a writer in response at
least in part to Persian rhetorical models during a comparably fertile time
of his literary tradition.

Perhaps no translation difficulty best represents the remarkable accommodation of Persian verse to Emerson's aesthetic than his relation to fragmentation. Stylistically, the *ghazal* as the primary form of Persian poetry according
to Davis resists the usual Western resolution of form. As he explains, the lack
of closure and failure to develop a subject leaves the reader with "the literary
equivalent of throwing one's hands in the air" ("Not Translating" 316). This
indeed seems quite different from the familiarly satisfying formal conclusions
in Western poetics. In this respect, early English translators calling the *ghazal*
the "Persian sonnet" especially exemplify an appropriative poetics of translation
far beyond Emerson. As referenced in Kane's study, Emerson inherently adopts
comparable tension to the *ghazal* in his original English prose by juxtaposing
disparate epigrams against his essays. Such a representative rhetorical tendency
seems to have allowed Emerson a better intuitive grasp of fragmentation in
the form, despite limited access to academic writing about Persian poetry as

compared to Davis's erudition in the twentieth and twenty-first centuries. His summation that "for the most part" Persian poets "affect short poems and epigrams" (*CW* 8:127), like the highlighting of his own fragmented renderings as well as his contextual notes on the foreign source poetry, thus reflect considerable understanding of Iran's verse tradition.

Davis and Emerson even more closely cohere in their respective English translations around the use of rhyme, which constitutes another definitive characteristic of Persian verse. Within inherently fragmented couplets, recurring phrasing plus a monorhyme in each second line of the *ghazal* establishes aural as opposed to thematic order. In their critical writing about Persian verse, both poet-translators remain especially attentive to such a formal characteristic. While Emerson again had the benefit of writing at a time that still favored rhyme, Davis as a Western neoformalist has acquired the requisite ear and skill with English meter to capture a sense of the original source poems through sound. Considering the origins of Persian verse translation in English with William Jones as well as contemporary models exemplified by Ladinsky, Rohrer, and Barks, both Davis and Emerson surface as more authentic outliers through their respective retentions of rhyme.

While Davis notes that the kind of monorhyme on which Persian thrives remains relatively nonexistent in English, elsewhere he curiously refers to songs of Bob Dylan as closely approximating the verse of Hafez. Though not specifically referencing rhyme, his comparative praise of how the American Nobel Laureate "hovers at the paraphrasable" (*Faces of Love* xlii) inherently gestures toward musicality as well as recurring lyrics with some rhyming pattern. To briefly expand on Davis's reading, a song like "Shelter from the Storm," wherein meanderingly varied phrases connect through rhyme to the same refrain, "Come in, she said, I'll give you, shelter from the storm," begins to mirror the formal impulse of the *ghazal*. Considering Emerson's rhetoric at its most essential relation to his lyric vision, the rhyme of the transparent "eye/I" captures both sound and sense of Persian poetry much like Dylan's lyrics in relation to his music. It proves comparably tonic throughout much of Emerson's lyric vision.

Also in their more complex relation to rhetoric, Davis and Emerson share more of a stylistic relation to Hafez with a key part of speech in his original language. In Davis's introduction to his translations, he cites the ambiguity of the addressee in Persian verse, a ubiquitous problem of pronominal confusion between "you" or "he." Such indeterminacy allows Ladinsky and Barks to assume the voice of the poet addressing a contemporary English audience as well as to create a false depiction of heterosexual romantic love, wherein, as Davis notes, more often the addressee is actually "a young boy" (xxiii).

Emerson hardly troubleshoots this translation problem to much better effect, yet through his rhyme of self and vision he does reproduce, as if for the first time, an ambiguity of subject and object. Rhyming his Romantic presence through transparency sufficiently empties it, clearing space for predecessor voices that in turn sound both like classical Persian poets as well as their more recent American poet-translators. Einboden's previously cited example of Emerson changing pronouns through the revision process of his English renderings offers practical support for the correspondence of his aesthetic to Persian verse.

Yet another tenable relation between predecessor and contemporary translator concerns the approach to stanza. Davis, like Emerson, at times breaks the lines of Persian couplets, where typically one-half line is as long as an English fourteener (*Faces of Love* lxviii). In part, as he explains, this is to create a comparable meter to the Persian:

> Strangely enough, this does, I think, give some notion of the rhythm of the Persian. The half-line itself in Persian often has a natural pause around its middle (corresponding to the caesura in an English verse line), and the equivalent of this is indicated by the break within the fourteener in the translations. (*Faces of Love* lxix)

For Davis this turns the verse of Hafez into a kind of English song with classical resonance:

> On Glory's highway
> Good Fortune's throne, I raise
> The wine-cup, and receive my friends'
> Warm welcome and their praise (*Faces of Love* 3)

Emerson too experiments with something akin to the ballad meter for Hafez:

> Of Paradise, O hermit wise,
> Let us renounce the thought;
> Of old therein our names of sin
> Allah recorded not. (*CW* 9:265)

Obviously, these attempts fall far short of the *ghazal*'s song produced through Persian rhyme and an indigenous metrical system. However, they both continue to recognize the integrity of rhyme and meter in the original, seeking to render their own versions that comparably resonate in an English poetic tradition.

At a more meta-analytical level, Emerson's brazen cut-and-paste approaches with his anthologizing practices of translations also help to re-create the spirit of the Persian form. His editing and publishing a variety of incomplete Persian poems by different poets in a single grouping such as his essay "Persian Poetry," as well as the haphazard combination of extended notes and translation drafts in *Notebook Orientalist*, mimics Davis's assessment of the *ghazal* as exemplified by Hafez: "the irresolvableness, the resistance to development or resolution, and therefore the lack of closure of the situation seem to be an intrinsic part of the poem's point" ("Not Translating" 316). Instead of honoring the form line by line in translation, Emerson effectively reorients the intertextual and dialogic functioning of the *ghazal*, playing with Western and Eastern allusions on his own American terms.

Emerson's all-encompassing Platonism that unifies if not obviates dif-ferences among national literary traditions, which in his *Notebook Orientalist* seemingly demonstrates the Persian lyric informed by allusions, further antici-pates Davis's intertextual analysis of Hafez. The comparative assessment of the fourteenth-century Persian poet offered by Davis closely imitates Emerson's previous Western summations:

> He can seem at times like Horace, in his simultaneous and para-doxical dependence on munificent patronage while advocating the joys of privacy and friendship away from centers of power . . . He can seem like the medieval troubadours of southern Europe in his linking of poetry and music . . . He can seem like Shakespeare in his abrupt switches of tone and scope of reference . . . [His] poems can remind us of the songs of Bob Dylan . . . (*Faces of Love* xli–xlii)

Such creative relations sound similar to Emerson claiming that Hafez possess the "attributes of Pindar, Anacreon, Horace, and Burns . . ." (*CW* 8:129) as well as his intertextually labeling "Firdusi, the Persian Homer" (*CW* 8:126). Davis's erudition, which includes knowledge of the Persian language, culture, and poetic tradition sorely lacking in his predecessor, also retrospectively justifies Emerson's early appropriative approach to Persian verse. The same philosophy that allows him to authenticate literature attributed to spurious sources based on aesthetic criteria gets uncannily supported by Davis's tracking of Hafez's own questionable claims on his literary past. Caring little if trans-lated words were actually ever said by Persian prophet Zoroaster as long as they offered "good sentences" (*JMN* 16:265), Emerson's appropriative practice gets partially vindicated by Davis explaining how it "has been suggested that

Hafez's Zoroastrians are more of a nostalgic fantasy than anything else—a way of saying 'very Persian, but very heterodox'" (*Faces of Love* xxxii).

One difficulty Davis addresses that makes Persian verse especially difficult to render truly has no real solution: the presence of pedophilia in the work of classical poets ("Not Translating" 312). To a certain extent, Emerson at least sees such an irreconcilable problem coming in his renderings. Even if he weren't overtly aware of such a translating dilemma, his approach nevertheless offered a way to subvert it. To avoid facing such an offensive subject, Persian translators tend to follow Emerson's authoritative interventions, derived from von Hammer-Purgstall's earlier decisions, as to what gets rendered for presentation to English readers. Despite misrepresenting the classical Persian canon, his early process of excerpted selection and editing of translations can thus be viewed as comprising a viable rhetorical strategy useful to his inheritors. As though responding to how Persian poets esteemed male beauty since they couldn't see the female body publically displayed (Kane 127), Emerson changes the "saki" who is frequently identified as a wine boy upon whom poets project their sexual desire (*Faces of Love* xxviii) either to "Butler" or, in his imitation of the Persian poets, to "Bacchus." When the boy does surface in his work, it is only to affirm a sense of joy or set up safely extended philosophical speculation. Later in "Bacchus," for example, he has Hafez declare, "Give me, boy, the Kaisar cup, / Which rejoices heart and soul" (*CW* 9:258). His Hafez translation beginning "Boy bring the bowl full of wine," leads to such didactic admonitions as "mourn for nothing, since past is past" (*PN* 204–205).

Yet considering that 90 percent of the time the beloved mentioned by Persian poets is a boy (Shamisa 34), the overdetermined heteronormative renderings of Rohrer, Ladinsky, and Barks, who so quickly revert to assumptions of husband and wife, warrant critical commentary. As Davis further explains, translators "fudging the issue" when interpreting the indeterminately gendered Persian pronoun in English as feminine end up "bowdlerizing the texts." Even the contemporary acceptance of homosexuality in the receiving English reading culture fails to help, since the original source poetry denotes relations between an older man and a minor ("Not Translating" 312). Though avoiding specific concerns with pederasty, Emerson here too can be seen as anticipating the subversion of this especially ethical concern, as evidenced by his continual stressing the moral sentiments that underpin Persian verse in addition to his decision of what lines to publish in English.

As an acclaimed Persian scholar and translator, given Davis's convincing arguments for not translating Hafez into English, his contradictory decision to eventually render verse of the poet into English proves especially curious. Despite a reasoned checklist making equivalence between languages and traditions seemingly impossible, his own brazen attempt to transcend such difficulties implicitly appeals to Emerson's Platonically informed precedent. If according to Davis's concluding point Hafez belongs among those poets that "cannot be translated because what they express draws so deeply on the culture's specific ethnic soul that it is not communicable in any other terms" ("Not Translating" 317), then Davis himself deciding to bring him into English after publishing the essay against translation ultimately opts for a version of Emerson's more radical domestication of foreign verse, albeit one that he attempts to inform with as much historical and linguistic background from the original source as possible. In the act of so thoroughly introducing what underpins the resistance to translating Hafez in his essay, he has started to expose the importance of the poet's original verse, as if attempting, even while avoiding, a literary rendering more aligned with Emerson's subversion of equivalence. His concluding paragraph interjects the following paraphrase of Goethe while mentioning that most readers remain relatively unaware of the integral value and originality in a representative poet's national literature. It is as though Davis intends to get to the ultimate source of resistance, to the spirit and letter of the text, a task that most fail to achieve:

> Goethe has a remark somewhere that few people realize that a poet's most felicitous effects are often embedded in the rules of language itself, and we can extend this observation to the conventions of poetry that grow up in a linguistic community. It is the poet able to realize and utilize such conventions most effectively who can seem the most inspired and gifted; what to others is learnt, and obviously so, seems to be what he has been given, his natural mental landscape, the ethos within which he luxuriates and flourishes. ("Not Translating" 317–318)

Despite reiterating how such literature of foreign nations remains impossible to accurately depict in translation, Davis surreptitiously renders a metaphorical comparison between German and Persian traditions, going through the former like Emerson before him to arrive at the English into which he translates. Though Davis does not write or translate poetry in the essay, he nevertheless has drawn a rather thorough outline of such a "natural mental landscape," foregrounding the Persian tradition onto which Hafez writes. Like Emerson before him with the *Notebook Orientalist*, Davis has, in fact, written an extensive translator's note, even without offering his own translation in his essay.

Tellingly, as Davis introduces "a set of strategies considered intrinsically poetic in Persian" such as "the inferiority of the speaker" and the "praise of addressee" ("Not Translating" 314), he removes himself from his usual role of a translator, even after being asked by a publisher to faithfully apply his expertise to the classical poetry (310). He holds the subject of translating Hafez on such a pedestal that he has obviated his presence in relation to the Persian master, claiming that not just he, but all of the other "poor poet-translators who metaphorically lie bleeding at his feet" (318), prove unworthy of the task. Such a move parallels the humble, often self-abased voice of the speaker in the verse of Hafez as experienced in the turn from the first line to the second in his *ghazal* couplets. The criteria in the essay regarding hyperbole and the presence of the humble if nonexistent speaker used to distinguish Persian from English verse effectively reveals the extent to which Davis has moved toward the former, even while substantiating a litany of reasons why the latter denies him full access:

> In fact, one might say that the Persian and English sensibilities here make directly opposing demands of verse: the more extreme the praise, the more poetic the poem is considered to be in Persian, and the closer to absurdity and distasteful flattery it is considered to be in English. ("Not Translating" 314–315)

Throughout his essay "On Not Translating Hafez," Davis has reduced himself as a Persian translator to lying at the seminal Persian poet's feet, much like Emerson's own recurring reversion to something akin to the Sufi's self-reduction, or *malámati*. Whether unconsciously or not (which invites further speculation, if "resistance" is to be taken with its Freudian implications), Davis has invented an especially apt pun upon his own penchant for metrics (he himself is a formalist poet) and the metrical feet of the great Persian bard (who, it should be stressed, established himself as an incomparable master of the pun). If by Emerson's admission he proves no visual match for Hafez, who "sees too far" and "sees throughout," then Davis metaphorically lies at the feet of the same Persian poet, extreme in his praise of his inimitable foreign predecessor. Given his own critical standard and sensibility, he sounds much more Persian than English. If we consider his project of resistance as close as he himself considers the verse of Hafez, contrary to the title of his essay it also sounds like he has made himself ready to translate his chosen poet. To a certain extent, he has already begun.

While Davis attempts to foreground with scholarship the difficulty of an ideal creative translator's invisibility, he starts to demonstrate Emerson's paradoxical transparency rendered visible through text. The mixed metaphor indigenous to Persian verse cited by Davis as yet another rhetorical trait making it irreconcilable to the English tradition aptly exemplifies the essential disruption of Emerson's influence. If for Davis "To refer to a person as a walking cypress tree (*sarve-e-ravan*) is only absurd in English" ("Not Translating" 315), then what of an all-seeing and walking eyeball on Boston Common that remains invisible? The thwarted figurative relation between Davis and Emerson again recalls Pease's identification of the latter's problematic self-defining trope as a catachresis (49). Insofar as the transparent eyeball challenges what Davis describes as "a literalism about English metaphor which strongly resists the mixed metaphor and labels it a mistake of taste" ("Not Translating" 315), it accommodates "the delicacy, charm, and wonder" of the rhetorical figure in Persian poetry at an especially essential, if not reductive level, of the poet-translator. Emerson's gaze at the East thus becomes inadvertently corrective through the distortion (to again use the English rendering of Freud's term) of translation for Davis, who by opting to translate Hafez after all his laments discovers like his nineteenth-century predecessor how to practically transcend theoretically impossible problems of Persian verse translation.

Though not a translator into English, the Indian-born poet Agha Shahid Ali from a Kashmiri Shia' family who more comprehensively introduced the form of the *ghazal* to English readers in the later twentieth century, ironically achieves a much closer stylistic equivalence to the Persian verse tradition than many of those officially attempting to translate the poems of Rumi, Hafez, and other classical poets from Iran. In addition to his own incomparable English *ghazals*, he critically introduced a set of rules governing the form, influencing other Western poets to write their own original versions in English, some of which he anthologized in his edited collection *Ravishing Disunities: Real Ghazals in English*. Unlike Pound's appropriative reinventions of axioms derived from the Eastern traditions to develop Western modernism, Shahid Ali foregrounds rules he extracts from Persian verse titled "Basic Points about the Ghazal" (*Disunities* 183–184) so close to the original source poems within which they function that he seemingly compels *ghazals* written in English to remain antithetical to a Western sensibility. Shahid Ali's strictures that each couplet remains "autonomous, thematically and emotionally complete in itself" and his insistence on a rigid "scheme of rhyme" and "refrain"—which he introduces by their original Arabic literary terms of *qafia* and *radif*—along with such conventions of the poet "signing" the last couplet (*Disunities* 2–3), effectively achieves a meta-formal translation beyond a specific source text. Though attentive to the integrity of form, his approach to the *ghazal* in this respect also extends back to Emerson's Platonically all-unifying and all-conflating approach to translation, transcendently defining it with stylistic equivalence.

Shahid Ali's return to the *ghazal* as hybrid poet in his adopted country of America begins to expose Emerson's seemingly transparent "third space" between traditions, even while subjected to its influence. Employing a sense of the "third space" used early in this study, Nishat Zaidi applies Homi Bhabha's theory informing such a formative location to show how Shahid Ali uses the Persian form in English to position his "hyphenated identity," thereby empowering his marginalized status (55–56). Much of Shahid Ali's own life circulated around his native India and his adopted country of the United States (where he received both his MFA and PhD), as well as his mother's Persian background (Zaidi 56). Though uniquely marginal in his identity and poetics, his formative literary background, which includes the traditions of Persian, English, and Urdu, nevertheless mirrors Emerson's predecessor accommodation of foreign and domestic influences. Zaidi's claim that Shahid Ali's India affords him "rich cultural resources" of "plurality, compositeness, and eclecticism" (55–56) surely seems warranted, yet his verse simultaneously continues to reflect Emerson's all-encompassing vision that foresaw the American importation of Indian and Persian literature into English. Zaidi's description of Shahid's aesthetic could easily be mistaken for that of Emerson's: "He does not use the linear time frame of history but prefers an elliptical movement using contrapuntal mythical terrain, where one voices echoes several voices across time and space . . ." (57). Though certainly making the *ghazal* form distinctive in English with the cultural complexity uniquely informing his own identity, Shahid Ali must also impose the Western verse tradition upon it by using "strict metrical forms . . . to express Subcontinental ideas, Kashmiri themes, and Urdu sentiments" (Zaidi 59) in ways that paradoxically also reflect his American predecessor.

As hybrid poet he would avoid a "unidirectional appropriative hegemonic interpretation of the 'other' by the center on its own terms," yet his corrective aspiration toward a "reciprocity of influence" (Zaidi 60) nevertheless mirrors his American precursor's *a priori* arrival as all-encompassing and accommodating transparency. Paradoxically, what makes his introduction of the Persian form of the *ghazal* in English most authentic to its foreign origins is Emerson's seeming artifice. While Davis may prove correct in his claim that national literatures such as the verse of Hafez don't effectively translate into other languages and traditions, Shahid Ali in his English explanations and rhetorical demonstrations of *ghazals* in which the Persian poets wrote shows how the form nevertheless invites imitation at least in part on the receiving culture's terms. They may stray far from equivalence, but American poet-translators nevertheless often appear especially compelled to become hybrid versions of their foreign predecessors, following Emerson's early attempts to figuratively transplant Mecca into his own nation as if for the first time. Though such attempts might critically fail, they nevertheless recur not so much because of the elusive challenge posed by the task, but more as a result of Emerson's expansive predecessor claim upon foreign sources in the American tradition. However unconsciously, even exacting scholars like Davis and formalist hybrid masters schooled in Persian poetics like Shahid Ali invariably must in a sense work more toward becoming Emerson than Hafez or Rumi.

Similar to Emerson before him, Shahid Ali in his rhetoric welcomes a montage of intertextual allusions and quotations, from modernist poets like e.e. cummings (*Ishmael* 54) who emerge out of the earlier American tradition to such sacred Western texts as the Bible (*Ishmael* 53). Despite Eastern allusions to the "Ganges" (*Ishmael* 64) or "Mughal ceilings" (*Ishmael* 82), contrary to Zaidi's claims of his "reaction against the attempt of the West to accommodate Third World culturalism," Shahid Ali indeed must to some extent participate "in its marketplace pluralism" (Zaidi 61). A comparable aesthetic allows Emerson to make claims on his foreign predecessors by inverting allusions in his Persian mirror, wherein Shahid Ali accommodates American verse in his strictly defined *ghazals*. This means he begins to become his own foreign (i.e., American) predecessors who extend back to the first significant American poet-translator to engage the Persian tradition in the nineteenth century. Also like Emerson, in a single poem of foreign imitation, as opposed to actual literary translation, he tends to simultaneously conflate time along with several literary traditions, as if looking the other way through his American predecessor's Platonically reflective telescopic gaze. Though introducing a critique (in a short essay much like that offered by Davis) mostly of American poets "claiming to write *ghazals* in English" who end up "far from the letter and further from the spirit" (*Disunities* 1) of the original Persian form, he too tends to revert to American mimicry.

Shahid Ali's most anthologized *ghazal* aptly shows how despite his attempts at authentic stylistic equivalence to Persian poetics, an influence defined by Emerson intervenes as a kind of American corrective:

Even the Rain

What will suffice for a true-love knot? Even the rain?
But he has bought grief's lottery, bought even the rain.

"our glosses / wanting in this world" "Can you remember?"
Anyone! "when we thought / the poets taught" even the rain?

After we died—*That was it!*—God left us in the dark.
And as we forgot the dark, we forgot even the rain.

Drought was over. Where was I? Drinks were on the house.
For mixers, my love, you'd poured—what?—even the rain.

Of this pear-shaped orange's perfumed twist, I will say:
Extract Vermouth from the bergamot, even the rain.

How did the Enemy love you—with earth? air? and fire?
He held just one thing back till he got even: the rain.

This is God's site for a new house of executions?
You swear by the Bible, Despot, even the rain?

After the bones—those flowers—this was found in the urn:
The lost river, ashes from the ghat, even the rain.

What was I to prophesy if not the end of the world?
A salt pillar for the lonely lot, even the rain.

How the air raged, desperate, streaming the earth with flames—
to help burn down my house, Fire sought even the rain.

He would raze the mountains, he would level the waves,
he would, to smooth his epic plot, even the rain.

New York belongs at daybreak to only me, just me—
to make this claim Memory's brought even the rain.

They've found the knife that killed you, but whose prints are
      these?
No one has such small hands, Shahid, not even the rain.
      (*Ishmael* 53–54).

Remaining formally as true to the source poetry as any translator of
classical Persian verse, such as Elizabeth Gray, whose renderings he esteems
for their relative stylistic equivalency (*Disunities* 4), he nevertheless displaces
the ubiquitous Persian trope of wine in all of its figurative connotations with
a Western mixed drink featuring "Vermouth." The "bergamot" mentioned
grows near the coast of Italy, as well as in France and the Ivory Coast. In just
one line and with just one allusion, the poet already refashions the Persian
form in Emerson-like cosmopolitan verse. While the river "ghat" referenced

proves closer to his ethnic Indian home, mention of the "Bible" as well as the Old Testament figure "lot" favors the Judeo-Christian tradition much like Barks and Ladinsky, even while elsewhere he cites the Islamic influence on his writing in the form (*Disunities* 2). While Persian poetry that came to define the *ghazal* the way Shahid Ali understands it generally quotes the *Qur'an* as well as predecessor Persian poets, he begins both lines of the second couplet with words from an Adrienne Rich poem titled "Poetry" (66). As if starting to play with his own strictures against any enjambment whatsoever, he breaks Rich's lines within his, even while maintaining end stops in his poem. Rich curiously has written *ghazals* herself. Though Shahid Ali concedes her needing to break from rhyme in her translations of Ghalib, he becomes somewhat critical of the way she and others in her original *ghazals* "simply did not bother with the form" (*Disunities* 11). Ironically, however, even by attempting to subsume her line breaks within what he reiterates as both rules number 1 and 2 under "Basic Points about the Ghazal" (*Disunities* 183), his inclusion of yet another American poet still begins to thematically impinge on his insistence of stylistic equivalence.

Honoring the form as much as possible while allowing an inevitable shift in meaning at least in part toward a predecessor American poet-translator *a priori*'s arrival in the nation to which he immigrates, Shahid Ali just as Emerson before him would inhabit figurative transparency. Like Emerson arriving on Boston Common as if for the first time, Shahid Ali claims "New York belongs at daybreak to only me, just me—," allowing the fantasy of rain clearing away all memory, and consequently any literary influence, even his foreign one. Reckoning with Emerson having first subsumed the hybrid space he would inhabit, he thus problematizes his own criteria he cites for the *ghazal* as "cultural unity—created by the audience's shared assumptions and expectations . . . a contrapuntal air" (5).

While honoring recurring rhyme and refrain, as well as other conventions he cites under "Basic Points about the Ghazal" such as mention of the poet's name or persona in the concluding couplet (*Disunities* 183), his own English verse can't help but betray some of the form's indigenously Persian qualities. What Emerson correctly reads as the "signing" of the *ghazal*'s last couplet as a kind of "copyright" (*CW* 8:134) in the context of the American tradition means that Shahid Ali invariably must displace the Persian source tradition he would attempt to imitate in English. In citing without quotation marks the lines by e.e. cummings in his final conclusion, he inhabits the formal tension between unenjambed lines found in the *ghazals* of Hafez, even while circulating around a very different cultural unity. cummings, influenced by Emerson to the point of memorizing his poems (Reef 9), begins taking

ownership of this poem, his understatedly famous line in the American tradition simultaneously putting an end to the words and the life of his imitative
author. Returning to the etymological origins of the Persian form as the cry
of the gazelle, by placing lines from the American poet in the position of
the beloved, Shahid Ali goes figuratively hunting for the American tradition
in an inherently hybrid form. The tracked "prints," however, like metrical
feet upon the knife lead back to cummings and ultimately to Emerson. In
the concluding couplet of another *ghazal* he self-defines "Shahid" as " 'The
Beloved' in Persian," the language in which he considers the form taking shape
and the tradition that foregrounded the beloved as the love-object leading to
the divine (*Ishmael* 81). Attempting to capture the *ghazal* within his formal
constraints, the hunter ends up becoming the hunted, prey to an American
inversion of foreign influence that originates with Emerson. Prior to the
rhyme and refrain of the form in the last line, of which Shahid Ali attempts
to take critical ownership in the West, the poet thus finds himself defined by
the American tradition's prior displacement of the Persian influence.

Like Davis as Persian translator, Shahid Ali as imitator of the *ghazal*
form paradoxically gets closer to the foreign source when somewhat creatively
following Emerson away from it. To take the "cult of pederasty" that Davis
cites as one of the "most obvious purely cultural problems that a translator
of medieval Persian poetry must inevitably face" ("On Not Translating" 312),
both the most exacting equivalent renderings as well as the loosely interpretive
imitations of classical verse avoid broaching the subject. Emerson through von
Hammer-Purgstall selects safe excerpts to introduce to their respective Western
audiences and also made such aforementioned changes from "saki" or "wine
boy" to "Butler," inviting other creative English interventions. Writing in the
voice of Sa'di, upon whom he projects his self-reliant philosophy, he begins
for example to subvert the authority of the source poet. As has been shown,
he goes further, channeling the words of his ideal Persian predecessor's son
who delivers the good news of a transcendence from beyond the grave as a
kind of allegory for the intoxicating mysticism typically brought by the wine
boy. Though the correspondence only goes so far, it nevertheless reveals how
Emerson offers an example of possibly capturing a certain sense of the source
text beyond taboo themes. Together with his theory of quotation, Emerson
allows for playful re-imaginings of original foreign verse.

From the style of the modern American poet influenced by Emerson
who favored radical play with free verse and comparably reduced the self even
while foregrounding it with a lower case "i," Shahid Ali carries the figurative
renewal of his literary inheritance into his concluding couplet. The title of

cummings's excerpted poem alone, "somewhere i have never travelled, gladly beyond," connotes the innocence of Emerson's transplanted Mecca in "Experience," and mention of "her first rose" (65) aligns virginity with nature. In the penultimate stanza, the power of the beloved's "intense fragility" proves greater than anything else "we are to perceive in this world." Despite the innocent love object's female identification, truer of course to the more modernly familiar Western tradition, she nevertheless becomes somewhat comparatively representative of the *saki* in Persian poetry. "Wine and boys," explains Davis, "are associated together in the figure of the wine-server . . . who, it is implied, is also often an object of desire to the speaker of the poem" (*Faces of Love* xxvii–xxviii). Though pederasty involving the wine boy must remain problematically literal, as Davis goes on to mention, "The interpretation of Persian poetry that apparently deals with secular love and wine as being in reality mystical and Sufi in its subject matter was well established by the fourteenth century" (*Faces of Love* xxix). True to the final couplet of the *ghazal*, Shahid interposes his own name in the third person. Through such self-objectification, he displaces the presumably young and virginal female beloved with childlike Romantic playfulness, effectively refashioned as if into a Persian wine boy. This makes the "prints" associative of metrical feet upon the penetrating "knife" that killed him playfully "small" while transcendently transporting them beyond the climatic death of the named poet. That "the voice of [his] eyes are deeper than all roses" (65) renders the perception, however inadvertently, deep into the realm of the Persian tradition, insofar as it penetrates beyond one of the most ubiquitous floral tropes in all of Sufi mystical poetry.

Even while advocating for what Jason Schneiderman calls an "historical dignity that had been denied the form in the west" (10), Shahid Ali thus invests his *ghazal* lines with the words of American writers such as Rich and cummings. Detaching much of the form from its Persian content, by filling couplets with frequent quotation from Western writers his *ghazals* revert to a kind of Emersonian imitation. Anecdotally, the Emerson scholar Robert Habich reports how years ago working in the writing center while in graduate school at Pennsylvania State University with fellow student Shahid Ali, the poet demonstrated a remarkable talent for mimicking the varied accents of his American students. Such performativity resembles the aforementioned Sufi mystics teaching the parrots to talk behind the mirror while further echoing Emerson's Persian imitations. Adhering to his own admonition to honor the lack of enjambment between couplets in this respect certainly insures stylistic authenticity in the form, even as it invites such American mimicry with Emerson's textual interventions:

One should be able to pluck a couplet like a stone from a necklace,
and it should continue to shine in that vivid isolation, though it
would have a different lustre among and with the other stones."
(*Disunities* 2–3)

Though retaining the integrity of the couplet so that it can "continue to shine"
in English, he nevertheless imbues it with the "lustre" of American voices.
Zaidi's argument for the cultural integrity of *ghazals* from his native Urdu
that "explore new meanings (*maʿani*) in the old themes" (62) strongly recalls
Emerson's assessment regarding "the old and the new," wherein he states
that "there is no thread that is not a twist of these two strands" (*CW* 8:94).
Shahid Ali in this respect introduces what he considers the oldest verse form
in which poets still write (*Disunities* 1), yet with lines threading through it
from the much newer American verse tradition.

Shahid Ali further centers his own hybrid identity in Emerson's "third
space" to make his "other half" an "expression" of other voices, thereby
returning to a comparable Platonic unity of language and traditions. Along
with lines of American verse, like Emerson he intertextually weaves a variety
of global allusions together. Defining the *ghazal* where he translates his own
name in the final couplet "In Arabic," he ironically writes the entire poem
in English. Such dialogic tension informs many of the lines, if not most of
his *ghazals*. "A language of loss?" he asks in the first couplet. "I have some
business in Arabic" (*Ishmael* 80). A few couplets later, further expressing the
loss not just of the essential language found in the *Qurʾan* but the very literary tradition of the Persian form to which it connects as essential allusion,
lines unravel in a trajectory from an ancient Eastern classicism to modern
Western decadence: "This much fuss about a language I don't know? So one
day / perfume from a dress may let you digress in Arabic" (*Ishmael* 80). Two
couplets after alluding to T.S. Eliot, Shahid Ali returns to the Persian and Arab
traditions by mentioning the well-known love story of Laila and Majnoon, just
as earlier he inserts more of his own aesthetic background with the lines: "At
an exhibition of miniatures, what Kashmiri hairs! / Each paisley inked into a
golden tress in Arabic" (*Ishmael* 80). In the same poem into which he threads
such authentic cultural material, however, he cites the further transnational
intertextual weaving of Lorca's "*qasidas* stiched seamless in Arabic" (*Ishmael*
80). Like Lorca before him, who appropriated the *ghazal* to represent his
native Grenada, Shahid Ali thus braids the form into his own hybrid setting.

In a penultimate couplet, he again switches traditions as well as linguistic references, juxtaposing "Hebrew" and "Arabic" around a reference to the
Israeli poet Amichai (*Ishmael* 80–81) as if to model poetic coexistence among

Arabs and Jews in a form indigenous to Iran. Though seemingly surrender-ing so much lost in translated and imitated English, Shahid Ali concludes by figuratively historicizing the transformation of the *ghazal* from Arabic into Persian, as it's in the final couplet where he self-references as "beloved" a lat-ter manifestation of the form that first started to take shape in the Arabian tradition. Simultaneously, as though rendering a meta-translation of the form itself into English, he further tracks the inherent hybrid appropriation of the form in the Spanish tradition through Lorca as well as the Hebrew through Amichai. Though attempting to offer a needed correction to the form he so values, he therefore tends to demonstrate much of Emerson's ideal Platonic unity wherein all languages and traditions ultimately cohere. Further identify-ing in the final couplet with a linguistic pun on his name "Shahid" as both "witness"[1] in "Arabic" and "beloved" in "Persian" (*Ishmael* 81), he carries the history of the form into his own identity in English. Such a Romantic insistence upon a displaced self, while returning both to the Persian and Arabic origins of the *ghazal*, orients him around Emerson's rhetorical tradition. Subjected as hybrid "beloved" to the American poetry he attempts to inhabit, he must bear "witness" to Emerson's predecessor vision. In this respect, Lewisohn's furthering the ambiguity of the poet's given name as "seer" (43) suggests a Sufi poet "who beholds in the mirror of human beauty" ("Prolegomenon" 49) while self-reflecting on the figurative site of the original American poet who first looked to the East to see him coming.

In attempting to negotiate a successful formal equivalence of the Persian *ghazal* in English, Shahid Ali like Davis thus must revert in part to translation practices reminiscent of those delineated by Emerson. Honoring the originating language and adhering to stylistic properties as much as pos-sible, given their erudition and poetic skill as formalists, they return to the influence of Emerson's early appropriation. As figurative first arrival in the American tradition, the early poet-translator anticipated the Persian poets of the thirteenth and fourteenth centuries, who he in turn transformed. Fol-lowing the thread of his own theory of quotation that so informs his foreign renderings and imitation, which intertwines with the verse of contemporary English translators, the individual *ghazal* couplets that Shahid Ali critically insists upon as separate jewels warrant reinterpretation. Though they might indeed at times reflect signifiers of the originating Persian or Arab literary traditions, they are ultimately threaded through an influence extending back to lines of Emerson's earlier American rhetoric.

Notes

Introduction

1. Albert von Frank notes how previous attention to Emerson's engagement with the Persian tradition has been subsumed under the more general "oriental" influences," which he attributes to the nineteenth-century Transcendentalists' welcoming an array of Eastern ideas, including "Hinduism, Confucianism, and the mystical tradition of Islam known as Sufism" (*CW* 9:lxviii). Such a conflation of spiritual ideas can be seen as further demonstrating Emerson's aesthetic informed by Platonism.

Chapter 1

1. Abu Bakr al-Kalabadhi further cites that Sufis may have acquired their name because of "purity (*safā*) of their hearts" while offering further speculation regarding their standing within the "first rank (*saff*) before God." They also were considered among the "people of the Bench (*suffah*), who lived in time of God's Prophet" (*Doctrine* 5).

2. Richardson's tracking of Emerson's reading practices further shows the specific juxtaposition of Persian and Platonic philosophy when noting how he revisited words of the Persian prophet Zoroaster a few months after studying the Neoplatonist Porphyry and during the same month he was rereading Plato's *Phaedrus, Meno,* and *Symposium* (346).

3. "Through his studies with his Professor of Greek, Edward Everett, his work on his essay on Socrates, the urging of his Aunt Mary (many of whose rambling letters he copied verbatim into his journal), and miscellaneous readings, he seems to have laid the first foundations of his new philosophy in Platonic idealism without actually reading much of Plato" (Spiller, *CW* 1:v).

4. See Einboden (*Islamic Lineage* 194 n30).

5. "Osman" is also used at times by Emerson as a model for James Very (*JMN 1838–1842*, 503).

6. Much of his early interest in the Persian prophet additionally stems from Pythagoras as well as Platonus (Richardson 351).

7. See also Joseph Slater's exhaustive note about Emerson's relation to the history of the *Desatir*, which includes a viable source from which Emerson quite possibly learned about the long debate over the veracity of the text's origins (*CW* 3:185–187 n34–35).

8. Theodore Parker (211–212).

9. Much like the Sufi poet opposed to the strictures of the mullah, Emerson argued that religion could not really benefit from "conventional preaching but only by living discourse" (Richardson 290).

10. For a detailed outline of Emerson's reading of Sufi poets and philosophy, see Ekhtiyar's "The Chronological Development of Emerson's Interest in Persian Mysticism."

11. See von Frank's note about Howard Carey's early reading about how "the tree of life in Genesis is also the tree of life in the Apocalypse and that its leaves are for 'the healing of the nations' (Revelation 22:2) . . ." (*CW* 9:632).

Chapter 2

1. In his reading of Emerson's transparent eyeball as "the opposite of narcissism," Richardson deems his transformation as the "mysticism of a commonly occurring and easily accepted sort" (228). Though the desired union with the divine through the beloved of the Sufi mystics appears rather distinctive from such a qualification, the attempt to negate the self in part through referencing the struggle to overcome it proves especially comparable to much of Persian Sufi poetry.

2. Ghazal 68, translated by the author.

3. Quoted in Lewisohn (*Hafez and his Genius* 76).

4. Even prior to Emerson's reading of Sa'di, Richardson cites his early interest in Zoroaster as "the first person to have institutionalized the pure and noble religion of nature in a cult or church" (351). In this respect a focus on the earlier Persian prophet's relation to nature further anticipates the emphasis on the natural world in Sufism.

5. Consider, too, in the context of such light imagery in the Sa'di translation Emerson's description of his son in a letter to Lidian as "the far shining stone that made home glitter to me" (*Letters* 3:12). Such an image especially resonates with both Emerson's physical removal of Waldo's tombstone as well as the figural extraction of a comparable stone before the grave of Sa'di's son.

6. Bernofsky has generously contributed the following rough unpublished English trot from von Hammer's German translation, which Emerson used for his renderings:

At Sanaa I lost a son,
No youth is so handsome/beautiful and fresh as Jussuf,
No cedar yet stood within this grove,
No wonder that roses blossomed from the dust,
I spoke: Lord! Die of shame at my command,
Despairing I climbed down to the tomb,
I wandered/went astray in this cramped horrific place,
When I came to myself from the deep pain,
"If this thick darkness so terrifies you,
"If you want the night of the grave to be bright as day,
The hordes believe that golden harvest stands,
But Saadi knows, it is the fruit, the seed,
How can I say how this bewilders my head,
Which isn't being devoured by the grave's fish (i.e. worms),
The hand not uprooted by the storm,
That draws the grave's crepe across the rosy cheek!
The pure youth dies like a sinful graybeard,
And tore the stone away from his grave,
His eyes inflamed, entirely beside himself,
Then it seemed to me, that my beloved was calling:
"Be wise, go out into the daylight.
"Only good works alone can achieve this."
Where no one has strewn the seed
of the man who has planted and sowed.

7. "I staggered down to his tomb, / And tore away the stone away (†) there down arrow from <its mouth>" (*TN* 2:77).

8. It's worth noting that Emerson frequently used "angel" much like "darling" for young Waldo (Schneider 100).

9. "Ghazal 5" of Hafez (translated by the author).

Chapter 3

1. Significantly, it was a year after writing his poem "Saadi" that Emerson actually did significant research on the Persian poet, thereby suggesting he "had merely appropriated the name for a mediation on the figure of the ideal poet" (*CW* 9:lxix).

2. To again exemplify the relatability of Emerson's translations to his imitative attempts, in the former he erroneously equates Muhammad to Jesus as the son of God in approaches to prayer (Obeidat 85).

3. This quote comes from a collection of sentences attributed to the Imam Ali (Ockley 31).

4. Ekhtiyar further notes the following: "Late in 1841, Emerson's interest was drawn to the doctrine of 'Beautiful Necessity' and to the notion of Destiny; his eagerness led him again to the concept of 'variety' in Hinduism and to Oriental mysticism. In a Journal entry for 1841, he records that he found an analogy to the fact of life in the Asiatic sentences and that the Oriental genius has no dramatic or epic turn, but that antithetical contemplative delights in it as in Zoroastrian Oracles, in the Vedas, and in Manu" (59).

5. See Slater's notes on Emerson's transformation of this quote from the *Qur'an* into his own couplet (*CW* 2:243).

6. As quoted by Slater (*CW* 6:191–192 n38).

7. To exemplify the lyric tension embedded within the inability to pin down the master name with signification, consider the inherent resistance to any assigned preposition as cited by the Sufi mystic Hallaj:

"Before" does not outstrip Him, "after" does not interrupt Him, "of" does not vie with Him for precedence, "from" does not accord with Him, "to" does not join with Him, "in" does not inhabit Him, "when" does not stop Him, "if" does not consult with Him, "over" does not overshadow him, "under" does not support him . . . (Arberry, *Doctrine* 15)

Chapter 4

1. Originally appearing in Edward Emerson (399).

2. *The Topical Notebooks of Ralph Waldo Emerson* 2:27.

3. As cited by Emerson in his rather loose translation of a related poem from Hafez, which Buell considers relatively close in correspondence (152–153).

4. "The nymphs of Paradise in Islamic teaching" (*CW* 9:264).

Chapter 6

1. "Shahid" or "witness" can be seen as relating to Hafez's Sufistic vision informed by the "contemplation of the divine . . . beholding the divine in the mirror of human beauty" (Lewisohn, "Prolegomenon" 43). In this respect, Shahid Ali can be considered as subtly referencing the classical Persian tradition, following his Persian inheritor who mastered the *ghazal* form.

Works Cited

al-Din Muhammad Davani, Jalal. *Akhlaq-i Jalali* (*The Jalalian Ethics*). Translated by W.F. Thomson. London: Oriental Translation Fund, 1839.

Ahmad, Mahnaz. "Walt Whitman and Hafiz: Expressions of Universal Love and Tolerance." Aminrazavi, pp. 153–162.

Alfanso, Ricardo. "The Influence of Anxiety or Postmodernity in Emerson." *New Literatures of Old: Dialogues of Tradition and Innovation in Anglophone Literature.* Edited by Jose Ramon Prado-Perez and Didac Llorens Cubedo. New Castle: Cambridge Scholars, 2008, pp. 46–63.

al-Kalabadhi, Abu Bakr. *The Doctrine of the Sufis.* Translation and Introduction by A.J. Arberry. Cambridge: Cambridge UP, 1935.

Ali, Imam. "Sermon of Glorification." Trans. Khazeh Fanana Pazir. bahai-library.com/imam-ali_khutbat_iftikhar. Accessed August 17, 2018.

Ali, Kazim. *Resident Alien: On Border Crossing and the Undocumented Divine.* Ann Arbor: U of Michigan P, 2015.

Ali, Agha Shahid, Ed. *Ravishing DisUnities: Real Ghazals in English.* Hanover: Wesleyan UP, 1998.

———. *Call Me Ishmael Tonight: A Book of Ghazals.* New York: Norton, 2013.

———. *A Nostalgist's Map of America.* New York: Norton, 1991.

Aminrazavi, Mehdi, Ed. *Sufism and American Literary Masters.* Albany, NY: SUNY P, 2015.

Anvar, Leili. "The Radiance of Epiphany: The Vision of Beauty and Love in Hafiz's Poem of Pre-Eternity." *Hafiz and the Religion of Love in Classical Persian Poetry.* Edited by Leonard Lewisohn. New York: I.B. Tauris, 2010, pp. 123–142.

Auden, W.H. "Frost." *The Dyer's Hand and Other Essays.* New York: Random House, 1990, pp. 344–346.

Avery, Peter. "Foreword: Hāfiz of Shirāz." *Hafiz and the Religion of Love in Classical Persian Poetry.* Edited by Leonard Lewisohn. New York: I.B. Tauris, 2010, pp. ix–xviii.

Azadibougar, Omid, and Simon Patton. "Coleman Barks' Versions of Rumi in the USA." *Translation and Literature*, vol. 24, no. 2, Summer 2015, pp. 172–189.

Baldock, John. *The Essence of Rumi.* London: Arcturus, 2005.

Bane, Theresa. *Encyclopedia of Beasts and Monsters in Myth, Legend, and Folklore.* Jefferson: McFarland, 2016.

Barks, Coleman. "Rumi's Poetry: 'All Religions: All This Singing, One Song.'" Blog for *The Huffington Post.* www.huffingtonpost.com/coleman-barks/rumi-and-some-new-ways-to_b_777382.html. Accessed August 17, 2018.

———. "Chat Transcript: Coleman Barks on Rumi." www.beliefnet.com/wellness/2001/06/chat-transcript-coleman-barks-on-rumi.aspx?p=4. Accessed August 17, 2018.

Barnstone, Willis. *The Poetics of Translation: History, Theory, Practice.* New Haven, CT: Yale UP, 1995.

Bayat, Mojdeh, and Mohammad Ali Jamnia. *Tales from the Land of the Sufis.* Boulder: Shambhala, 2001.

Benjamin, Walter. "Task of the Translator." *Selected Writings: 1913–1926.* Edited by Marcus Bullock and Michael W. Jennings. Vol 1. Cambridge: Belknap, 1996, pp. 253–263.

Benton, Joel. *Emerson as a Poet.* New York: Mansfield and Wessels, 1883.

Bhabha, Homi K. *The Location of Culture.* New York: Routledge, 1994.

Bloom, Harrold, *The Anxiety of Influence: A Theory of Poetry.* London: Oxford UP, 1966.

———. "The Central Man: Emerson, Whitman, Wallace Stevens." *Massachusetts Review.* Vol. 8, 1966, pp. 23–42.

———. *The Poems of our Climate.* Ithaca: Cornell UP, 1987.

———. "Bacchus and Merlin: The Dialectic of Romantic Poetry in America". *The Ringers in the Tower: Studies in Romantic Tradition.* Chicago: U of Chicago P, 1971, pp. 290–321.

Bly, Robert. *The Angels Knocking on the Door: Thirty Poems of Hafez.* New York: Harper Collins, 1999.

Borges, Jorge Luis. *Jorge Luis Borges: Selected Poems, 1923–1967.* Edited by Norman Thomas di Giovanni. Translated by Mark Strand. London: Penguin, 1972.

Brodsky, Joseph. "On Grief and Reason." *On Grief and Reason: Essays.* New York: Farrar Straus Giroux, 1995.

Brooks, Cleaneth, and Robert Penn Warren. *Conversations on the Craft of Poetry: With Robert Frost, John Crowe Ransom, Robert Lowell, Theodore Roethke, a Transcript of the Tape Recording Made to Accompany Understanding Poetry.* New York: Holt, Rinehart, and Winston, 1961.

Brooks, Van Wyck. *The Flowering of New England, 1815–1865.* New York: Dutton and Company, 1936.

Brujin, J.T.P. *Persian Sufi Poetry: An Introduction to the Mystical Use of Classical Persian Poems.* New York: Routledge, 1997.

Buell, Lawrence. *Emerson.* Cambridge: Belknap, 2003.

Bulfinch, Thomas. *Age of Chivalry or King Arthur and his Knights.* Edited by J. Loughran Scott. Philadelphia: David McKay, 1900.

Burkhardt, Titus. *Introduction to Sufi Doctrine.* Bloomington, IN: World Wisdom, 2008.

Canteins, Jean. "The Hidden Sciences in Islam." sunnirazvi.net/sufism/more/hidden.htm. Accessed August 17, 2018.

Carpenter, Frederic. *Emerson and Asia.* New York: Haskell House, 1968.

Cameron, Sharon. "Representing Grief: Emerson's 'Experience.'" *Emerson's Essays*. Edited by Harold Bloom. New York: Chelsea House, 2006, pp. 125–154.

Cervantes, Miguel de. *Don Quixote*. Translated by J.M. Cohen. New York: Penguin, 1950.

Chittik, William. "The Pluralistic Vision of Persian Sufi Poetry." *Islam and Christian Muslim Relations*, Vol. 14, 2003, pp. 423–428.

Ciabbatari, Jane. "Why is Rumi the Best Selling Poet in the U.S." *BBC Culture*. October 21, 2014.

Claro, Andrés. "'Transportation is Civilization': Ezra Pound's Poetics of Translation." Lecture. www.academia.edu/27216096/Transportation_is_Civilisation_Ezra_Pounds_Poetics_of_Translation. Accessed August 17, 2018.

Cox, James. "R.W. Emerson: The Circles of the Eye." *Emerson: Prophecy, Metamorphosis, and Influence*. Edited by David Levin. New York: Columbia UP, 1975.

cummings, e.e. *Selected Poems*. New York: Liveright, 1994.

Cranch, Christopher Pearse. *Illustrations of the New Philosophy: Drawings*. Houghton Library. Cambridge: Harvard University, 1837–1839.

Curiel, Jonathan. "Poet Follows His Own Muse in Translating Sufi Mystic: His Rumi Books Are Surprising Best-Sellers." *San Francisco Chronicle*. April 4, 2002. www.rumi.net/Rumi_SFC.htm. Accessed August 17, 2018.

Darr, Robert. Review in *Mawlana Rumi Review*, vol. 1, 2010. Archetype, pp. 42–147.

Davis, Dick. "On Not Translating Hafez," *New England Review*, vol. 25, no. 1–2, 2004, pp. 310–318.

———. *Faces of Love: Hafez and the Poets of Shiraz*. New York: Penguin, 2013.

Derrida, Jacques. "*Différance*." Translated by Alan Bass. *Margins of Philosophy*. Chicago: U of Chicago P, 1982, pp. 3–27.

Dickinson, Emily. *Emily Dickinson Selected Letters*. Edited by Thomas Johnson. Cambridge: Harvard UP, 1958.

Dimock, Wai Chee. *Through Other Continents: American Literature Across Deep Time* Princeton, NJ: Princeton UP, 2003.

Dunston, Susan. "East of Emerson." *Emerson for the Twenty-First Century: Global Perspectives on an American Icon*. Edited by Barry Tharaud. Newark: U of Delaware P, 2013, pp. 107–130.

Edmonson, Phillip. "The Persians of Concord." *Sufism and American Literary Masters*. Edited by M. Aminrazavi. Albany, NY: SUNY P, 2015, pp. 213–220.

Einboden, Jeffrey. *The Islamic Lineage of American Culture: Muslim Sources from the Revolution to Reconstruction*. Oxford: Oxford UP, 2016.

———. *Islam and Romanticism: Muslim Currents from Goethe to Emerson*. London: Oneworld, 2014.

Ekhtiyar, Mansur. "The Chronological Development of Emerson's Interest in Persian Mysticism." *Sufism and American Literary Masters*. Edited by M. Aminrazavi. Albany, NY: SUNY P, 2015, pp. 55–74.

Elling, Rasmus. "Taking the Islam out of it: Coleman Barks." *Tidsskrift for Mellemonstens litteratur*. Vol. 5, 2003, pp. 24–50.

Emerson, Edward, Ed. *Complete Works of Ralph Waldo Emerson*. Vol. 9. New York: Houghton Mifflin, 1904.

Emerson, Ralph Waldo. *The Journals and Miscellaneous Notebooks of Ralph Waldo Emerson*. Edited by William H. Gilman, Ralph H. Orth, et al. 16 vols. Cambridge: Harvard UP, 1960–82.

———. *The Collected Works of Ralph Waldo Emerson*. Edited by Alfred R. Ferguson, Joseph Slater, et al. 10 vols. Cambridge: Harvard UP, 1971–2013.

———. "Manuscript Translations." *Ralph Waldo Emerson: Essays and Lectures*. Edited by Joel Porte. New York: The Library of America, pp. 465–549.

———. *Complete Sermons of Ralph Waldo Emerson*. Edited by Albert J. von Frank et al. Vol. 4. Columbia: U of Missouri P, 1992.

———. *The Poetry Notebooks of Ralph Waldo Emerson*. Edited by Ralph H. Orth, Albert J. von Frank, et al. Columbia: U of Missouri P, 1986.

———. *The Letters of Ralph Waldo Emerson*. Edited by Ralph L. Rusk and Eleanor Tilton. 10 vols. New York: Columbia UP, 1939–1996.

———. "Notebook Orientalist." *The Topical Notebooks of Ralph Waldo Emerson*. Vol. 2, pp. 37–121.

———. "Poetry and Imagination." *Letters and Social Aims*. Vol. 8. New York & Boston: Houghton Mifflin, 1889, pp. 7–64.

———. "Preface." Musle-Huddeen Sheik Saadi. *Gulistan or Rose Garden*. Translated by Francis Gladwin. Boston: Ticknor and Fields, 1865, pp. iii–x.

———. *Topical Notebooks of Ralph Waldo Emerson*. 3 vols. Edited by Ralph H. Orth, Susan Sutton Smith, Ronald A. Bosco, and Glen M. Johnson. Columbia: U of Missouri P, 1990–1994.

Ernst, Carl. *Following Muhammad: Rethinking Islam in the Contemporary World*. Chapel Hill: U of North Carolina P, 2003.

Fenollosa, Ernest. *The Chinese Written Character as a Medium for Poetry*. Edited by Haun Saussy, Jonathan Stalling, and Lucas Klein. New York: Fordham UP, 2009.

Furlanetto, Elena. "The Rumi Phenomenon Between Orientalism and Cosmopolitanism: The Case of Elif Shafak's The Forty Rules of Love." *European Journal of English Studies*, vol. 17, no. 2, 2013, pp. 201–213.

Geldard, Richard. *The Spiritual Teaching of Ralph Waldo Emerson*. Northumberland: Lindisfarne, 2001.

Gerando, Joseph de. *Historie comparée des systèmes de philosophie*. Paris: Alexis Eymery, 1822.

Geoffrey, Eric. *Introduction to Sufism: The Inner Path of Islam*. Translated by Roger Gaetani. World Wisdom, 2010.

Guénon, Rene. *Symbolism of the Cross*. Translated by A. Macnab. London: Luzac, 1975.

Hafis Mohammed Schemsed-din. *Der Diwan von Mohammed Schemsed-din*, Translated by Barron von Hammer. Stuttgart and Tubingen, Cota, *1812–1813*.

Hafiz-i-Shirazi. *The Divan, Written in the Fourteenth Century*. Translated by Wilberforce Clarke. Calcutta: Government of India Central Printing Office, 1891.

———. *Green Sea of Heaven: Fifty ghazals from the Divan of Hafiz*. Translated by Elizabeth T. Gray, Jr. Ashland, OR: White Cloud, 1995.

Hammer-Purgstall, Joseph. *Geschichte der schönen redekünste Persiens, mit einer blüthenlese aus zweyhundert persischen dichtern*. Wien: Heubner und Volke, 1818.

Hawthorne, Nathaniel. *The Scarlet Letter: A Romance*. Edited by John Stephen Martin. Ontario: Broadview, 2004.

Hodder, Alan. "Asia." *Emerson in Context*. Edited by Wesley Mott. New York: Cambridge UP, 2014, pp. 40–49.

Holmes, Oliver Wendell. *The Writings of Oliver Wendell Holmes: Memoirs of R. W. Emerson and J.L. Motley*. Cambridge: Riverside Press, 1892.

Ilahi-Ghomshei, Husayn. "The Principles of the Religion of Love in Classical Persian Poetry." In Lewisohn, *Hafiz and Religion*, pp. 77–106.

Ives, Charles. *Essays Before a Sonata*. New York: Knickerbocker Press, 1920.

Jahanpour, Farhang. "Emerson on Hafiz and Sa'di: The Narrative of Love and Wine." In Aminrazavi, *Sufism and American Literary Masters*, pp. 117–152.

———. "Ralph Waldo Emerson and the Sufis: From Puritanism to Transcendentalism." *Journal of Globalization for the Common Good* (2007). www.globethics. net/gel/4050599. Accessed August 17, 2018.

Jung, Hwa Yol. *Transversal Rationality and Intercultural Texts: Essays in Phenomenology and Comparative Philosophy*. Athens: Ohio UP, 2011.

Kalyani, Chitra. "Coleman Barks on Rumi: Bridge to the Soul, a Conversation on the Bridge." Archive Islam, 11 December 2007. archive.islamonline.net/?p=6018. Accessed August 17, 2018.

Kane, Paul. "Emerson and Hafiz: The Figure of the Religious Poet." *Religion and Literature*, vol. 41, no. 1, 2009, pp. 111–139.

Kashani, Aryanpur, *Odes of Hafiz*, Translated by Abbas Aryanpur Kashani. Costa Mesa: Mazda, 1984.

Katouzian, Homa. *The Poet of Life, Love, and Compassion*. Oxford: One World, 2006.

Kasravi, Ahmad. *Dar Paramun-e-Adabiyat*. Tehran, 1325/1946, pp. 53–61.

Kenner, Hugh. *The Pound Era*. Berkeley: U of California P, 1973.

Kern, Robert. *Orientalism, Modernism, and the American Poem*. Cambridge: Cambridge UP, 1996.

Khan, Hazrat Inayat. *The Sufi Message of Hazrat Inayat Khan: The Mysticism of Sound, Music, the Power of the Word, Cosmic Language*. Cairo: Library of Alexandria. 2000.

———. "Selflessness. Inkisar." Chapter 8, Vol. 8: *The Art of Being*. wahiduddin.net/ mv2/VIII/VIII_2_8.htm. Accessed August 17, 2018.

Khanam, Farida. *Sufism: An Introduction*. New Delhi: Goodword Books, 2006.

Khojastehpour, Adineh, and Behnam Fomeshi Mirzababazadeh. "A Poet Builds a Nation: Hafez as a Catalyst in Emerson's Process of Developing American Literature." *Kata: A Bilingual Publication on the Study of Language and Literature*, vol. 16, no. 2, 2014, pp. 109–118.

Kristeva, Julia. "Word, Dialogue, and Novel." *Desire in Language: A Semiotic Approach to Literature and Art*. Edited by Leon S. Roudiez. Translated by Thomas Gora et al. NY: Columbia UP, 1980, pp. 64–91.

Lacan, Jacques. *Écrits. A Selection*. Translated by Alan Sheridan, London: Tavistock Publications, 1977.

———. *Écrits*. Paris: Seuil, 1966.

————. *The Four Fundamental Concepts of Psycho-Analysis.* New York: Norton, 1981.

————. *Le Séminaire Livre IV. La Relation d'objet.* Edited by Jacques-Alain Miller, Paris: Seuil, 1991.

Ladinsky, Daniel. *The Gift: Poems by Hafiz the Great Sufi Master.* New York: Penguin, 1999.

————. *A Year with Hafiz: Daily Contemplations.* New York: Penguin, 2011.

————. *I Heard God Laughing, Poms of Hope and Joy: Renderings of Hafiz by Daniel Ladinsky.* New York: Penguin, 1996.

————. "My Portrait of Hafiz." Review. 18 April 2005. www.amazon.com/review/RST KIIS25ZD79. Accessed August 17, 2018.

Lahouti, Hassan. "Franklin D. Lewis." Ketab-e Mah-e Addabiyat va Falsafeh, 79, 1383/ 2004, 50–3, p. 50.

LaRocca, David, and Ricardo Miguel-Alfonso, Eds. *A Power to Translate the World: New Essays on Emerson and International Culture.* Hanover, NH: Dartmouth College Press, 2015.

LaRosa, Ralph. "Invention and Imitation in Emerson's Early Lectures." *American Literature,* vol. 44, no. 1, 1972, pp. 13–30.

Lasch, Christopher. *The True and Only Heaven: Progress and its Critics.* New York: Norton, 1991.

Lawler, Andrew. "Walking Around in the Heart. Coleman Barks on Rumi, Sensuality, and the Path with no Name." *The Sun,* no. 382, 2007, pp. 4–9.

Lederer, Florence. *The Secret Rose Garden of Sa'd ud din Mahmud Shahbistari.* Translated by Florence Lederer. London: John Murray, 1920.

Lewis, Franklin. *Rumi: Past and Present, East and West: The Life, Teachings, and Poetry of Jalal al-Din Rumi.* Oxford: OneWorld, 2000.

Lewisohn, Leonard, Ed. *Hafiz and the Religion of Love in Classical Persian Poetry.* New York: I.B. Tauris, 2010.

————. "Prolegomenon to the Study of Hāfiz." In Lewisohn, *Hafiz and Religion,* pp. 3–76.

————. "English Romantics and Persian Sufi Poets." In Aminrazavi, *Sufism and American Literary Masters,* pp. 15–45.

————. "The Religion of Love and the Puritans of Islam: Sufi Sources of Hāfiz's Anticlericalism." In Lewisohn, *Hafiz and Religion,* pp. 159–196.

————. "Hafez and his Genius." *The Angels Knocking on the Door: Thirty Poems of Hafez.* Translated by Robert Bly and Leonard Lewisohn. 2007, 67–86.

Lings, Martin. *What is Sufism?* Cambridge: Islamic Texts Society, 1999.

Loloi, Parvin. "Emerson and Aspects of Sa'di's Reception in Nineteenth Century America." In Aminrazavi, *Sufism and American Literary Masters,* pp. 91–116.

Lopez, Michael. "Conduct of Life: Emerson's Anatomy of Power." *The Cambridge Companion to Ralph Waldo Emerson.* Edited by Joel Porte and Saundra Morris. Cambridge: Cambridge UP, 1999, pp. 243–266.

Majercik, Ruth, Ed. and Trans. *The Chaldean Oracles.* New York: E.J. Brill, 1989.

Martinez Alfaro, Maria Jesus. "Intertexuality: Origins and Development of the Concept." *Atlantis,* vol. 18, 1996, pp. 268–285.

Maulsby, David Lee. *Emerson: His Contribution to Literature*. Medford: Tufts College P, 1911.

Marquet, Yves. "Imâmat. 'Résurrection et Hiérarchie selon les Ikliwân al-Sòafâ.'" *Revue des études islamiques*, no. 30, 1962, pp. 49–142.

Medhora, Dhunjeebhoy Jamsetjee, Ed. *The Desatir, or Sacred Writings of the Ancient Persian Poetry*. Translated by Mulla Firuz Bin Kaus. Bombay: Courier Press, 1818.

Meisami, Julie Scott. "Persona and Generic Conventions in Medieval Persian Lyric, with Illustration. *Comparative Criticism: An Annual Journal*. Edited by E.S. Shaffer. Vol. 12. Cambridge: Cambridge UP, pp. 125–152.

Melville, Herman. *Correspondence*. Edited by Lynn Horth. Chicago: Northwestern UP, 1993.

———. *Some Personal Letters of Herman Melville and a Bibliography*. Edited by Meade Minnigerode. New York: Brick Row, 1922.

———. *His Fifty Years of Exile (Israel Potter)*. New York: Sagamore, 1957.

Mindlin, Henry. "The Life and Work of Hafiz." In Ladinsky, *God Laughing*, pp. 75–88.

Mojaddedi, Jawid, Trans. *Rumi: The Masnavi. Book Two*. Oxford: Oxford UP, 2007.

Mumtaz Ali, Syed. "Sama Mystical Music." 7 January 2016. Canadian Society of Muslims. www.deenislam.co.uk/mix/sama.html. Accessed August 17, 2018.

Nadel, Ira. *Cathay: Ezra Pound's Orient*. New York: Penguin, 2015.

Naficy, Majid. "Coleman Barks and Rumi's Donkey." 13 December 2005. iranian.com/mnaficy.html. Accessed August 17, 2018.

Nemet-Nejat, Murat. "Review of Daniel Ladinsky's *The Gift: Poems by Hafiz the Great Sufi Master*." home.jps.net/~nada/hafiz.htm. Accessed August 17, 2018.

Nile, Green. "Ostrich Eggs and Peacock Feathers: Sacred Objects as Cultural Exchange Between Christianity and Islam." *Al Masaq: Islam and the Medieval Mediterranean*, vol. 18, no. 1, 2006, pp. 27–78.

Nute, Kevin. *Frank Lloyd Wright and Japan: The Role of Traditional Japanese Art and Architecture in the Work of Frank Lloyd Wright*. New York: Routledge, 1993.

Obeidat, Marwan. "Ralph Waldo Emerson and the Muslim Orient." In Aminrazavi, *Sufism and American Literary Masters*, pp. 75–90.

Ockley, Simon, Ed. *Sentences of Ali, Son in law of Mahomet, and his Fourth Successor*. London: Bernard Lintot, 1717.

Packer, Barbara. "Transcendentalism." *The Cambridge History of American Literature*. Vol. 4. Edited by Sacvan Bercovitch. Cambridge: Cambridge UP, pp. 87–136.

Parker, Theodore. "The Writings of Ralph Waldo Emerson," *Massachusetts Quarterly Review*, vol. 3, 1850, pp. 211–212.

Parsinejad, Iraj. "From Nicholson to Barks: A Look at English Translations of Classical Persian Literature." *Sokhan-e Eshq*, vol. 21, no. 2, 2004, pp. 18–25.

———. *A History of Literary Criticism in Iran*. Bethesda: IBEX, 2006.

Paryz, Mark. *The Postcolonial and Imperial Experience in American Transcendentalism*. New York: Palgrave, 2012.

Pease, Donald. "Emerson, Nature, and the Sovereignty of Influence." *Boundary 2: A Journal of Postmodern Literature and Culture*, vol. 8, no. 3, 1980, pp. 43–74.

Pound, Ezra. *The Spirit of Romance*. London: J.M. Dent and Sons, 1910.

――――. *Ezra Pound's Poetry and Prose. Contributions to Periodicals*. Edited by Lea Baechler, Walton Litz, and James Logenbach. Vol. 2. New York: Garland, 1991.

Pritchet, Frances. "Orient Pearls Unstrung: The Quest for Unity in the Ghazal." *Edebiyat*, vol. 4, pp. 119–135.

QTasfir.com. "The Meaning of Tuba." www.qtafsir.com/index.php?option=com_content&task=view&id=2297&Itemid=68. Accessed August 17, 2018.

Rajneesh, Bhagwan Shree. *Sufis: The People of the Path*. Vol. 1. New York: Osho, 2009.

Reef, Catherine. *e.e. Cummings: A Poet's Life*. New York: Clarion, 2006.

Renard, John. *Historical Dictionary of Sufism*. Lanham, MD: Rowman and Littlefield, 2015.

Rich, Adrienne. *Your Native Land, Your Life*. New York: Norton, 1986.

Richardson, Robert. *Emerson: The Mind on Fire*. Berkeley: UC Press, 1996.

Robbins, Michael. "Bedeviled by Books in Translation." *Chicago Tribune*, 30 July 2015. www.chicagotribune.com/lifestyles/books/ct-prj-reading-in-translation-20150730-story.html. Accessed August 17, 2018.

Rohrer, Matthew. *Surrounded by Friends*. New York: Wave Books, 2015.

――――. "Translations from Hafiz." *The American Poetry Review*, vol. 41, no. 6, 2012, pp. 151–158.

Rumi, Jalalludin. *The Essential Rumi: Translations of Coleman Barks*. Edison: Castle Books, 1997.

――――. *A Year with Rumi: Daily Reflections*. Translated by Coleman Barks. New York, Harper One, 2006.

――――. Trans. *Rumi: The Book of Love: Poems of Ecstasy and Longing*. Translated by Coleman Barks. New York, Harper One.

――――. www.masnavi.net/2/10/eng/2/1529. Accessed August 17, 2018.

――――. *The Mathnawi of Jallalu'ddin Rumi*. Vol. 5. Translated by Reynold Nicholson. Cambridge: Cambridge UP, 1925–1940.

――――. *The Quatrains of Rumi: Ruba`iyat-é Jalaluddin Muhammad Balkhi-Rumi: Complete Translation with Persian Text, Islamic Mystical Commentary, Manual of Terms, and Concordance*. Translated by Ibrahim Gamard and Rawan Farhadi. San Rafael: Sophia Perennis, 2008.

Sa'di. *The Gulistan or Rose Garden of Sa'di*. Edited by David Rosenbaum. Translated by Edward Rehatsek. New York: Putnam, 1965.

――――. "Iranian Poetry 'Bani Adam' inscribed on United Nations Building Entrance." *Zaufishan*. 17 September 17 2011. www.zaufishan.co.uk/2011/09/iranian-poetry-bani-adam-inscribed-on.html. Accessed August 17, 2018.

Sanborn, Geoffrey. *The Sign of the Cannibal: Melville and the Making of a Postcolonial Reader*. Durham: Duke UP, 1998.

Sari, Nil. "The Simurgh: A Symbol of Holistic Medicine in the Middle Eastern Culture in History," *Proceedings of the 37th International Congress of the History of Medicine*. September 10–15, 2000, Galveston, Texas, 2000, pp. 156–158.

Schimmel, Annemarie. *Mystical Dimensions of Islam*. Chapel Hill: U of North Carolina P, 2011.

————. *A Two-Colored Brocade*. Chapel Hill: U of North Carolina P, 1996.

————. "Hafiz and his Critics." *Studies in Islam*, vol. 16, 1979, pp. 253–285.

————. *The Mystery of Numbers*, Oxford: Oxford UP, 1993.

Schmidt, Leigh Eric. *Restless Souls: The Making of American Spirituality*. Berkeley: U of California P, 2012.

Schneider, R. *The Public Intellectualism of Ralph Waldo Emerson and W.E.B. Dubois*. New York: Palgrave MacMillan, 2010.

Schneiderman, Jason. "The Loved One Always Leaves: The Poetic Friendship of Agha Shahid Ali and James Merrill." *American Poetry Review*, vol. 43, no. 5, 2014, pp. 11–12.

Schulte, Rainer, and John Biguenet. *Theories of Translation: An Anthology of Essays from Dryden to Derrida*. Chicago: U of Chicago P, 1992.

Sedarat, Roger. "Ghazal #1" by Hafez. *Cerise Press: A Journal of Literature, Arts, and Culture*, vol. 4, no. 10, 2012. www.cerisepress.com/04/10/hafez-ghazal-1. Accessed August 17, 2018.

————. "Middle Eastern-American Literature: A Contemporary Turn in American Studies." In LaRocca and Miguel-Alfonso, *A Power to Translate the World: New Essays on Emerson and International Culture*, pp. 310–325.

Seelarbokus, Chenaz. "Thoroughly Muslim Mystic: Rewriting Rumi in America." *Muslims and American Popular Culture*. Santa Barbara: Praeger, pp. 267–288.

Sells, Michael. *Mystical Languages of Unsaying*. Chicago: U of Chicago P, 1994.

Seyed-Gohrab, Ali-Asghar. "The Erotic Spirit: Love, Man, and Satin in Hafiz's Poetry." In Lewisohn, *Hafez and Religion*, pp. 107–122.

Shamisa, Sirus. *Sar-e ghazal dar sh'er-e farsi az aghaz ta emruz* (Tehran: Entesharat-e Ferdowsi, 1362/1983). As quoted in Davis's *Faces of Love*, p. xxiii.

Stepaniants, Marietta. *Sufi Wisdom*. Albany, NY: SUNY P, 1994.

Suhrawardi, Yahya ibn Habash. *The Philosophy of Illumination*. Translated by John Walbridge and Hossein Ziai. Provo, UT: Brigham Young UP, 1999.

St. André, James. "Relay." *Routledge Encyclopedia of Translation Studies, 2nd Edition*. Edited by Mona Baker and Gabriela Saldanha, pp. 230–232.

Thoreau, Henry David. *The Writings of Henry David Thoreau. Journal, IV. May 1, 1852–February 27, 1853*. Edited by Bradford Torrey. Boston and New York: Houghton Mifflin, 1906.

Toury, Gideon. *Descriptive Translation Studies and Beyond*. Philadelphia: John Benjamins, 2012.

Trivedi, Harish. "Translating Culture vs. Cultural Translation." *In Translation: Reflections, Refractions, Transformations*. Edited by Paul St.-Pierre and Prafulla C. Kar. Delhi: Pencraft International, 2005, pp. 277–288.

Tuerk, Richard. "Emerson as Translator: The Phoenix." *Emerson Society Quarterly*, no. 63, 1961, pp. 24–26.

Vaughan, Robert Alfred. *Hours with the Mystics. Vol. 1*. London: Gibbings, 1893.

Verma, Kumar Jainendra, and Farhat Bano Beg. "The Reception of Classical Persian Poetry in the Anglophone World: Problems and Solutions." *Socrates*, vol. 2, no. 1, 2012, pp. 39–49.

Versluis, Arthur. *American Transcendentalism and Asian Religions*. Oxford: Oxford UP, 1993.

Waugh, Winston. *Sufism*. Maitland, FL: Xulon Press, 2005.

Weisbuch, Robert. "Post-Colonial Emerson and the Erasure of Europe." *The Cambridge Companion to Ralph Waldo Emerson*. Edited by Joel Porte. Cambridge: Cambridge UP, 1999, pp. 192–217.

Whitman, Walt. *Leaves of Grass*. Glasgow: Wilson and McCormick, 1884.

Yao, Steven. *Translation and the Languages of Modernism*. New York: St. Martin's, 2003.

————. "Translation." *Ezra Pound in Context*. Edited by Ira Nadel. Cambridge: Cambridge UP, 2010, pp. 33–42.

Yarshater, Ehsan. "Hafez i: An Overview." *Encyclopedia Iranica*. vol. 11, fascicle 5. New York: Bibliotheca Persica Pres, 2003, pp. 498–500.

————. "Persian Poetry in the Timurid and Safavid Period. *The Cambridge History of Iran: The Timurid and Safavid Period*. Edited by Peter Jackson and Lawrence Lockhart. Cambridge: Cambridge UP, 1986, pp. 965–994.

Yohannan, J. D. "Emerson's Translations of Persian Poetry from German Sources." *American Literature: A Journal of Literary History, Criticism, and Bibliography*, vol. 14, no. 4, 1943, pp. 407–420.

————. "The Influence of Persian Poetry upon Emerson's Work." *American Literature: A Journal of Literary History, Criticism, and Bibliography*, vol. 15, no. 1, 1943, pp. 25–41.

Young, Robin. "Why is the Muslim Mystic, Rumi, America's Best Selling Poet?" *Here and Now*. 18 January 2011. www.wbur.org/hereandnow/2011/01/18/rumi-poetry. Accessed August 17, 2018.

Zaidi, Nishat. "Center/Margin Dialectics and the Poetic form the Ghazals of Agha Shahid Ali." *The Annual of Urdu Studies*, vol. 23, 2008, pp. 55–65.

Zarrīnkūb, ʿAbd-al-Ḥosayn. "Fatalism." 15 December 1999. www.iranicaonline.org/articles/fatalism. Accessed August 17, 2018.

Index